D1228533

studies in

MULTIMEDIA

State-of-the-Art Solutions in Multimedia and Hypertext

studies in

MULTIMEDIA

State-of-the-Art Solutions in Multimedia and Hypertext

Proceedings of the 1991
Mid-Year Meeting
of the American Society for Information Science

San Jose, California, April, 1991

Edited by
Susan Stone and Michael Buckland

ASIS Monograph Series

Published for the American Society for Information Science
by Learned Information, Inc.
Medford, NJ
1992

Library of Congress Catalog Card Number: 92-53056

ISBN: 0-938734-59-1

Price: $39.50

The opinions expressed by contributors to this publication do not necessarily reflect the position or the official policy of the American Society for Information Science.

Book Editor: James H. Shelton
Cover Design: Sandy L. Brock
Book Design: Patricia Keegan and Shirley Corsey

Printed in the United States of America

PREFACE

The "Multimedia" theme for the 1991 American Society for Information Science midyear meeting had already been chosen when I was asked to chair the Technical Program Committee. I confess that I was pleasantly surprised by the richness and variety of the contributions.

Authors of formal papers were invited to offer their work for consideration for inclusion in a publication on the meeting's theme. The present volume, therefore, is not a proceedings of the meeting; rather, it represents papers drawn selectively from those presented. I hope that this process of selection and publication will provide a useful precedent for future ASIS midyear meetings.

I wish to express gratitude to the several poeple who made the meeting and this volume possible. Clifford Lynch and William Paisley served as members of the Technical Program Committee. Richard Hill, Peter Solomon, and other ASIS staff were responsible for organizing the meeting. In particular, appreciation is due to Susan Stone, who was primarily responsible for the editing of this volume.

Finally, I would like to thank the staff at Learned Information, Inc., and especially James Shelton, for bringing this volume to production.

MICHAEL BUCKLAND

TABLE OF CONTENTS

Indexing and Thesaurus Design

CHAPTER 1

Updating the Art and Architecture Thesaurus for Use in Object and Image Documentation

Joseph A. Busch

INTRODUCTION

The process of constructing and applying a thesaurus is based on an analysis of literature in a given subject area. Over time, the topical interests and perspectives evolve, along with research and development, analytical techniques, hypotheses, theories, and resources. Thus the way researchers and reporters write about the topic and the language they use in this work inevitably change. A thesaurus that aims to provide a controlled vocabulary on a subject must also change or else diminish its usefulness.

TYPES OF CHANGES TO THESAURI

A thesaurus consists of terms and information about them. Thesaurus terms include the main or entry term, as well as lead-in terms or synonyms and spelling variations. Information about terms includes a definition or scope note, and term warrant or source information. Another sort of information particular to a thesaurus describes the relationships between terms or the syndetic structure of the thesaurus. These include information about the hierarchical relationships between terms—the broader (BT) and narrower (NT) term relationships; information about the cross references between terms—the related term (RT) relationships; and information about the lead-in terms—the use for (UF) relationships. In this thesaurus model, all terms are viewed as equal, that is, all are terms or potential entries. The type of term and its particular meaning (as in the case of homonyms) is specified through the relationships of one term to one or more other terms. Figure 1 depicts this thesaurus information model.

As a thesaurus changes, changes may occur to either the term information or to information about its relationship to other terms. Changes to term information are more or less like text editing, that is, text is added, edited, or deleted. Term relationships may also be added or deleted, and in some cases changed. A relationship is changed when a term is moved from one hierarchic or synonymic parent to another.

ART AND ARCHITECTURE THESAURUS CASE STUDY

The Art and Architecture Thesaurus (AAT) is an operating project of the J. Paul Getty Trust Art History Information Program (AHIP). The AAT is in the process of constructing and maintaining an exhaustive thesaurus of indexing terms that cover all aspects of Western art and architecture, and associated concepts. The AAT is organized hierarchically into seven broad categories or facets, and 43 hierarchies. The first edition of the AAT was published by Oxford University Press (OUP) in 1990 as printed volumes [1] and as a computer file. [2] The AAT is also distributed in the USMARC authorities format and it has been implemented as an authority file by the Research Libraries Group on the RLIN system using the USMARC format to transfer the AAT data records. Currently, the publicly distributed AAT contains terms in the topical areas of architecture, photography, drawings, and associated concepts. However, the production database at the AAT offices in Williamstown, Massachusetts and the AHIP offices in Santa Monica, California contain work-in-progress, which is an online real-time database management system application.

Term Information

CHANGE	TERM STRINGS	NOTES	SOURCES (WARRANT)
ADD	X	X	X
EDIT	X	X	X
DELETE	X	X	X

Relationships

CHANGE	BT/ NT	UF	RT	SEE RT	TRANS-LATION
ADD	X	X	X	X	X
MOVE	X	X	N/A	X	N/A
DELETE	X	X	X	X	X

Figure 1. Thesaurus Information Model

The AAT is a large data management endeavor. The database currently contains approximately 26,200 descriptors and node labels; 56,625 lead-in terms and relationships; 200 related term relationships; 10,650 scope notes; and 155,500 sources for terms. Approximately 38,000 database transactions on the AAT system have taken place during the past six months. From the editorial point of view, approximately 7,700 thesaurus changes have been recorded since data was sent to OUP some 15 months ago. The problem since then has been to devise methods to trap, track, and report changes so

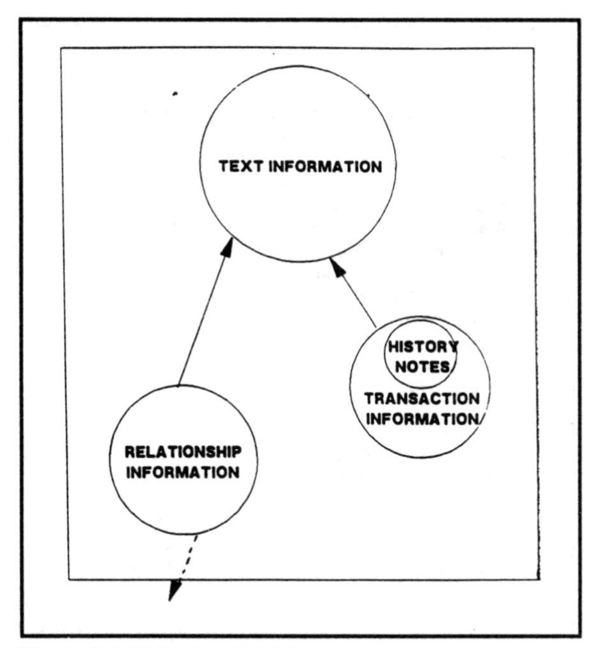

Figure 2. AAT Database Model

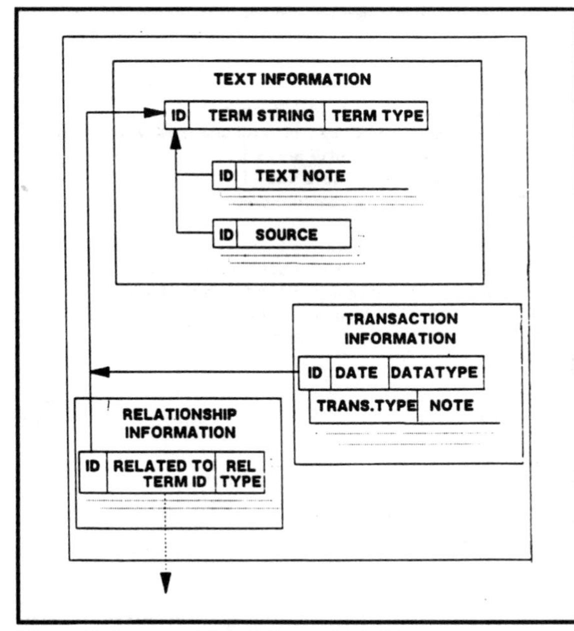

Figure 3. Decomposition of Types of AAT Data

that the AAT publication can be supplemented and the electronic files updated. To manage this prodigious effort, AHIP has designed a database using the thesaurus model presented above.

Figure 2 illustrates the AAT database model for managing thesaural information. In this model, a third type of information — transaction information— has been added. Transaction information is automatically generated when the AAT editors add or change text or relationships information as specified by the AAT editorial policies. Such editorial transactions are called history notes. History note transactions represent approximately 20% of the database transactions on the AAT system. To facilitate the editorial goals of the AAT, the application provides a controlled environment where the AAT editors are permitted to add, edit, or delete system-generated history notes. Finally, a supplement generation program further conflates redundant history notes according to a set of rules.

Figure 3 presents a closer look at the AAT data model illustrating how each type of information is decomposed for storage, retrieval, and processing in the AAT database. Figures 4 and 5 illustrate views of AAT data built up from the attributes and tables in the database. Figure 4 is an example of a detail record which can be viewed online for any descriptor in the AAT system. The detail record represents a fairly complete presentation of the data which can be included for a descriptor in the AAT system. Figure 5 is an example of a view of the same record which would appear in the next AAT supplement. This supplement will only include data which has been changed since January 1, 1990.

```
dwellings
SN: Building or portions of a building designed
    exclusively for residential occupancy by one
    family, but not including hotels or other buildings
    intended for use by transients.
HN: September 1990 lead-in term added
    September 1990 lead-in term changed, was 'home'
    June 1990 descriptor moved
    June 1990 scope note added
BT: <single built works by function>
UF: domestic architecture
    domestic facilities
    domiciles
    habitations
    homes
    residences
    residential buildings
    residential facilities
 Term as Found in Sources:
    dwellings                        m p W
    dwellings                        m p CIT
    dwellings                        m p LCSH
```

Figure 4. Example of AAT Online Detail Display for Descriptor "Dwellings"

```
dwellings
HN: September 1990 lead-in term added
    September 1990 lead-in term changed, was 'home'
    June 1990 descriptor moved
    June 1990 scope note added
BT: <single built works by function>
UF: homes
    residential facilities
SN: Building or portions of a building designed
    exclusively for residential occupancy by one
    family, but not including hotels or other buildings
    intended for use by transients.

                    ...
homes
USE dwellings

                    ...
residential facilities
USE dwellings
```

Figure 5. Example of Supplement Display for Descriptor "Dwellings"

IMPACT OF THESAURUS CHANGES

Changes to a published thesaurus impact its use both in indexing new materials and in retrieval from a target database that has used the thesaurus as a resource for indexing. Changes to a thesaurus may: 1) change the terms available for indexing, 2) change the indexing instructions or guidelines, and 3) change the cross-references available to find ap-

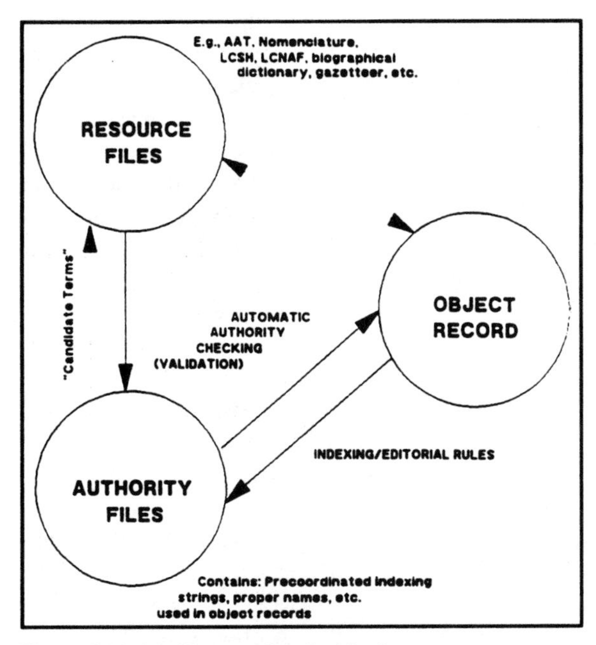

Figure 6. Model of Integrated Authorities System

propriate indexing terms.

In retrieval, the searcher may encounter old terms as well as new terms in the same database. This situation can lead to inconsistent data and reduced or confusing results from a database search. There are several options when thesaurus terms are changed: 1) change all affected indexing in the database retrospectively, 2) make no retrospective changes but apply the up-to-date thesaurus for all new indexing (that is, apply superimposition), or 3) change retrospective indexing as much as possible, taking advantage of the thesaurus structure.

Some retrospective changes can be processed automatically where a one-for-one change occurs to a term string. For example, a one-for-one change can be made automatically when a term is switched with its used for (common spruce UF white pine is switched to white pine UF common spruce). Some retrospective changes, however, require human judgment, such as in splitting one term into two (common spruce is split into white pine and white fir). In these cases, an application database can be helpful in generating summaries and lists of affected entries. One-off conversions and global changes are often feasible methods to update a database. While consistent data is highly desirable, the costs and benefits of making retrospective changes to indexing will typically be the determining criteria.

INTEGRATED AUTHORITIES SYSTEMS

The best way to achieve consistent data is through the design, development, and implementation of production database systems that use integrated authority files. An integrated authority system automatically validates terminology when it is entered into a database. Invalid entries may be flagged as candidates to be reviewed by a database editor later. Regardless of the retrieval scheme—Boolean/proximity or automatic ranked output based on probable relevance [3]—the more consistent the data, the bet-

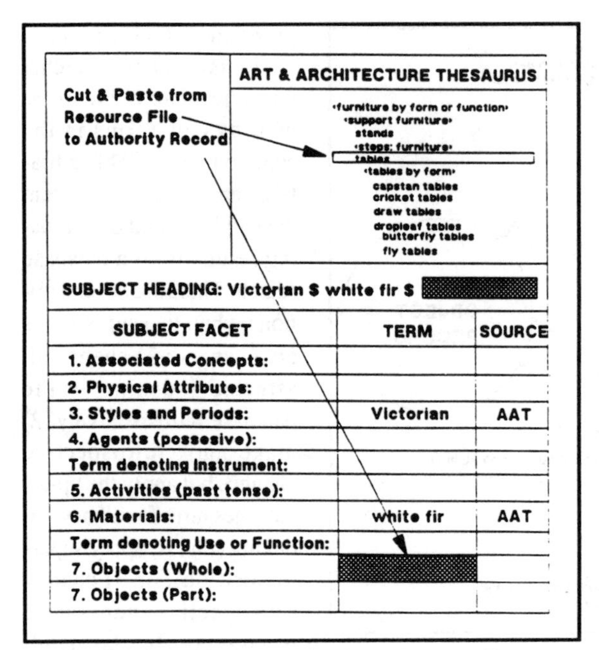

Figure 7. Building a Subject Heading from a Resource File

Cut & paste from authority file to object record

SUBJECT HEADING: Victorian $ white fir $ tables

SUBJECT FACET	TERM	SOURCE
1. Associated Concepts:		
2. Physical Attributes:		
3. Styles and Periods:	Victorian	AAT
4. Agents (possesive):		
Term denoting Instrument:		
5. Activities (past tense):		
6. Materials:	white fir	AAT
Term denoting Use or Function:		
7. Objects (Whole):	tables	AAT
7. Objects (Part):		

FIELD	VALUE
1. Artist:	Greene & Greene
2. Class:	furniture
3. Short Title:	table
4. Date:	1910
5. Subject:	Victorian white fir tables
6. Owner:	Gamble House (Pasadena, CA)
7. Shape:	rectangular
8. Applied Materials:	white fir

Figure 8. Building an Object Record from an Authority File

ter the recall. As described in the previous section, integrated authority files provide for automatic updating of authority controlled values in the records in many cases. Integrated authority files can also improve the speed of indexing new materials once the authority files reach a critical size.

Resource files are off-the-shelf products. They contain source vocabularies for authority files. In some cases they may be appropriate for direct application in database records; in other cases they may provide a resource which will be constructed into more complex entries through pre-coordination according to indexing or other editorial rules. Some examples of resource files are the AAT, Nomenclature, [4] Library of Congress Subject Headings (LCSH), Library of Congress Name Authority File (LCNAF), Union List of Artist Names (ULAN), [5] biographical dictionaries, gazetteers, etc. Figure 6 depicts a model of an integrated authorities system. Figures 7 and 8 present a closer look at such an integrated system. Figure 7 shows how a subject heading has been decomposed into facets and then constructed according to indexing rules. In this example, appropriate terms are cut and pasted from the AAT into the subject authority file. Each facet has rules determining which AAT hierarchy contains appropriate resource terms for this attribute. The resource and authority files may be linked so that changes to an AAT term are automatically reflected in the subject authority, or not. Instead, the system might automatically report on subject authority records that are affected by changes to AAT terms so that the database editor can determine which changes are made automatically and which will be processed by hand. Figure 8 shows how an object record in the database has been decomposed into fields and then filled in by cutting and pasting from the appropriate authority file.

NOTES

1. *Art & Architecture Thesaurus* (New York, NY: Oxford University Press, 1990).

2. *Art & Architecture Thesaurus: Electronic Edition* (New York, NY: Oxford University Press, 1990).

3. Charles R. Hildreth, *Intelligent Interfaces and Retrieval Methods for Subject Searching in Bibliographic Retrieval Systems* (Washington, DC: Cataloging Distribution Service, Library of Congress, 1989), 41.

4. *The Revised Nomenclature for Museum Cataloging: a Revised and Expanded Version of Robert G. Chenhall's System for Classifying Man-made Objects* (Nashville, TN: American Association for State and Local History, 1988).

5. *Union List of Artist Names* (Santa Monica, CA: Vocabulary Coordination Group, Getty Art History Information Program, 1988).

Joseph A. Busch
Getty Art History Information Program
401 Wilshire Boulevard
Suite 1100
Santa Monica, California

CHAPTER

2

GEOGRAPHIC INDEXING TERMS AS SPATIAL INDICATORS

Linda L. Hill and Edie M. Rasmussen

INTRODUCTION

Geographic information systems, which have applications in many fields for the display and analysis of geographic data, have considerable potential as user interfaces to a bibliographic database. Such an interface would provide an alternative to word-based retrieval for geographic concepts. The work reported in this chapter compares word-based and spatial representations as access points to geographic information. To provide context for the study, we discuss problems associated with geographic index terms and the potential value of spatial indicators in the context of a visual interface. It should be emphasized that the area of interest here is access to bibliographic information in which geographic concepts form an important part of the subject description, rather than access to "geodata" such as maps and satellite images. This leads to the problem of an appropriate geographic representation for text-based information; the traditional solution is to assign geographic index terms.

For many bibliographic databases, access to information by geographic location is a particularly important avenue for retrieval. This situation is typified by databases such as *Petroleum Abstracts*, a database of information on petroleum exploration and production, *GeoRef*, a database of geological information, and *Enviroline*, a database of environmentally-related materials. In these and similar cases, a vocabulary of geographic indexing terms provides access to geographic concepts.

Nonetheless, many problems are associated with geographic access. Since no standardized geographic indexing vocabulary exists, each database producer develops its own terminology and structure for the specific mission and coverage of the database. Lack of standardization is only part of the problem; there are also problems associated with the geographic terminology itself. These include changes over time and from language to language, the vague nature of many geographic terms (expressions such as "Northern B.C." or "Mississippi River Valley," which have no exact physical reference), and the use of identical names in different places. [1-3] Geographic searching presents several problems for the user: the need to identify the exact terminology the database employs; the problem of matching a target location when the indexing term describes a larger, smaller, or overlapping area; and the difficulty in identifying areas for which no specific terminology exists, e.g., oceanic locations. Problems such as these make it very difficult to search geographic concepts well.

One can imagine a solution in the form of a visual interface, in which the user simply points to or outlines the specific area of interest on a map enclosing it. Geographic information systems, which exist in other fields, are a potential solution to the problems presented by information retrieval using geographic concepts.

GEOGRAPHIC INFORMATION SYSTEMS

The field of cartography has been revolutionized by the application of computer technology to the production and manipulation of maps. Digital maps are routinely available, in some cases replacing print versions. A logical next step is the addition of location-linked information to the digitized maps. This geographic information (for example, archeological sites, population densities, environmental data) can be linked to specific locations (points, lines, or regions) on the earth. Recent advances in computer hardware and software make this integration possible in a single system. Such a system is referred to as a *Geographic Information System*, or GIS, which may be functionally defined as "a data base system in which most of the data are spatially indexed, and upon which a set of procedures operates in order to answer queries about spatial entities in the data base."[4]

Some applications of these systems are in environmental monitoring, local planning, petroleum exploration, and epidemiology. Typically, the data on which these systems are based is factual in nature and can be accommodated in a relational database structure. Commercial software is available, notably ARC/INFO, [5] that integrates map images with relational databases.

Two potential applications of GIS systems for information retrieval are:

- Provide access to a map collection through a "spatial index," which would locate the maps or other images associated with an area identified by pointing to it on a screen image.
- Act as a linking mechanism between an area identified on a map image and related bibliographic information.

In the U.K., two studies funded by the British Library have dealt with the first application, the development of GIS systems (*Mapfinder* and *CARTO-NET*) to find physical maps. [6, 7] In the U.S., the Research Libraries Group has designed a system to access "geodata"—maps, photographs, surveys, atlases, etc., [8] though no prototype exists. *ImageQuery*, an image database developed at Berkeley, also has a geographic retrieval component. [9]

As discussed above, the linking of factual information to spatial images is of wide interest in areas such as the environment, exploration, and planning. For a bibliographic application, designers face a more complex situation. Large databases exist, containing textual rather than formatted data, that employ their own word-based geographic indexing. The use of a geographic information system as an interface for such bibliographic files requires a suitable mapping of the geographic indexing to a spatial representation. The spatial representation must be suitable for manipulation by GIS software and must accommodate retrieval based on point, line, and polygon matches and varying degrees of overlap.

SPATIAL REPRESENTATIONS IN THE LITERATURE

Figure 1 is an example of an exemplary study area map from a geoscience research document. It shows with an index map the general location of the study area. The enlarged area includes latitude and longitude coordinates, scale, outlines of political subdivisions and geological provinces, and the point locations of the cores that the author

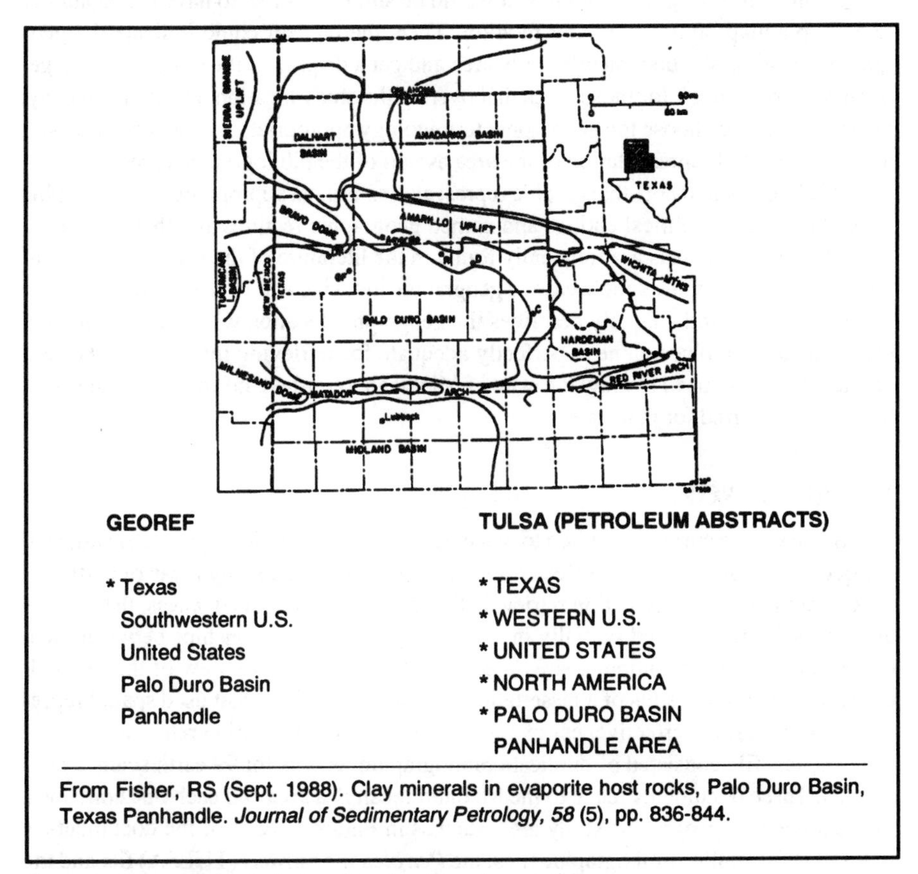

DALHART BASIN
ANADARKO BASIN
TEXAS
AMARILLO UPLIFT
BRAVO DOME
PALO DURO BASIN
HARDEMAN BASIN
RED RIVER ARCH
MATADOR ARCH
Lubbock
MIDLAND BASIN
GEOREF
* Texas
Southwestern U.S.
United States
Palo Duro Basin
Panhandle
TULSA (PETROLEUM ABSTRACTS)
* TEXAS
* WESTERN U.S.
* UNITED STATES
* NORTH AMERICA
* PALO DURO BASIN
PANHANDLE AREA
From Fisher, RS (Sept. 1988). Clay minerals in evaporite host rocks, Palo Duro Basin, Texas Panhandle. *Journal of Sedimentary Petrology, 58* (5), pp. 836-844.

Figure 1. Representative Study Area Map from Geoscience Article

discusses in the article. Clearly, this map pinpoints what geographic location the article addresses.

A search for this document would be wonderfully direct if it could be located from a bibliographic file by calling up a map of the world, zooming into this area of the southwest and, by circling the target area, have the system find the document and all others relevant to the same area. Instead, to find this document by geographic area requires use of the geographic terminology of the bibliographic records. This terminology functions rather well when a recognized place name exists for the area or general area and when the number of retrieved records is manageable for selection of the truly geographically relevant documents. But even with recognizable place names, format differences often exist between files and, in most cases, the geographic terminology really doesn't represent the specific locations of the studies. Rather, the terminology represents larger areas that enclose the study location.

From an indexing point of view, it would be similarly direct to have the capability to call up a map on the computer monitor. Then, the indexer could indicate the geographic location of a document's study area and get a display of the system's valid geographic terminology for those areas that overlap the study location. From this display, the indexer could choose the geographic terminology appropriate for the record as well as create a spatial representation of the area as part of the bibliographic record.

It is important to note that graphic representation is most appropriate for geographic areas that overlap political entities and named geographic features and that are irregularly shaped. Such areas are frequently found in the literature of the earth and environmental sciences. For the simple case of geographic indexing and retrieval, where a place name accurately and uniquely describes the geographic location with a universally accepted name, the place name is perfectly adequate for retrieving information. For example, there is no need to draw the state of Michigan to retrieve information that is collected and reported for that state.

CURRENT WORK

Since we are currently limited to place names for most bibliographic retrieval, [10] the question arises as to their effectiveness in representing the study areas of earth science documents for information retrieval. To test place name effectiveness, these study areas must be represented spatially in such a way that the relationships between them can be analyzed with computer software. What follows is an overview of the methodology and the main results of a dissertation research study [11] that used spatial representations to test the effectiveness of geographic text for information retrieval.

The test file consisted of duplicate bibliographic records for 99 earth science documents. These documents relate to the Mediterranean Sea area and each one contains a map showing its geographic study area, such as in Figure 1. Each of the documents is indexed in two online bibliographic files: the *Petroleum Abstracts* (TULSA) file and the *GeoRef* file. ORBIT records from these two files were used. *Petroleum Abstracts* is pro-

- Identify and list geographic text
- Digitize study area maps
- Overlap analysis of cell maps; distance measurement between non-overlapping cell maps
- Rank documents on the basis of spatial similarity
- Rank documents on the basis of various treatments of the geographic text
- Determine correlation between spatial reference set and text-basied ranked lists
- Determine two measures of precision for relevant records
- Develop optimal search strategies for three target areas and derive recall and precision values for retreived sets

Figure 2. Summary of the Analysis Process

duced by a unit of The University of Tulsa. It is a closed file, available by subscription only, that serves the exploration and production segment of the petroleum industry. It contains an extensive set of geographic indexing terms. *GeoRef* is produced by a unit of the American Geological Institute. It is the most comprehensive geoscience bibliographic file in general use.

The records, and thus the documents, were chosen by identifying duplicate indexing in *GeoRef* and *Petroleum Abstracts*, starting from the most recent additions to the file and using the records of both databases at the start. The documents represent recent geoscience articles about geological, geophysical, and geochemical exploration and analysis in the Mediterranean, and each one contains a map of the study area.

Figure 2 outlines the analysis process. First, geographic terminology—both index terms and free text—was identified and listed in data files, which were used to determine the co-occurrence of terminology in pairs of records within each bibliographic file.

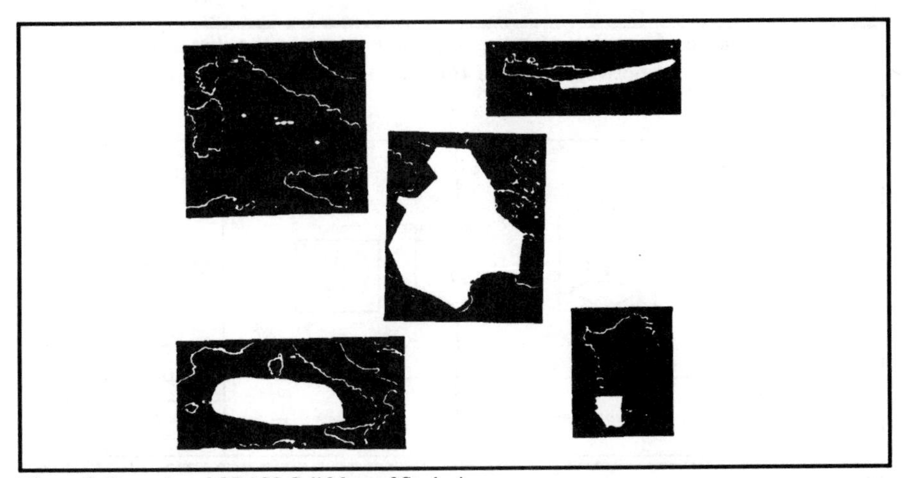

Figure 3. Examples of GRASS Cell Maps of Study Areas

Next, each study area map was digitized using the GRASS GIS software. GRASS is a product of the US Army Construction Engineering Research Laboratory (CERL) in Champaign, Illinois. It is a raster-based system, but it also can handle vector files. For this research, the outlines of continents and islands and other vector data were obtained from the *World Data Bank II* developed by the CIA.

It proved to be relatively easy to create GRASS *cell maps* to represent the documents' study areas. Figure 3 contains examples of the cell maps. Notice that there are no features within the areas; only the area occupied by the study area is represented. GRASS was used to analyze the overlap of the digitized study areas and, for nonoverlapping areas, to measure the distance between the nearest points.

Each document was used in turn as the target document. For each document, all other documents could then be ranked according to their geographic similarity to the target document using the scale in Figure 4. Overlapping areas have a positive value between 0 and 1 based on the similarity calculation of 2 times the intersection divided by the union—or 2 times (A and B) divided by (A or B). Areas sharing a common boundary have a value of 0. Nonoverlapping areas have negative values, which are the distances between the areas. Such ranked lists were created for each document in the test file as spatial reference sets with which to compare the relationships given by the geographic text.

The next task was to rank the documents for geographic similarity according to the co-occurrence of the geographic text in the bibliographic records. The variables involved and the treatments used for the text are shown in Figure 5.

First, each document had duplicate bibliographic records from *GeoRef* and *Petroleum Abstracts*. Second, the analysis could be based on index terms or free text; free text included individual words from the index terms as well as words from the titles and abstracts, when available. Third, terms could be weighted in various ways. Both

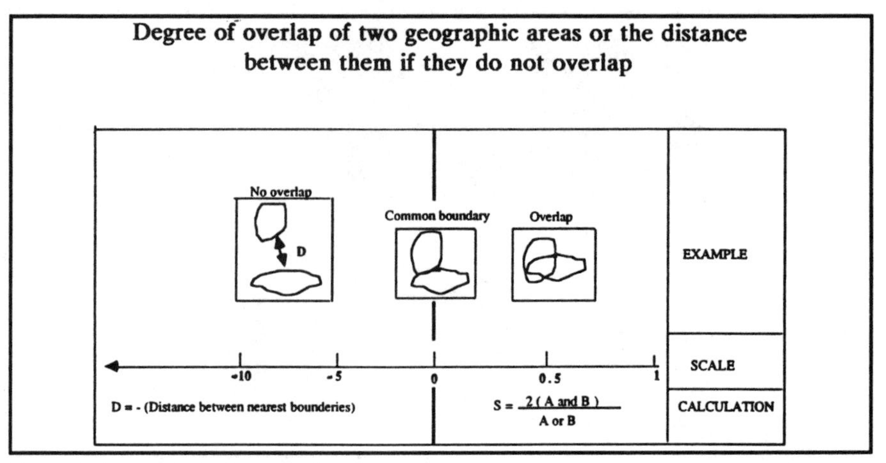

Figure 4. Geographic Similarity Scale

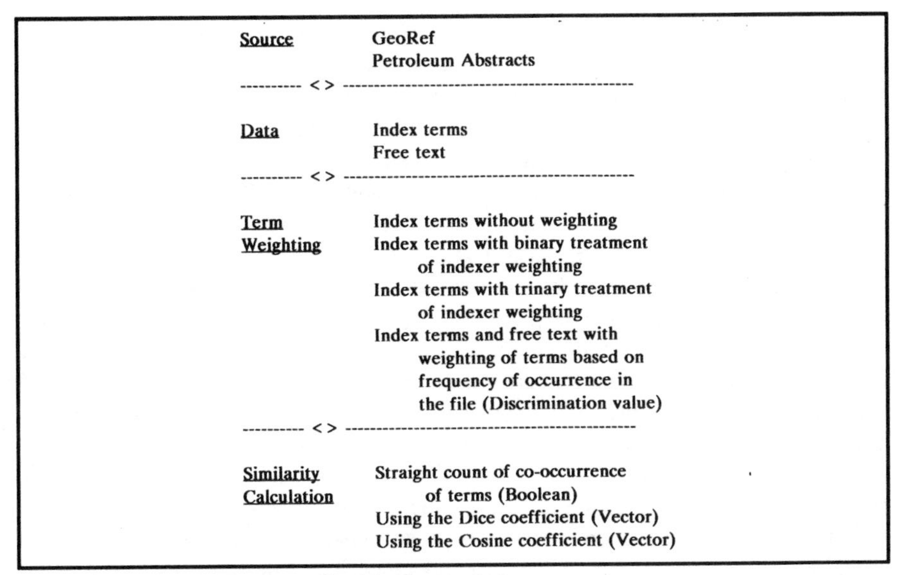

Figure 5. Variables and Treatments Used for Text Analysis

Petroleum Abstracts and *GeoRef* use binary weighting to indicate whether the index term represents a major or a minor document concept. This indexer-assigned weighting could be ignored so that the weighted term would equal the unweighted term or the weighting could be taken into account so that a match would occur only when a particular term had the same weight assigned in the records being compared. Both binary and ternary weighting of the index terms was applied. Binary weighting indicated simply that the term was weighted by the indexer or it was not. Ternary weighting assigned one of three values for each index term: 0 when the term was not present in the record, 0.5 when present but not weighted, and 1 when present and weighted by the indexer.

Finally, index terms and free text could be weighted according to their frequency of occurrence in the test file; that is, on their capacity to discriminate by linking like records while separating unlike records. Terms representing narrow concepts tend to separate records into small groupings; terms representing broad concepts tend to link large groups of records. Two discrimination value weighting calculations were used. The White & Griffith frequency weighting formula [12] assigns a decreasing weight to terms as their frequency of occurrence increases. Essentially, it is the inverse log of the frequency of occurrence. Terms that occur only once have a value of 0 since they apply to only one record in the file; 2 postings gives a weight of 3.3; 20 postings gives a weight of 0.8.

The Average Pairwise Similarity Weighting is a more complicated analysis, taking into account the context in which the term is used. It works by computing the average pairwise similarity value for the entire file with and without a particular term and using the difference between these values as the weight (based on the document centroid method of Salton, 1989. [13]) Thus, there is a range of values for terms used once, twice, three times, etc. Terms that are used a moderate number of times tend to have higher values than terms used either infrequently or very frequently.

The geographic similarity between documents, using the various text treatments, was calculated using three models. The Boolean model was a straight count of the co-occurrence of terms. For each document, the other documents fell into groups depending on the number of geographic terms that they had in common with the target record. The assumption was made that the more geographic terms that documents had in common, the more similar they are geographically. Two vector models were also used. Vector calculations factor in the total number of geographic terms assigned to the records and result in similarity values that are more continuous.The Dice coefficient was used because it is simple to apply and it is frequently used for information retrieval research. The cosine coefficient was used for discrimination value weighting.

The results of these treatments were sets of ranked lists based on the geographic similarity of documents according to the co-occurrence of geographic terminology in the bibliographic records under various treatments of the text. Each document was used in turn as the target document and all other documents were ranked in relation to it.

The next step was to run a correlation analysis of each text-based ranked list in comparison to the spatially-based ranked list for each document using the Spearman Rank Correlation Coefficient. This analysis measures the common variance between two ranked lists. If the rankings were in the same order exactly, the correlation value would be 1.00. If the rankings were exactly reverse of one another, the value would be -1.00. A completely random relationship between the two lists would result in a value of 0. A value of 0.5 between two lists would indicate that 25% of the variance between the lists can be attributed to common causes. A value closer to 0 than 1 indicates a weak correlation between the lists.

RESULTS

Figure 6 shows the range of correlation values for the six categories of text treatment. The results have a plus or minus 0.03 boundary on error. Each range represents six median values based on averaging each document as a target document for each treatment of text. The best of these, 0.38, indicates a weak correlation between the text-based lists and the spatially-based lists, meaning that, at best, a 14% common variance exists with the spatially-based lists.

Figure 6 also lists the top performers. There are interesting differences in the performance of different sets of terms and different treatments. In general, free text performed better than index terms. Vector treatment improved the performance of *GeoRef* vocabulary more than *Petroleum Abstracts*; the reason for this is not clear. Frequency weighting did not improve the performance of the text as much as expected; it may be that the test file was too small for the pairwise similarity method to work well. The resulting weights for this method were very small.

RESEARCH RESULTS

Correlation Values

Unweighted Index Terms	0.23 - 0.35
Indexer-Weighted Index Terms (Binary)	0.19 - 0.23
Indexer-Weighted Index Terms (Trinary)	0.23 - 0.32
Free Text	0.28 - 0.37
White/Griffith Inverse Frequency Wtg.	0.29 - 0.38
Average Pairwise Similarity Weighting	0.25 - 0.33

- < > -

Sorted Correlation Values for Text Treatments

GeoRef Free Text, White/Griffith	0.38
Petroleum Absts. Free Text, Straight Count	0.37
Petroleum Absts. Unweighted Index Terms, Str. Count	0.35
GeoRef Free Text, Cosine Coefficient	0.35
GeoRef Free Text, Dice Coefficient	0.34
Petroleum Absts Free Text, pairwise Sim. Wtg.	0.33
Petroleum Absts Trinary Wt. Index Terms, Cosine	0.32
Petroleum Absts Trinary Wt. Index Terms, Dice	0.31
Petroleum Absts Index Terms, White/Griffith	0.31
GeoRef Free Text, Pairwise Sim. Wtg.	0.31
Petroleum Absts Unweighted Index Terms, Cosine	0.30
Petroleum Absts Free Text, White/Griffith	0.30

Figure 6. Research Results

There are interesting differences in the performance of the geographic text of the two bibliographic files and also in the structure of their controlled vocabularies, their auto-posting practices, their term weighting practices, the presence of abstracts in the *Petroleum Abstracts* records but not in *GeoRef*, and in the number of single-posted terms in the records (73% of the *GeoRef* geographic index terms in the test file were used only once). On average, the two sets of test records have the same number (5) of geographic terms per record, even though *Petroleum Abstracts* has 4 times more index terms of all types on average than *GeoRef*. The number of geographic terms for particular documents, however, varies greatly.

The research didn't attempt to measure the effect of the various file features on the retrieval performance. It is clear that the advantage of free text lies primarily in the fact that it avoids the formatting differences of the index terms by using the individual words in the index terms. The geographic words from the titles and abstracts, in these records, were only secondary contributors to the effectiveness of the free text.

Because it may be asking too much of geographic text to represent accurately all of the geographic relationships in a file, e.g., similarity between nonoverlapping areas as well as between overlapping areas, an attempt was made to see if text could at least rank overlapping documents highly on the ranked lists. Any overlap between the areas of documents was considered to make the two documents mutually relevant, no matter how small the similarity value. This meant, for example, that a document whose study area is the whole Mediterranean area was relevant to all of the other, smaller areas in the Mediterranean, with the similarity values varying directly with the size of the smaller areas.

These calculations showed that weighted index terms perform only slightly better in identifying relevant documents. The range of correlation values was 0.24 to 0.30 for the binary treatment and 0.26 to 0.35 for the ternary treatment of weighted index terms. Unweighted terms and free text did not have higher correlation values. It seems that text is not any better at identifying relevant documents than it is at identifying the overall geographic similarity of the documents in the test file.

One phase of the research was to find out, through case studies, the predictability of geographic terminology for a given geographic area through the development of optimal search strategies for three target areas. As with most case studies, the revelation of why and how rather than what is of most interest. The factors adversely affecting recall and precision in these case studies were of two types: the variability of the textual representations within the files and the imprecision of the geographic terminology. The variability led to a lack of predictability. The imprecision was exemplified by the lack of specific place names for each irregular study area and the impossibility of indexing all of the enclosed geographic features and areas when dealing with a large geographic area. The use of a broad geographic place name does not precisely represent the smaller areas within it. This is in contrast to spatial representation, where the representation of a large area automatically represents all smaller areas within it.

The most important problems affecting the predictability of the geographic text to describe an area were:

- Inconsistency in the assignment of indexing terms: using Cyprus Ridge on some records but not on others that also discussed the area.

- Inconsistency in the format of the terminology: failing to standardize the spelling of the Levant or Levantine Basin.

- Lack of overlap in the assignment of index terms and consequent missed links between related terms: not using both Cyprus Ridge and Cyprus on the same record to alert the searcher to the existence of the other term.

- Inadequate cross references in the thesauri: *GeoRef* was the chief offender here—only 44% of its geographic terminology in the test records resides in its thesaurus. It permits the creation of terms at any time by the indexers. When a term and its variants has been used sufficiently (10 times), the indexers consider putting it in the thesaurus.

SUMMARY

This research project provides data to support the notion that textual representation of geographic study areas for information retrieval purposes, when those areas cannot be represented by specific and unique place names, is ineffective. This result indicates what we can expect of text when it is representing even less clearly delineated concepts in information retrieval environments.

Spatial representation of geographic concepts has obvious advantages. Systems have been developed that can provide the starting point for the development of a graphic retrieval interface for bibliographic files, but design considerations of data storage models, matching algorithms, and display capability and characteristics have to be resolved. We need to add users to the equation and conduct studies to test their comfort and success with a graphic retrieval interface. We don't even know as much as we should about how and under what circumstances people link information geographically, how often map illustrations are used to represent the geographic study areas, and what portion of the literature of any discipline has a significant geographic component. We need to know how consistent indexers are in drawing the boundaries of study areas and how their different renditions will affect retrieval. And, we need to investigate the potential for extracting value-added information from a bibliographic database by a map-based display of a retrieval set—say a set of documents discussing a particular geologic formation, the occurrence of earthquakes, or the sightings of particular flora or fauna. Patterns of geographic occurrence could reveal new intelligence about the subject that was not obvious from the individual records.

On the indexing side of the process, we need to gain some experience in trying to represent a set of geographic terminology spatially. There are many problems here, perhaps more intractable than the retrieval side of the picture.

NOTES

1. A. Griffiths & M. Lynch, *Geographical Information Systems : A Library Perspective.* British Library Research & Development Department Project SI/G/700. (Sheffield, UK: Department of Information Studies, University of Sheffield, 1987).

2. Linda L. Hill, "Geographic indexing for bibliographic databases," *Resource Sharing and Information Networks*, 4(2), 1989, 1-12.

3. Daniel O. Holmes, "Computers and geographic information access," *Meridian*, 4 (1990) 37-49.

4. T.R. Smith et al, "Requirements and principles for the implementation and construction of large-scale geographic information systems," *International Journal of Geographical Information Systems*, 1(1), 1987, 13-31.

5. S. Morehouse, "ARC/INFO : A geo-relational model for spatial information," *Proceedings. Auto-Carto 7. Digital Representations of Spatial Knowledge.* (Falls Church: ASP/ACSM, 1985), 388-397.

6. E.V. Brack et al, *Mapfinder: The Use of Computer Graphics in an Automated Map Retrieval System: Final Report.* British Library Research & Development Department Project SI/G/700. (Sheffield, UK: Department of Information Studies, University of Sheffield, 1987).

7. Barbara Morris, "CARTO-NET: Graphic retrieval and management in an automated map library," *Bulletin of the Geography and Map Division of the Special Libraries Association*, 152 (1988), 19-35.

8. Research Libraries Group, *The GEODATA Project : Summary*. [Unpublished project description, 1988].

9. Holmes.

10. Coordinate representations, such as are provided by *GeoRef* for some of its records, are not included in this overview. The full research report [14], however, does include a discussion of coordinate representations and specifically the coordinate representations of the test records.

11. Linda L. Hill, "Access to Geographic Concepts in Online Bibliographic Files: Effectiveness of Current Practices and the Potential of a Graphic Interface." University of Pittsburgh dissertation. (Pittsburgh, PA: University of Pittsburgh, 1990).

12. Howard D. White & Belver C. Griffith, "Quality of indexing in online data bases," *Information Processing & Management*, 23(3), 1987, 211-224.

13. Gerard Salton, *Automatic text processing: The transformation, analysis, and retrieval of information by computer*. (Reading, MA: Addison-Wesley, 1989), 281-284.

14. Hill, "Access to Geographic Concepts".

ACKNOWLEDGMENTS

Funding for this research was provided by the Internal Grants Program of the University of Pittsburgh. *Petroleum Abstracts* and *GeoRef* both contributed the bibliographic records that were used for the test file. Their contributions are gratefully acknowledged.

Linda L. Hill *
Petroleum Abstracts
University of Tulsa
Tulsa, Oklahoma

Edie M. Rasmussen
School of Library and Information Science
University of Pittsburgh
Pittsburgh, Pennsylvania

* Ms. Hill is now at Information International, NASA STI Program, Code JTT, Washington, DC 20546

CHAPTER
3

INDEXING IN HYPERTEXT DATABASES

Yasar Tonta

WHAT IS HYPERTEXT?

As Franklin puts it, "defining hypertext is much like describing beauty: part of it is inherent in the eye of the beholder." [1] Nevertheless, hypertext can be defined as "non-sequential reading and writing." Hypertext systems contain frames of text, pictures, sound, and animation that are organized nonlinearly in a network of linked frames. From any frame, users can access a variety of other frames containing text or other media. [2] Users follow various sequences of frames and links to retrieve the information they require or add new frames and connections between them.

The term "hypermedia" defines hypertext systems that include not only text but also sound, images, animation, and audio-visual data in digitized forms. The terms hypertext and multimedia in this chapter apply to both hypertext and hypermedia systems.

Hypertext origins go back to the 1940s when Bush outlined his vision of Memex, which was to have some hypertextual features such as linking and associating different parts of documents in a way that would facilitate what he called "associative thinking." [3] Twenty years later, inspired by Bush's ideas, Nelson coined the terms hypertext and hypermedia to describe the associative linking of information into large networks. [4]

Today, various hypertext systems, most of them experimental, have been developed in different areas such as education and publishing. Because hypertext systems are a relatively new phenomenon (the oldest hypertext system is less than ten years old), systems developed tend to be small in size with relatively unsophisticated information retrieval capabilities. Furthermore, some teething problems need to be addressed before hypertext systems can be used in a variety of disciplines.

PROBLEMS WITH HYPERTEXT SYSTEMS

Conklin summarizes the problems with hypertext systems under two headings: *disorientation* and *cognitive overhead*. [5]

Disorientation is the tendency to lose one's sense of location and direction in a nonlinear document. Browsing through nonlinear documents creates a general feeling of being lost or of losing context. Foss, in working with NoteCards, has identified one of these disorientation problems as "the embedded digression problem" (when users following a chain of cross-references become distracted from the main task and never return) and another as "the art museum phenomenon" (when users, so deluged by information, cannot summarize what they have seen). [6] To help users stay oriented, Foss has developed support mechanisms such as history graphs and twin cards. [7]

Cognitive overhead occurs when users confront many alternatives in reading hypertext documents. For example, each node may be linked to several other nodes and users may not be able to figure out which line to follow. Users therefore must exert additional effort and concentration to maintain several tasks or trails at one time.

Marchionini and Shneiderman [8] and Carando [9] point out the difference between searching for facts and browsing. Unlike database systems, hypertext systems are not designed for fast and efficient fact retrieval. Rather, they support unhurried and informal information seeking. These opposing interaction styles may frustrate users expecting a different kind of support. Marchionini and Shneiderman contrast these two objectives. In the first instance, users searching for a fact want a swift and efficient way to reach their goal; that is, to extract information. Such users may be professional on-line searchers or users just in a hurry (for example, software engineers who need a fact quickly). The second type of information seeker may wish to browse through system knowledge, unconcerned with efficient search performance; these may be users with a long-term commitment to the domain of interest, who believe that random knowledge acquired during information examination will be useful in the future.

Many researchers emphasized that there is a thin line between order and "chaos" in presenting information in hypertext systems. [10] Hypertext systems tend to fragment information, which makes its management difficult. The reality is that we are developing what van Dam calls "docu-islands" of knowledge that are incompatible with one another. Just when it seems that compatibility problems of microcomputers have eased somewhat, new, more complex hyperdocument systems will make all those interconnections obsolete. [11]

Larson approaches the issue from an information retrieval point of view. He claims that many hypertext systems lack even rudimentary search capabilities that operate across multiple hypertext networks. Applying the same techniques used in personal information systems to large hypertext systems would create "chaos." Larson is more concerned with the "scale" issue and warns that "large hypertext databases will, of course, face all of the problems of large bibliographic databases. Yet, so far, there are no indications that hypertext researchers have considered such things as name authority or subject vocabulary control. Both of these will eventually need to be addressed if library-sized hypertext networks are to avoid scattering information that should be kept together." [12]

INDEXING IN HYPERTEXT SYSTEMS

Even though most hypertext systems use some kind of indexing for information retrieval, indexing in hypertext systems so far has not been a discrete research topic. Nevertheless, some researchers have briefly mentioned the indexing subsystem in their hypertext systems. Only a few authors [13-15] emphasized the importance of indexing in hypertext systems.

Bush, in his vision of Memex, asserted that the human mind "operates by association." He claimed that "with one item in its grasp, it snaps instantly to the next that is suggested by the association of thoughts, in accordance with some intricate web of trails carried by the cells of the brain." [16] (See also [17].) Bush suggested a new kind of information indexing—associative indexing—to incorporate the associative characteristic of the human mental process into the selection of information. Associative indexing is such that "whereby any item may be caused at will to select immediately and automatically another." In this way, the author or "associative indexer" of a document creates associative links or trails between items of information. The reader follows or navigates a trail from item to item, reviewing each item rapidly or slowly according to his/her needs. The reader can choose to navigate trails set up by the authors of the information or create a new web of associative trails reflecting the reader's particular point of view about the information store. [18]

Weyer's "Dynabook" [19] is one of the earliest pieces of research on electronic books that also deals with indexing problems. Weyer compares three different electronic books (Book A, B, C) with different search capabilities. He describes a simple dynamic book (Book C), based on a world history textbook, implemented in the Smalltalk programming system and used by students to answer questions. Book B and Book C had some indexing capabilities as well. Students were more successful in searching Book C than Book A and Book B and they liked some of the design features in Book C such as fast access to subject terms, term highlighting, and simultaneous access to subject index and text. (see also. [20]

Egan et al. describe "SuperBook," which is "a new presentation system designed to improve the usability of existing machine readable documents". [21] They present a series of behavioral studies that directly compare how people find information in conventional printed documents and the same documents in SuperBook form.

The authors believe that "people fail to find desired information in textual databases" because of indexing policies. They are skeptical of the value of controlled vocabularies and state that indexing performed by subject experts does not necessarily improve users' performance over automatic techniques. They have enhanced their SuperBook system with what they call "rich indexing," stating that "rich indexing is implemented in SuperBook by means of full content indexing in which every occurrence of every work is indexed, and by aliasing. The latter technique permits users to establish their own search synonyms." [22] Despite their "rich indexing," the SuperBook creators soon admitted that a thesaurus might improve system performance even though they were originally skeptical about the value of controlled vocabularies. Their altered view is not surprising because full text databases with automatic indexing exhibit problems much worse than databases with controlled vocabularies. Blair and Maron found that the recall rate in a full text document database is shockingly low. [23]

Marchionini and Shneiderman think that, after all, links at every word to every word are clearly not desirable from the user's perspective nor that of system performance. [24] The trade-offs in machine overhead and user cognitive load (in the form of facing too many choices) must be weighed carefully. Designers should consider the targeted task domains and typical user population in deciding how fine the access points should be and what links among access points should be visible to users.

In SuperBook, in the authors' words, "other, more complex search mechanisms (e.g., full Boolean search) are not supported because previous research suggests that end users rarely use such mechanisms effectively." [25] One needs to be skeptical about the above statement. For full text indexing, some sort of Boolean search capability should be provided in order to reduce the information overload even though users may have some problems with Boolean operators. Boolean search capabilities have become an indispensable part of online catalogs and users are not totally unfamiliar with basic operators such as *AND* and *OR*.

It should be noted that the case study for SuperBook required the users to come up with answers to factual questions. In an actual information retrieval environment, the kind of questions asked could be quite different than factual questions. Authors' evaluation of SuperBook is based on how successful users were in finding relevant sections in the SuperBook. [26] This approach does not require index-using skills that are more sophisticated than the skills needed to use back-of-the-book indexing, which can hardly be compared with the indexing in large databases.

More recently, attempts have been made to build hypertext databases that are larger than electronic books or encyclopedias. [27-29] Research now underway in several institutions investigates the challenges and opportunities that large hypertext databases will offer. It will be interesting to see, from the indexing point of view, how well the indexing techniques developed for electronic books will "scale up" in larger hypertext databases.

The University of California, Berkeley has a variety of multimedia information sources scattered all over the campus. Some multimedia collections are housed in libraries (e.g., the Geography Department's Map Library and the Architectural Slide Library), while others are held by different departments in the campus (e.g., University Art Museum and Lowie Museum of Anthropology).

The UC Berkeley Image Database project aims to provide access to some of the school's image collections by means of an online catalog with tools for visually browsing surrogate images. Terms to index images are taken from the *Art & Architecture Thesaurus (AAT).* [30] The software developed for the prototype system is called *ImageQuery.* It allows users, as in traditional online catalogs, to enter search terms taken from the controlled vocabulary (*AAT*) and then to browse visually the resultant surrogate images associated with the search term. Besser points out that combining visual browsing capabilities with controlled vocabulary terms helps users find relevant images more quickly and efficiently, whereas using only index terms tends to retrieve many images, some of which are not quite relevant. [31] (See also [32].)

The National Archives of Canada developed an optical disc imaging system called *ArchiVISTA* (see Chapter 14) to provide access to 20,000 editorial cartoons and caricatures in its holdings. Images of cartoons and caricatures are accessible via subject, artist, publication, place, date, and unique item numbers. In addition, the description of archival records for images can also be retrieved from the bibliographic database by means of a minicomputer-supported database management system (MINISIS). [33]

The Film Repository at NASA's Johnson Space Center (JSC) "houses a collection of more than 1 million negatives and transparencies, as well as around 10,000 motion picture and audio reels, documenting all aspects of the manned space flight program in this country since 1958." [34] JSC has recently decided to establish intellectual control over the storage and retrieval of images in this collection. Researchers at JSC first digitized some images and then concentrated on developing a "visual thesaurus" to streamline access to images in the database. The terms included in the visual thesaurus come mainly from the card catalog for the image collection. The *NASA Thesaurus* was used for further enriching the visual thesaurus. Hierarchical relationships between the terms were also identified (e.g., broader, narrower, related terms).

The visual thesaurus provides browsing facilities for each term and brings up the corresponding image(s). Personal Librarian was chosen as the data retrieval engine for this project. This software application offers relatively advanced retrieval capabilities and is not based on Boolean logic. It weights the terms and ranks the images in the order of their relevance to the search query. The retrieval performance of the Personal Librarian proved to be satisfactory during the preliminary experiments. [35] Marchionini and Shneiderman argue: "Present systems may support browsing strategies attractive to end users but inefficient for fact retrieval. To compensate, cumbersome analytical strategies that take advantage of indexing to improve retrieval may be supported; however, the overall design may become complex. Analytical strategies include consulting thesauri before search, using Boolean connectives, and systematically iterating queries." [36]

It is interesting to note that users prefer using indexes when searching in hypertext databases. Allison and Hammond found that the index in their "Hitch-Hiker's Guide" was used by 79 percent of student users. [37] Index use was found to be much higher in the Marchionini and Shneiderman study. [38] When subjects were asked to perform efficiently in searching for specific factual information in a Hyperties database, they overwhelmingly (14 of 16 subjects) chose the alphabetical index.

Indexing in existing hypertext systems, however, is not satisfactory and more sophisticated indexing techniques should be tried. Nielsen reports: "... big hypertexts will be the most useful ones and it is therefore important to address the issues of overview in large information spaces. We are currently working on methods for assigning relevance to links based on an information retrieval measure of similarity between the two linked nodes as well as an estimate of the user's current interests. However, it is yet too early to judge the usability of such methods for real work. If such metrics can be tuned to correspond to users' actual intentions it would be possible to filter out links with ratings below some cutoff point." [39]

Marchionini and Shneiderman summarize the search features that should be implemented in hypertext systems:

> Search features like Boolean connectives, string search, proximity limits, and truncation facilitate rapid access to information, but cause additional cognitive load on the part of the user and substantial preprocessing of the database itself. Systems that provide only browsing features allow casual, low cognitive load exploration, but are typically inefficient for directed search tasks or fact retrieval. Defining a hybrid system that guides discovery seems an appropriate compromise, but involves a number of trade-off decisions. How deeply the database is indexed, whether some automatic controlled vocabulary is included, and how feedback is summarized and even formatted on the screen affect the strategies users will apply. If every word is indexed, the possibility of information overload increases. Therefore, features for filtering such as frequency of occurrence per node or support for *NOT* operators must be enhanced. If a controlled vocabulary is included, automatic thresholds must be established, or the user must be prompted to apply the controlled vocabulary or be alerted to its effects. For example, in an encyclopedia, a query that retrieved more than 50 articles could automatically trigger a narrowing function. [40] (See also [41, 42].)

Lynch discusses some of the potential problems in large hypertext databases. [43] As database size grows, the number of links between terms will increase tremendously. This will in turn increase the number of links to follow, thereby creating potential "disorientation" and "information overload" problems. Lynch does not see automatic indexing as a solution for large hypertext databases, because the method will generate many terms and assign many links to a given occurrence of a term. He also finds the tree structure of small hypertext databases inadequate to locate information in large hypertext databases "both because the access points may not have a natural hierarchical structure and because the number of tree nodes that it may be necessary to transverse to reach a useful starting point may be large." [44] Lynch offers the following techniques to tackle retrieval problems in large hypertext databases and to assist users in identifying relevant material from large result sets: keyword and phrase searching, Boolean queries, proximity searching, term weighting, and result ranking.

Salton and Buckley investigated the applicability of automatically generating content links in hypertext databases. [45] They tried to generate automatic content links between terms based on the global term and phrase matches and tested the usefulness of this method. They suggested that further research is needed in this area, although the preliminary results they obtained are somewhat promising.

Regarding indexing and classification, Farmer warns that the library profession, as the prime collectors and organizers of information, needs to look at how hypermedia will affect traditional cataloging and classification: "In the future, cataloging codes may include sections on how to set up webs of information; what types of relationships should be expressed; how to guide users through a hypermedia database; and how to create their own links and trails. New cataloging standards, which define the structures and relationships that can be imposed on a hypermedia document, may need to be developed." [46]

ISSUES AND FUTURE DEVELOPMENTS

Indexing for small size hypertext databases such as electronic books and encyclopedias is quite different from that of large hypertext systems. Existing hypertext systems have indexes similar to back-of-the-book indexes, which do not "scale up" to large hypertext systems. Larson describes this "scaling up" issue as the "order of magnitude" problem. [47] If the size of the hypertext database gets bigger, the database needs to be rearranged. Indexing principles used in small databases simply do not work for large databases.

Larson points out that hypertext systems attempting to support very large databases of multimedia information face additional problems: "The problems of cataloging and indexing nontextual materials are well-known, and simply putting a collection of such materials into digital form does not address the problem." [48]

Hypertext databases should support a multitude of data types such as text, sound, images, animation, and audio-visual data. New data types such as point data, raster data, vector data, and spatial and temporal data should also be supported in hypertext databases. For instance, many satellite and remote sensing instruments produce a regular array of point measurements. Similarly, data on topographical maps are represented as vectors. It is suggested that one approach to representing this type of data in hypertext databases will be to use existing thesauri of geographical regions and place names that include the cartographic coordinates of places. [49]

The volume of multimedia data that is to be fed by satellites, the Earth Observing System (EOS), and sensors is mind-boggling. It is expected that 1950×10^9 bytes of raw data will be received every day from these stations. Furthermore, the amount of multimedia data will reach 1.0×10^{16} bytes in 15 years! Providing access to such large volumes of multimedia data requires sophisticated indexing techniques. For instance, in order to find "all the images of Lake Tahoe taken by, say, Orbit Platform #1 for the period June-September 1986," spatial data and time need to be indexed. Furthermore, performing this search requires indexes on the result of a function and not the raw value. "Indexing functions for images and text often return a collection of values for which efficient access is desired." [50, 51]

Automatic indexing of images, unlike text, may not be possible for some time to come. Satisfactory image recognition software has yet to be developed. This lack will exacerbate the indexing problems in large-scale multimedia databases. As voice recognition software gets better, it might be possible to index recognized words automatically. [52]

Currently it appears that supporting visual browsing capabilities with controlled vocabularies such as *AAT* improves retrieval effectiveness in image databases. Developing specialized "visual thesauri" for other disciplines might help solve indexing and retrieval problems in other multimedia databases as well. In conclusion, as van Dam put it, designing hypertext systems needs people "who . . . can think about classification and indexing." It is librarians and information workers who could provide safer journeys in tomorrow's colossal information spaces.

NOTES

1. Carl Franklin, "Hypertext Defined and Applied," *Online* 13 (May 1989), pp. 37-49.

2. Carolyn L. Foss, "Tools for Reading and Browsing Hypertext," *Information Processing & Management 25* (1989), pp. 407-418.

3. Vannevar Bush, "As We May Think," *Atlantic Monthly* 176 (July 1945), pp. 101-108.

4. Ray R. Larson, "Hypertext and Information Retrieval: Towards the Next Generation of Information Systems," *ASIS '88: Proceedings of the 51st ASIS Annual Meeting, Atlanta, Georgia, October 23-27, 1988*. Ed. by Christine L. Borgman and Edward Y.H. Pai. (Medford, NJ: ASIS, 1988), Vol 25, pp. 195-199.

5. J. Conklin, "Hypertext: An Introduction and Survey," *IEEE Computer* 20 (1987), pp. 17-41.

6. Foss, "Tools for Reading."

7. Patricia Carando, "Shadow—Fusing Hypertext with AI," *IEEE Expert* 4 (Winter 1989), pp. 65-78.

8. Gary Marchionini and Ben Shneiderman, "Finding Facts versus Browsing Knowledge in Hypertext Systems," *IEEE Computer* 12 (January 1988), pp. 70-80.

9. Carando, "Shadow."

10. Torrey Bayles, "A Context for Hypertext: Some Suggested Elements of Style," *Wilson Library Bulletin* 63 (November 1988), pp. 60-62.

11. Ann F. Bevilacqua, "Hypertext: Behind the Hype," *American Libraries* 20 (February 1989), pp. 158-162.

12. Larson, "Hypertext."

13. Ibid.

14. Clifford A. Lynch, "Hypertext, Large Databases, and Relational Database Management Systems," in *National Online Meeting Proceedings*. (Medford, NJ: Learned Information, 1989), pp. 265-270.

15. Linda Farmer, "Hypertext: Links, Nodes and Associations," *Canadian Library Journal* 46 (August 1989), pp. 235-238.

16. Bush, "As We May Think."

17. Lauren B. Doyle, "Indexing and Abstracting by Association," *American Documentation* 13 (October 1962), pp. 378-390.

18. Farmer, "Hypertext."

19. Stephen A Weyer, "The Design of a Dynamic Book for Information Research," *International Journal of Man-Machine Studies* 17 (July 1982), pp. 87-107.

20. Stephen A Weyer and Alan H. Borning, "A Prototype Electronic Encyclopedia," *ACM Transactions on Office Information Systems* 3 (January 1985), pp. 63-88.

21. Dennis E. Egan et al, "Formative Design Evaluation of SuperBook," *ACM Transactions on Information Systems* 7 (January 1989), pp. 30-57.

22. Ibid.

23. David C. Blair and M.E. Maron, "An Evaluation of Retrieval Effectiveness for a Full-Text Document Retrieval System," *Communications of the ACM* 28 (March 1985), pp. 289-299.

24. Marchionini and Shneiderman, "Finding Facts," p. 78.

25. Egan et al, "Formative Design," p. 37.

26. Ibid, pp. 40-41.

27. I. Ritchie, "Hypertext—Moving Towards Large Volumes," *The Computer Journal* 32 (December 1989), pp. 516-523.

28. Peter Cooke and Ian Williams, "Design Issues in Large Hypertext Systems for Technical Documentation" in *Hypertext: Theory into Practice.* Ed. by Ray Mcaleese. (Norwood, NJ: Ablex, 1989), pp. 93-104.

29. Kenneth Utting and Nikole Yankelovich, "Context and Orientation in Hypermedia Networks," *ACM Transactions on Information Systems* 7 (January 1989), pp. 58-84.

30. Toni Petersen, "Developing a New Thesaurus for Art and Architecture," *Library Trends* 38 (Spring 1990), pp. 644-658.

31. Howard Besser, "Visual Access to Visual Images: The UC Berkeley Image Database Project," *Library Trends* 38 (Spring 1990), pp 787-798.

32. Howard Besser and Maryly Snow, "Access to Diverse Collections in University Settings: The Berkeley Dilemma," in:*Beyond the Book: Extending MARC for Subject Access.* Ed. by Toni Petersen and Pat Molholt. (Boston, MA: G.K. Hall, 1990), pp. 203-225.

33. Gerald Stone and Philip Sylvain, "ArchiVISTA: a New Horizon in Providing Access to Visual Records of the National Archives of Canada," *Library Trends* 38 (Spring 1990), pp. 737-750.

34. Gary A. Seloff, "Automated Access to the NASA-JSC Image Archives," *Library Trends* 38 (Spring 1990), pp. 682-696.

35. Ibid.

36. Marchionini and Shneiderman, "Finding Facts," p. 71.

37. Lesley Allison and Nick Hammond, "A Learning Support Environment: the Hitch-Hiker's Guide," in Ray Mcaleese, ed. *Hypertext: Theory into Practice.* (Norwood, NJ: Ablex, 1989), pp. 62-74.

38. Marchionini and Shneiderman, "Finding Facts."

39. Jakob Nielsen, "The Art of Navigating Hypertext," *Communications of the ACM* 33 (March 1990), pp. 297-310. Quotation from p. 300.

40. Marchionini and Shneiderman, "Finding Facts," pp. 78-79.

41. Ben Shneiderman, "User Interface Design for the Hyperties Electronic Encyclopedia," in *Proceedings of Hypertext '87, (November 13-15, 1987, Chapel Hill, North Carolina.* (New York: ACM, 1989), pp. 199-204.

42. Xianhua Wang and Peter Liebscher, "Information Seeking in Hypertext: Effects of Physical Format and Search Strategy," *ASIS '88: Proceedings of the 51st ASIS Annual Meeting, Atlanta, Georgia, October 23-27, 1988.* Ed. by Christine L. Borgman and Edward Y.H. Pai. (Medford, NJ: ASIS, 1988), Vol. 25, pp. 200-204.

43. Lynch, "Hypertext."

44. Ibid, p. 267.

45. Gerard Salton and Chris Buckley, *On the Automatic Generation of Content Links on Hypertext.* Technical Report TR 89-993. (Cornell University, Department of Computer Science, 1989).

46. Farmer, "Hypertext," p. 238.

47. Ray R. Larson, "Indexing and Intellectual Access in Multimedia Databases," Seminar presented at UC Berkeley, 12 October 1990.

48. Larson, "Hypertext," p. 197.

49. Ibid.

50. Clifford Lynch and Michael Stonebraker, "Extended User-Defined Indexing with Application to Textual Databases," in *Proceedings of the 14th International Conference on Very Large Databases, Los Angeles, California, August 29-September 1, 1988.* Ed. by Francois Bancilhon and David J. DeWitt. (Palo Alto, CA: Morgan Kaufmann, 1988).

51. Information presented in this paragraph comes from Professor Michael Stonebraker's seminar series at UC Berkeley (Spring 1991), and from an unpublished proposal.

52. Larson, "Indexing."

ACKNOWLEDGMENTS

I am grateful to Professors Ray R. Larson and Michael K. Buckland for their comments on an earlier draft of this chapter.

Yasar Tonta
School of Library and Information Studies
University of California, Berkeley, CA 94720

Documents and Images

CHAPTER
4

ADDING AN IMAGE DATABASE TO AN EXISTING LIBRARY AND COMPUTER ENVIRONMENT: DESIGN AND TECHNICAL CONSIDERATIONS

Howard Besser

INTRODUCTION [1]

Until now, most image databases have been implemented as standalone systems in isolated environments. Developers were therefore able to design without the constraints imposed by exterior systems and without adhering to standards and protocols.

With increases in storage capacity and in the telecommunications bandwidth, multiuser image databases are becoming financially feasible. Libraries and computer centers are beginning to consider offering online access to collections of images as part of their services.

If we want to start thinking seriously about delivering images within an online retrieval system, what are the issues to consider? This chapter provides an outline of several key items of concern. First, it briefly describes what is meant by "image collections" and discusses why these collections have either not created image databases at all or have done so on single-user, closed box systems. Next, this chapter thoroughly examines past problems with creating multiuser image databases and shows how both technological barriers and vocabulary control problems are beginning to clear up. Finally, it identifies some implementation concerns and ways of helping alleviate some of the remaining problems.

IMAGE COLLECTIONS AND THEIR ENVIRONMENTS

Libraries, museums, and archives often have substantial collections that are important for their visual aspects. The collections include slides, photographs, diagrams, charts, manuscripts, and ethnographic objects covering a wide variety of disciplines. Examples of collections that the author has worked with include architecture slides, art objects (Japanese scrolls), geographic materials (maps and coordinate-based images), old manuscripts, anthropological objects, historical photographs, instructional resource materials, and library special collections.

It is important to note a number of facts about collections such as these. First, many collections contain a vast number of objects. For example, slide collections usually have 500,000 items, and it is not unusual for Natural History Museums to have one million items. Additionally, these collections appear in a wide variety of disciplines, and each often has its own set of required information or controlled vocabulary. For example, geographic material needs coordinates, art often requires vocabulary from the Art and Architecture Thesaurus, biology material may require vocabulary from MeSH, and any of these may require particular local information (such as a professor referring to it as his/her "introductory set"). The organizations managing these collections provide varying degrees of access to them, ranging from uncataloged materials, to card-catalog access, to online library catalog-type access, to full-fledged image databases.

IMAGE DATABASE IMPLEMENTATIONS

There are distinct technical problems in delivering an image database to multiple simultaneous users. These have led developers to favor the single-user systems based around analog/videodisc technology.

Until recently, virtually all image databases have been standalone (closed box) systems, though this situation is likely to change. [2] The typical current set-up requires that each user have his or her own workstation and own videodisc player. Analog images are stored on a videodisc and displayed on a television monitor, while textual information is stored in a digital database on a computer disk and displayed on a workstation screen. The computer and the videodisc player are physically connected, and the videodisc frame number is stored on the computer database, linking the images and the text.

Although these standalone systems appear rather primitive from the point of view of networking or shared resources, they are extremely advanced in their implementation of graphic user interfaces. Systems have been developed that display a large amount of information in a compact and easy-to-understand way. Videodisc-based systems also offer the advantage of large storage capacity (up to 108,000 images per platter).

Even more important, standalone systems allow the designer to tailor the amount of information to a specific collection and expected user needs. By tightly controlling the way in which a user can approach the information, the designer can provide a much more attractive and intuitive user interface. And a designer who does not have to worry about different types of external use no longer has to adhere to standards or provide "hooks" for other applications.

In the past, technical barriers made it impossible to implement image databases in shared-user environments. Each of the two basic models for multiuser image databases has posed its own problem. The analog image storage model (represented by Project Athena's parallel analog and digital networks) has required an incredibly complex (and expensive) infrastructure. The economies of scale that make multiuser set-ups cheaper per user served do not operate in an environment that requires a computer workstation, videodisc player, and two display devices for each user.

The digital image storage model, on the other hand, has required vast amounts of storage space (as much as one gigabyte per 30 images). The cost for such enormous storage space had made this model prohibitive as well; but plunging storage costs are finally making this alternative viable.

If storage costs no longer pose an impediment, what *do* we need to consider in building digitally stored multiuser image databases? Perhaps the key problem stems from the wide variety of display devices that one is likely to find in any given environment. To create an interface which will work in a user-friendly way on a mixture of devices is not an easy task.

Librarians and vendors creating online public access catalogs have had to deal with problems of screen design and presentation on a variety of display devices. Many of these have recently begun to extend this work to include Z39.50 implementations. But the problems posed by bit-mapped workstations have received scant attention in the library and information science literature.

Interface designers for library catalogs have not yet begun to consider problems posed by attempting to display a single database on workstations that may have different screen aspect ratios and sizes, different types of color phosphors, or different numbers of mouse buttons. Nor have they dealt with problems posed by window management systems, including issues regarding window size and placement. But for the most part, the technical problems posed by image databases center around the large file sizes for images, and the problems these large files cause for storage, transmission, display, and response time.

IMAGE DATABASE BASIC SYSTEM REQUIREMENTS

The key problems posed by image databases are rooted in the huge storage space needs of each image file. We will confine our remarks here to still images, after noting that moving images obviously require even much larger (24-30 still images per second) storage capacities, and cause a number of other problems (mostly due to the added dimension of time).

A normal digital color image that fills the screen of a standard megapel workstation (such as a SUN, MicroVax, NeXT, or RT) will take up 1 megabyte of storage for an 8-bit image or 3 megabytes for a "true color" 24-bit image. Lossless compression algorithms might bring storage down to 1/3 to 1 megabyte per image, but not much further. [3, 4] But, for certain kinds of objects, 15 megabytes [5] and as much as 30 megabytes might be required. [6, 7]

These requirements create tremendous strains on systems in terms of storage, system resources, and telecommunications. The fundamental problem is storage (see Figure 1). Using an image size of 1/3 to 1 megabyte, only 1,000 to 3,000 images can be stored on a 1-gigabyte disk. Storing smaller images, of the size of a PC screen, would increase the storage four-fold, to 4,000 to 12,000 images/gigabyte (compared to 108,000

WORKSTATION FULL SCREEN IMAGES

Bits / Image	Image Size	Compressed Size	# of Images / Gigabyte
8	1M	.33M	3,000
24	3 M	1M	1,000

Figure 1.

on videodisc). Fortunately, storage capacities are climbing very quickly, but perhaps not quickly enough to make digital storage viable for a large image collection in the immediate future.

Just retrieving an image from a disk takes much time (see Figure 2). To read the image off the disk under ideal circumstances can take from 2/3 second to more than a second. When multiple users are trying to access the disk at the same time, the process is much slower—the requests have to be handled serially (one after the other). And putting the disks in a jukebox (which will probably be required in order to achieve the necessary storage capacity) will add another 5 to 10 (serial) seconds to each request just to remove the disk from its storage slot and position it over the read head.

The key telecommunications problem posed by images relates to transmission time. As can be seen in Figure 3, anything slower than T-1 speed is impractical for images of 1 megabyte or larger. For instance, even a 56-kilobit line would take 3 minutes to transfer a 1-megabyte file. And these figures assume ideal circumstances that ignore the possibility of other users contending for network bandwidth, disk access time, or the time for remote display. Obviously, current common telephone transmission rates are completely impractical—few users would be willing to wait the hour necessary to transmit a single image at 2400 baud.

Other strains on the system include the large amount of system resources necessary

SAMPLE AVERAGE IMAGE TRANSFER TIME

Drive	Avg Disk Access Time	Transfer Rate	Access / Delivery Time for 1 M Image
Sony WDD300 WORM	250 milliseconds	2400 KB/second	0.67 Seconds
Hitachi OD101 WORM	80 milliseconds	1000 KB/second	1.08 Seconds
Sony D501 erasable	95 milliseconds	680 KB/second	1.57 Seconds
Cannon M-O erasable	92 milliseconds	1000 KB/second	1.09 Seconds

Figure 2.

IMAGE TRANSMISSION TIME

Speed (bits)	Transmission Time (1 M Image)	Transmission Time (1/2 M Image)
1200 bps	139 minutes	69 minutes
2400 bps	69 minutes	35 minutes
9600 bps	17.4 minutes	8.7 minutes
56 Kb	2.97 minutes	1.49 minutes
T-01 (1.544 Mb)	6.5 seconds	3.2 seconds
Ethernet (10 Mb)	1 second	0.5 seconds
T.3 (45 Mb)	0.2 seconds	0.1 seconds
FDDI (100 Mb)	0.1 seconds	0.05 seconds
SUN bus (320 Mb)	0.015 seconds	0.007 seconds

Figure 3.

to move these huge files around within a workstation, and the amount of time (sometimes more than 10 seconds) that it takes to paint the screen.

Until now, it has been impractical to consider actual implementation of image databases due to the prohibitive cost of technology for even a moderate-sized collection. And it's been difficult to do serious research on image databases because we haven't been able to create one large enough test. But increased speed, higher capacity disk storage, increased RAM for frame buffering, and better compression algorithms are creating an environment conducive to more image research that likely will soon produce applications.

THE CONTENT SIDE: MARC, AACR2, AND VOCABULARY STANDARDS

Now we will turn briefly to nontechnical problems and examine the vocabulary and standards used to describe images. First we will look at problems related to the only standard format designed specifically for audio-visual materials, and then briefly examine several current projects in the area of vocabulary control.

Probably the most confusing issue for vocabulary describing images is "depiction." When we have a slide or a photograph of an object, what should we catalog and describe, the slide or photograph or the object depicted in it? If we have a collection of slides taken of paintings, are the dimensions of each exactly 35 mm? AACR2 suggests that the main entry be the photographer. But this may not be good practice for photographs that have become part of the collection solely because of what they depict (i.e., photographs of the Sistine Chapel in an architecture slide collection). Collection managers (and their users) would, instead, expect the main entry for these to be under the object depicted.

Though MARC-AVM is the only format designed specifically for visual materials, most museums and slide libraries find the system completely inadequate. It was initiated by the Society of American Archivists in 1986 and designed mainly for historical archives.

As explained elsewhere, [8] managers of small collections find AVM confusing and overblown for their needs. Many find it repetitive for most records. For example, the 008/15-17 field is used for *Country of Production (single entry),* the 044 field for *Country of Producer (single entry),* the 257$A field for *Country of Producing Entity,* and the 260$A field for *Place of Publication.* And motion picture credits are divided between the 508 and 511 fields. One UC Berkeley librarian lamented, "MARC/AVM makes you find data to put in for things that you don't care about, and you have to be really creative to try to squeeze in some of the data that you find necessary and MARC/AVM doesn't care about."

A number of small collections that regard AACR2 and MARC as beyond their needs have turned to simple relational database management systems that can maintain 6 to 12 fields per record. At the same time, the limitations of AVM for museum collections impelled the call for another MARC format more attuned to museum needs. The Museum Computer Network has received an NEH grant to create a Computerized Index to Museum Information (the CIMI project).

Another major issue concerns whether to provide one record for each image or collection-level records for groups of images. A library probably doesn't want its online public access catalog "polluted" by a branch's collection of 1/2 million relatively unique slides, yet the reference librarian for that slide collection wouldn't find it useful to have only one MARC record for 25,000 Michelangelo slides. But for the manager of the image collection, the incentive to enter item-level records into machine-readable form lies in the tools that will then become available for retrieval and, eventually, circulation. The manager has little or no incentive to enter collection level records (which will be absolutely useless for circulation). But the construction of an item-level catalog would be such a long and arduous task that the collection manager would never think of being able to complete it.

The sort of image collections under discussion here face a number of problems in the areas of vocabulary control and standards. It has long been recognized that general standards (such as Library of Congress Subject Headings) are not very useful for special collections. Until recently, there have been no tools to insure terminology consistency both within a single collection and between similar collections at different institutions. The lack of standard descriptive terminology—even within a single discipline—has led to a "Tower of Babel" vocabulary. But in recent years, promising work has been done in art-related fields, with projects such as the Art & Architecture Thesaurus, the Syracuse Museum terminology project, and the Getty-sponsored Art Terminology task force. And for some time other disciplines have each been developing their own sets of terminology, usually arranged in a syndetic structure. These include MeSH (medical), Chenhall's Nomenclature (history, anthropology, archeology), and NAMID form and genre (films, videos).

Until very recently, many managers of small image collections have questioned why they should conform to standards at all. In the library world, the major motivating force for adherence to standards was shared cataloging and the savings that could be realized through copy cataloging from a central source. On the surface one would think that these image collections (many of which have unique items) would not benefit from sharing collection information with other institutions and, consequently, would not be motivated to adhere to standards. But a closer look shows a number of areas of commonality, any one of which might be shared with other institutions. Authority lists can obviously be shared. Many apparently unique items are just slight variants of records that are likely to exist in other institutions, such as another view of the same depiction (e.g., a famous building), a detail of a painting already cataloged, a specimen of the same type of plant, or one object in a series where someone else has cataloged others in the same series. In addition, the records of other institutions can serve as a useful reference source, as OCLC demonstrates with its EPIC system.

IMPLEMENTATION CONCERNS

Now that we have looked at some of the technical problems (such as storage, transmission, display, and format), how can we begin to address these if we still want to deliver images to a set of users?

X-Windows

One very useful tool is the X-Windows window manager. X-Windows is designed to operate on a wide variety of hardware platforms, and systems designers can use it to support a single user interface that should run on most workstations. This server-client relationship allows many different users to share the same resources without overloading the central server with display and interaction services. It also permits a wide variety of hardware platforms to access the file-server in functionally transparent ways.

X-Windows essentially "projects" the interface onto the user's display device, and the display device handles the display management and user interaction. With these functions offloaded onto the user's workstation, the image server can concentrate on image retrieval and manipulation. But X-Windows applications normally tie the information to the user interface employed to access it, preventing other applications from using the image data in different contexts.

Storage

As we have shown earlier, centralized storage of large image files creates access problems. Here we will suggest two methods, either of which is likely to make these problems less severe.

One way to alleviate the problem of access time (i.e., the serial queuing of multiple requests) is by distributing storage among a number of disk drives. This method could take the form of redundant copies of the images sitting on different disk drives, or of distributing a single set of images among different drives in such a way that simultaneous requests are likely to be answerable from different drives. Either of these methods will require some knowledge of use patterns. Carnegie-Mellon University's Project Mercury plans to implement a variant of this method.

Another way to minimize access time is through disk caching. This method could take the form of an initial transfer of images from a slower optical drive to a faster magnetic drive, or from a server to an individual's workstation. In either case, we would need to develop software to anticipate the next request for an image, based upon what has been requested previously. Let us take a very basic example. A user retrieves a set of 10 text records and begins pondering over which one(s) to use. Meanwhile, the system sends the first 5 of the associated images to magnetic disk (or perhaps even to local storage on the user's own workstation). In this way the system might position appropriate images into an area of quicker access while awaiting the user's decision.

Compression

Another key problem area to consider is that of image compression. Why should we compress? Because then we will use much smaller files for our image material, [9] creating far less of an impact on system resources. But we need to weigh the savings in storage space and network transmission against the systems resources it will take to compress and decompress the images. If we do choose to compress, the major issue is: How much can we compress, and how much are we willing to lose in the process?

Compression can be done in hardware, software, or a combination of the two. Compression is generally faster in hardware, but distributed systems consisting of a number of different hardware platforms may not be able to obtain decompression boards for all their supported platforms. Also, as more advanced compression algorithms become available, hardware-based compression systems will require that new cards be purchased and installed in all workstations. Compression in software, on the other hand, allows one to change algorithms with relative ease and cost-free, but it is generally slower than hardware-based compression.

For those already familiar with text compression techniques, we should first note that algorithms have always been less effective for continuous-tone images than for text or line drawings. There are a number of compression algorithm families (most of which are common to both text and images), but we will only mention a few of them here.

The most common techniques for text compression are the statistical algorithms such as run-length coding. These techniques use short symbols to represent frequently occurring patterns. The symbols achieve great compression for textual information but, by themselves, are not very useful for images.

Perhaps the most useful techniques for image compression belong to the transform family. These techniques rely upon a small amount of data to represent a larger block that is similar to it. A form of this is the two-dimensional discrete cosine transform (DCT), which has become the basis for an international standard adopted by the Joint Photographic Experts Group, ISO/IEC JTC/SC2 Working Group 8 (coded representation of picture and audio information). This standard, commonly known as JPEG, combines DCT coding with the removal of components that the human eye cannot see. It is designed specifically for natural scenes and continuous tones. Compression ratios can range from 25:1 to as much as 100:1 (depending on the amount of detail in the image and the desired level of quality). [10, 11] This standard is in its final stages of adoption, and chips implementing the standard have already begun to appear on the market. A related group (MPEG) is at an earlier stage adopting a similar standard for moving images. [12]

Other compression techniques which should be mentioned include the common CCITT Group III FAX (based upon run length coding), the newer Group IV FAX (which has made more of a provision for continuous tone images), and the proprietary Digital Video Interactive (DVI) which uses block pixel replication and interframe compression to compress moving image materials. [13, 14]

How much can we save through compression? That generally depends upon how much quality we are willing to lose. When loss is acceptable, some algorithms give up to 100:1 compression with only a moderate loss in image quality. One useful technique is "subjective redundancy," which uses visual psychophysics to try to remove information from the image in such a way that the human eye cannot perceive the difference.

Lossless compression tends to rely primarily upon the abbreviation of repeating patterns. It therefore works best with images having extensive blank space or large blotches of continuous color. CCITT Group 3 suggest that 2:1 is reasonable to expect from art-type works. Other techniques might achieve as much as 5:1 (depending on the image).

There are a number of compression-related questions that have not yet been adequately explored. For example, will images look better when captured at a very high resolution and then compressed with a moderate amount of loss, or when captured at a lower resolution and compressed using a lossless technique? With topology images, should decompression be done at the image server or at individual workstations? How long a decompression time delay are users willing to tolerate?

Display

How high a resolution do we need for various collections? The only significant study to date was done by the Getty Art History Information Program. [15] This study found that art historians cannot distinguish some quality differences at resolutions beginning at about 800 pixels, and are pretty much unable to detect any differences at HDTV levels (~ 1500). We need more such studies in other environments. We also need to recognize that browse (identification-level) images would be adequate for certain collections and certain groups of users, while much higher resolution will be needed for other combinations of users and collections.

Color balancing also poses a problem. The same image viewed on two similar workstations might be different due to ambient lighting or to the fact that color phosphors dull over time. Some manufacturers (such as Radius) provide a piece of equipment to properly adjust the color balance.

Another significant problem is that different display devices have different phosphors. A particular shade of "red" on one workstation does not necessarily correspond to that same shade of "red" on another workstation. We need to develop a standard that transfers RGB values to CIE coordinates, and to ensure that display manufacturers adhere to the standard.

Networking

As we have shown earlier, the vast size of these images causes a significant delay in moving the image files from centralized storage to a user's workstation. The issue of transmission time is not confined to response time; it also will impact general systems resources in a variety of ways.

Having a large number of users moving large image files around a network is sure to lower network performance, but no one knows by how much. We need to assess that impact. In the real world, networks don't really run at the speed vendors claim. The actual throughput is much less than the claimed rate due to overhead from routing strategies, attempts to avoid collisions, response to interference on lines, etc. And these transmission times get even slower as competition for bandwith rises. We have had little practical experience with saturated networks, but image transmission will create plenty of occurrences because of the huge file sizes. We can expect that sets of images forced to pass through a gateway or router (either at a point near the image server or somewhere else along the network path) are likely to back up there due to the gateway's handling as the images wait for enough bandwidth to pass onto the next part of the network.

Ideally we can assume that the National Research Education Network (NREN) will form a high speed transmission backbone within this decade. But we must remember that not everyone will have a direct connection to NREN. We also must consider how large-scale image delivery will affect local subnets and even the NREN backbone.

Image transmission becomes more viable as networks get faster and faster. But even FDDI speeds are not fast enough for handling a lot of traffic consisting of uncompressed multimedia documents. And, at least for the moment, running FDDI networks will cause bottlenecks at the user's workstation unless users begin to purchase the more expensive workstations (with FDDI capabilities).

Recently, telecommunications companies have announced plans to offer services that will drastically increase the transmission speed of images. Not surprisingly, services offered are targeted at multimedia applications. Large and small business firms may now purchase internetwork services (using SMDS) that achieve 45 MB speeds continuously across the country. At present, the cost of such services are prohibitive to most businesses, but the cost is decreasing as more telecommunications companies offer the service. The entry of large commercial players into this market assures that more research will be done into the problems created by moving large images around a network.

Technical considerations and trade-offs

There are a number of areas in which the choice one makes in system design will greatly affect user satisfaction and system performance. We will just briefly mention several of these here.

Might we consider local storage instead of centralized storage? Duplicating the database at points close to the user (as analog videodisc-based systems often do), eliminates telecommunications overhead for central or shared storage. Response time is enhanced at the cost of redundant storage.

Do all the images have to be readily accessible in full resolution? Could small browsing images be fully accessible online and high resolution versions stored offline (on unmounted optical disks or tapes)? Or could users be required to go to a particular cluster in order to view high resolution versions of these images? This solution would minimize telecommunications and storage problems at the expense of access to full resolution images.

Can we be careful about storing the images closest to their areas of greatest use? This could take the form of redundant storage (see **Storage** above), distributing storage so that images are stored closest to workstations making the heaviest use, or even laying out data on disks such that items frequently viewed in conjunction with one another are physically adjacent (in order to minimize access time).

How long are our users willing to wait to view an image? Instead of citing only network speed, we need to examine the entire system. To obtain the total transfer rate, we need to look at the speed of the network, disk access, display time, decompression time, etc., as well as how any of these may be affected by bus throughput and CPU speed. Ultimately, our system design will not prove effective if response time is beyond our users' tolerance.

DESIGN CHARACTERISTICS

Today, most multimedia databases store their records in individual files by media type. A file might be a full bit-mapped image, a piece of music, or a frame or clip of film. Access is still primarily provided by textual information stored separately from the other media (which are treated merely as attributes that are involved only in the output stage).

This structure (see Figure 4) makes it relatively easy to modify many types of existing search strategies (boolean retrieval, similarity and clustering methods, weight functions, related terms using thesauri, ranking by relevance, etc.) to work with the image

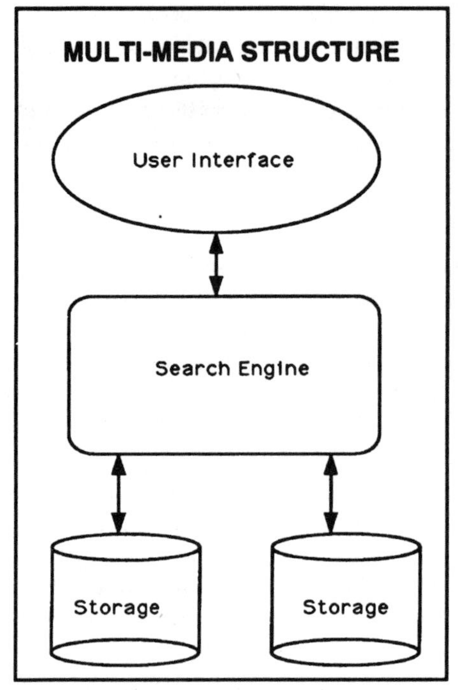

Figure 4.

collections. A designer begins with familiar techniques to create a database of textual information pertaining to the multimedia material. Then, the designer just needs to add additional fields with filename and datatype to the textual database, and provide software to retrieve and display the image. In effect, the implementation of a multimedia database becomes primarily a user interface problem. We will now turn to one such implementation and look at several design features.

Separation of the User Interface from the Database

The Berkeley Image Database System (*ImageQuery*) was designed for a networked campus environment, giving a large number of users remote access to several different image collections [16]. The prototype system allows users to

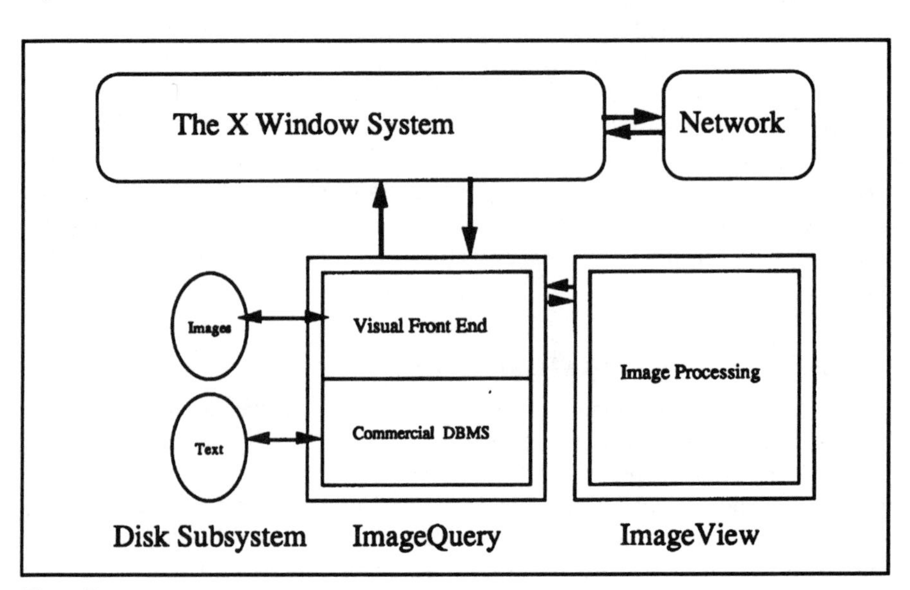

Figure 5.

browse through images in the University Art Museum, the Lowie Museum of Anthropology, the Architecture Slide Library, and the Geography Department's map collection. [17]

The software is structured in a modular format (see Figure 5) in order to take advantage of optimized commercial software. The Visual Front End handles iconic (mouse-based) input and display, and translates these into queries that are sent to a back-end database management system. This modular approach allows the database administrator to select which database management system to place on the back-end. (Options include a built-in, flat-file database and commercial DBMSs such as Ingres and Oracle. Eventually it would be advantageous to build an interface to a full-fledged bibliographic retrieval system.) The separation of image-handling from text retrieval tools allows the system to take advantage of commercial database management systems, on which programmers have spent the last decade developing techniques to optimize performance.

In principle, this system also lets others access the images and data for their own purposes, but only in a very rudimentary way. What will be needed is a well-defined set of standards that will allow others to use the same database while maintaining their own user interface. In this way we could make the interface independent of the data and realize some of the benefits that are promised by standards such as Z39.50.

LOCATING THE PROPER RETRIEVAL SET

We know from indexing experience with online public access catalogs that 60% precision is very good for well-indexed text material. We can expect even less precision with image retrieval due to the difficulty in describing an image adequately, even in 1000 words.

But because image files are so large, precision becomes even more important. Moving huge files around the system, clogging up storage devices and networks, is really not justifiable unless there is a better than 50% chance that the user might really want these.

We can offer two ways of helping to alleviate this problem: browse images and progressive transmission. As we have noted elsewhere, [18] low resolution surrogate browse images should greatly improve precision by allowing the user to visually determine whether a particular image is likely to be useful before actually retrieving the image itself. The movement of browse images through the system is far less taxing on system resources than the movement of high resolution images. This situation is not unlike what we already do with online public access catalogs—transmit brief records until the user asks for a complete record. Of course, eventual implementations of this method should also incorporate caching and anticipation of subsequent requests (as outlined previously in the section on **Storage**).

The likelihood that different users will have different resolution needs poses a dilemma. Few institutions will be able to afford to store an array of different quality versions of each image (from a vague monobit outline to a high resolution color image) and deliver exactly what the user requires. Browse images can be delivered quickly, but are not of sufficient quality for many users. Higher resolution images may be of sufficient quality for all users, but few would be willing to endure the lengthy response time.

An interesting solution to this problem might be progressive transmission, where iteratively better versions of the image are transmitted, giving users the chance to stop the transmissions whenever they become satisfied with the quality. This is roughly analogous to delivering every 10th pixel to the user's screen on the first pass, then every 5th pixel on the second pass, every third pixel on the third pass, etc. The first version transmitted will be a form of browse image, and may be good enough for the user to determine that it is not the desired image. Each subsequent version improves image quality, while using only the minimal system resources necessary to deliver an image of a particular quality. The drafts for CCITT group IV (FAX) standards incorporate progressive transmission features.

Another factor to consider relates to the different display techniques needed when a query retrieves a large number of hits. Obviously, users are just as poorly served when the system displays 1000 browse images as they are when it displays 1000 citations in an online public access catalog. We need to develop techniques to intervene when the retrieval set is too large. One obvious technique is to present a small subset of the total retrieved set and ask the user to rank them in order of preference. The system can then use common attributes of the highest ranking members of the small set in order to rank the entire larger set before presenting it to the user.

SUMMARY

This chapter has examined several of the problems involved in creating an image database, paying particular concern to the problems faced in adding a collection of images to an existing online multiuser environment. Although the problems remain great, we are finally beginning to see the technical and design breakthroughs needed to build and test the various aspects of an image database configuration. We have identified a number of those areas that still need empirical examination, and have suggested a number of approaches that are likely to prove fruitful.

NOTES

1. Portions of this chapter were presented originally as part of the OCLC Distinguished Seminar Series, February 27, 1991.

2. Howard Besser, "User Interfaces for Museums," *Visual Resources* 7 (1991): 293-309 (in press).

3. Michael Alexander, "Data storage: Grace under pressure," *Computerworld* (May 21, 1990): 17.

4. *Image Presentation Guide*, August 1988 (Santa Monica, CA: The Getty Art History Information Program), Mimeographed, 29.

5. William R. Nugent, *Electronic Imaging in High Resolution Gray Scale for Fine Art & Salon Photography* 1-7 (September 11-13, 1990). For Presentation at Optical Information Systems Conference, Crystal City, VA.

6. Michael Ester, "Image Quality and Viewer Perception," *Leonardo* (*Digital Image-Digital Cinema,* Supplemental Issue, 1990): 51-63.

7. Alexander, *op cit.*

8. Howard Besser and Maryly Snow, "Access to Diverse Collections in University Settings: The Berkeley Dilemma", *Beyond the Book: Extending MARC for Subject Access,* edited by Toni Petersen and Pat Moholt (Boston: G K Hall, 1990): 203-224.

9. Robin Raskin, "Multimedia: the next frontier for business," *PC Magazine* 9:13 (July 1990): 112.

10. Jon T. Beck, Mikko J. Oijala, and Lee M. Chen, "A real-time ISDN picturephone implementation using a single chip DSP," *Electronic Imaging '90 West: Advance Printing of Paper Summaries* (Waltham, MA: BIS/CAP International, 1990): 84-87.

11. S.E. Elnahas, R.G. Jost, J.R. Cox, and R.L. Hill, "Progressive Transmission of Digital Diagnostic Images," *Applications of Digital Image Processing,* VIII 575 (Aug 20-22, 1985): 48-55.

12. Raskin, *op cit.*

13. Alexander, *op cit.*

14. A. Wilson, "Packing pixels using image compression," *Computer Graphics World* 13:9 (September 1990): 74-75.

15. Ester, *op cit.*

16. Besser and Snow, *op cit.*

17. Howard Besser, "Visual Access to Visual Images: The UC Berkeley Image Database Project," *Library Trends* 4 (Spring 1990): 787-798.

18. *ibid.*

ACKNOWLEDGEMENTS

I am indebted to Charles DiFatta for the insights he provided to the networking portions of this paper. Discussions with Mr. DiFatta and Clifford Lynch were helpful in examining the design characteristics. Laurie Anderson provided research assistance. Steve Jacobson, Randy Ballew, and Ken Lindahl wrote the *ImageQuery* software. The UC Berkeley Institute for the Study of Social Change provided a workplace and computer equipment.

Howard Besser
School of Library & Information Sciences
University of Pittsburgh
Pittsburgh, Pennsylvania

CHAPTER
5

DIGITAL PRESERVATION: A JOINT STUDY

Anne R. Kenney and Lynne K. Personius

INTRODUCTION

Libraries and archives everywhere face a preservation crisis. The gradual degradation of book and paper production quality since the mid-nineteenth century, combined with exponential increases in book and periodical production, is causing the deterioration of library materials at an alarming rate.

Cornell University Library established a comprehensive preservation/conservation program in 1985. The six units of the Library's Conservation Department engage in a range of preservation activities, including assessment, repair, restoration, and reformatting. The Department responds to local user needs by producing preservation photocopies of brittle books while participating in joint projects with other major institutions in the Research Libraries Group (RLG) to preserve the nation's scholarly resources through preservation microfilming.

A reformatting technology that could combine the desirable qualities of photocopy and film would clearly add an enormously powerful weapon to the preservation arsenal. Thus it is that the digitizing, storing, transmitting, and retrieving of information on demand has the potential to revolutionize preservation technology. Digital image technology makes it possible to separate the medium for storage from the medium for use and access.

For the purposes of this chapter, we define digital image technology as the electronic encoding in digital image form of scanned documents. Whereas the digital image may be compressed for reasons of storage and transmission economy, the text contained in these images or original documents is not converted (for textual interpretation or indexing purposes) to alphanumeric form at the time of scanning (although the potential exists for such conversion, in whole or in part, from the digital images at some later time). When scanned documents are stored as digital images, they can be transmitted at any time across data networks, or converted into other formats, such as printed paper or microfilm.

Thus, digital image technology offers the potential for combining the storage and duplication characteristics of microfilm with the usability of paper facsimiles, and gaining transmission and distribution capabilities not previously available. Digital image technology promises higher quality paper facsimiles than can be produced with standard microform or light-lens photocopying processes.

The Xerox Corporation has developed such technology. The new Xerox technology holds great promise of meeting the requirements of digital preservation for a considerable body of documents that have become, or are in danger of becoming, brittle; and for providing access to such digitally preserved images by producing "paper-on-demand" printed versions and by distribution of the digital images across data networks.

A pilot project is underway to test the applicability of digital image technology to preservation and access. It is a joint effort among Cornell University Library, Cornell Information Technologies, the Commission on Preservation and Access (CPA), and the Xerox Corporation. The CPA contract ensures that the results of the prototype activities shall be made available to the research library community as a whole, so that the potential of digital preservation and access can be more fully evaluated.

PROJECT GOALS

As its general purpose, this project aims to evaluate digital technology and to report on the feasibility of its use for the preservation and access of library materials. The project will result in the digitizing of 1,000 volumes from the Cornell University Library, the production of an equal number of archival quality paper facsimiles, and the testing of access capabilities presented by this new technology. The specific objectives of this project include:

1. **Digital preservation.** Evaluate the process, requirements, benefits and costs of the technology as a means of producing and storing full digital image files for preservation. Determine the benefits and costs of scanning material now with possible transfer to film by Cornell (outside the scope of this project), versus microfilming now and scanning later. Test the feasibility of producing paper copies and microforms on demand as a contribution to the national preservation program.

2. **Production of paper facsimiles.** Test the suitability and cost-effectiveness of new Xerox technology for production of permanent durable paper facsimiles. Perform a systematic analysis and comparison with current technologies for this purpose, in terms of quality and permanence of output, work flows, and costs.

3. **Selection for digital preservation.** Develop criteria for selecting materials appropriate for digital preservation. The characteristics of materials most suitable for digital preservation will be identified based on the experience of faculty and librarians, evaluation of search and retrieval capabilities, and comparison of graphic image quality with that of other media. In addition, during the latter phases of

this project the selection process itself will be evaluated in light of the production capabilities of this new technology.

4. **Bibliographic access to digitally stored materials.** Use or modify existing cataloging conventions for describing digitally stored information. Make recommendations to national bibliographic utilities to insure that this material is readily highlighted in a display of search results.
5. **Electronic Full Image Access.** To be available only in the local library environment.

TARGET COLLECTIONS

Half of the 1,000 volumes to be digitally preserved will come from the Mathematics Library. Cornell's Mathematics Collection is one of the finest in the country, rated at Level 5 in the RLG Conspectus in 32 categories. Level 5 represents a comprehensive collection in which a library endeavors, so far as is reasonably possible, to include *all* significant works of recorded knowledge. This project will reformat 500 mathematics monographs, including the works of significant authors and those volumes that have contributed substantially to the development of the discipline. Each title has been carefully selected for its historical and intellectual significance based on faculty review and citation studies. Although these mathematical classics are in poor condition, they are heavily used locally and much requested by scholars in other libraries throughout the world. Only complete volumes will be used and the librarian and faculty are aware that the original volumes will be disbound and cut in the process. This collection was identified as Cornell's top preservation priority in a February 1989 report to New York State.

ACCESS TO DIGITAL IMAGES

Completion of phases 1 through 4 of the project will result in 1,000 books (documents) being stored in digital form on optical disk. These images will reside on an optical jukebox controlled by a network-attached file server, the Image Server. In addition to the images themselves, the Image Server will maintain a database, the Document Structure File, that defines and describes the documents. This database will specify the images that make up a document; contain some information about the contents of particular images (table of contents, body of text, index, etc.); and store some optional textual description of the document or particular images. The Xerox-provided scanning workstations will communicate directly with the Image Server using Xerox software. The technicians who operate the scanning stations will be able to update images and the Document Structure File, and also to request the printing of a either all or part of a document.

Access by library patrons or other library staff to the digitized material will be the focus of later phases of the project. Phase 5 is concerned with "local" access, which is defined as access from within a library facility. In this phase, a Xerox-provided workstation running Xerox software will be installed in the library. The software is similar to that used for the scanning stations, except that no update of images or the Document Structure File will be permitted. Patrons will be able to search for, view, and request printing of images from the workstation just as the scanning technicians do. A number of experiments are planned for this phase which will provide information on the utility of various functions to library patrons.

Phase 6 is concerned with "campus" access, which is defined as the ability for any patron with a workstation connected to the Cornell network to request delivery of a printed copy of a document. Unlike local access, which assumes a workstation equipped with special hardware to decompress and display images and with Xerox's software to communicate with the Image Server, campus access will provide much more limited availability through an intermediary network server, the Request Server. The Request Server will communicate with both the Image Server and with a patron's workstation. It will provide patrons with information contained in the Document Structure File, but not with actual images. Rather, once patrons identify documents of interest, they may request that all or part of those items be printed and delivered to them. The Request Server will collect billing and delivery information, then forward a print request to the Image Server, which will send the actual images to the printer.

The next level of access would be "national," which would provide the same kind of access as campus access to library patrons beyond Cornell's environs. Beyond this project would be access to actual images or the ability to request printing at a remote printer.

Local Access

Local access is defined as the ability of a patron to use a library workstation to display and read digital images. Local access is being used now by library staff as part of the production process; images are viewed as they are created. Quality assurance is done using the interface delivered as part of the Xerox product, with images being retrieved and replaced as needed.

Using a public access workstation that will be set up in the library, patrons will be able to access the full digital images, to select either a digital document or some previously defined subset of it, and to request that a paper facsimile be produced and delivered. Xerox is providing the workstation and a modified version of the scanning software system that permits retrieval and viewing of images.

Local access intends to provide library patrons with the opportunity to read from a workstation. The experiment will have the following objectives:

- Test capability of ordering printed copies
- Evaluate the value to patrons of ability to view images directly

- Test use of the Document Structure File in access to books
- Experiment with "variant" Document Structure Files (in which patrons can construct their own local versions of the DSF)
- Evaluate the utility of images vs. printed copy.

Campus Access

The model envisioned for campus access to the stored images is that library patrons throughout the campus will be able to determine from the online catalog that a digital image exists, and then to communicate with a separate file server, the Request Server, to obtain a complete or partial printed copy of the item. The Request Server is being provided and its software developed by Cornell University.

When the images making up a book are captured, the action will be noted in the bibliographic record of the online catalog database. Help screens will be available in the online catalog indicating how to make a print request. The patron can then connect via the network to the Request Server and order a printed copy. Alternately, a patron who is interested only in stored images could bypass the online catalog and connect directly to the Request Server. Thus the patron can browse the copy of the Document Structure File stored there to learn for which documents images have been stored.

Any X Windows-capable workstation connected to the Cornell campus network will be able to make a print request. It is envisioned that each library in the Cornell Library system will possess at least one such workstation that is available for public use.

Request Server Functions

The Request Server will function as an intermediary between patrons who wish to request printed copies of images and the Image Server (network file server with attached optical jukebox). The functions the Request Server will perform are:

- Permit the patron to browse the author/title fields of the Document Structure File to determine for which books images have been stored
- Permit the patron to view the contents of the Document Structure File for a particular document to learn more about the contents of the images, including how many pages (images) the document has, or what parts of the document have been labeled as separate structures (table of contents, index, etc.)
- Permit the patron to request printing of all or part of a document
- Provide the patron with a cost estimate
- Collect delivery information (campus address)
- Collect billing information and perform authorization checking (eventual).
- Construct a print job request and forward it to the Image Server (which will construct the actual print job and send it to the printer).

A user interface is being designed and developed that will permit access to the imaged document index from the workstation, allow collection of accounting and delivery information, and provide a straightforward way to request the details of printing and binding options. A desire to have this interface work with the RLG interlibrary loan systems was expressed.

National Access

National access to the images created at Cornell will be accomplished using the RLG database as a national index. All image files will be cataloged in the RLG file. An individual at another RLG institution can discover that Cornell has available a wanted image by searching the RLG database.

For this project, the next step toward acquisition of a personal copy of the "book" will be to contact a local Interlibrary Loan (ILL) Department. Arrangements will be made using a traditional, in-place delivery procedure to acquire a printed copy of the work. The ILL department at Cornell will have equipment that permits its staff members to access the Request Server and request printed copies of books for delivery to other institutions.

PROJECT STATUS

The Cornell/Xerox/Commission on Preservation and Access Joint Study in Digital Preservation has been in operation since January 1990. The first three phases of the project, (Planning, Experimental Test Bed, and Prototype Production) were complete as of April 1991. Cornell and Xerox have collaborated in developing workstation hardware and software specifically designed to meet the needs of a technician doing preservation scanning. All of the necessary equipment to accomplish the project has been delivered and is operating successfully. At this point, books are being scanned and stored, and their images cataloged. The scanning workstation and the DocuTech printing workstation necessary to accomplish this project are in place. Attention is now turning toward improving efficiency and speed in the processing and handling of material. Development and delivery of the image storage facility and development of the server needed to offer access to images are planned.

Anne R. Kenney
Cornell University
Ithaca, New York

Lynne K. Personius
Cornell University
Ithaca, New York

CHAPTER

6

CONVERSION OPTIONS FOR DOCUMENT IMAGE SCANNING

Thomas R. Kochtanek

INTRODUCTION

Information management in today's organizations must find solutions to problems associated with the need to organize and access huge amounts of unstructured data, including both text and images. Sources of such information include the publishing industry, document collections within businesses and libraries, newspaper archives, full text databases, and public information agencies. Technological advances, lowering costs for converting and storing print in electronic formats, and improved access software have provided a base from which to build second order information systems. These systems offer access to a wider array of data and information, including nontraditional unstructured information sources.

One issue in providing access to unstructured information involves the conversion from traditional paper-based sources to electronic representations amenable to computer systems. This issue has attracted the attention of many system vendors and of office automation vendors as they compete for their share of the expanding market.

MARKET TRENDS

The growth of document scanning is illustrated in Table 1. Rapid market growth has stimulated competition among several vendor categories. Major systems vendors such as IBM, Digital Equipment, Hewlett-Packard, Bull, Wang, NCR, and Unisys already offer, or plan to offer, hardware/software platforms for document conversion systems. Office automation vendors, including Kodak, 3M, and Bell & Howell, now market solutions for document imaging and conversion systems. And companies with more focused product lines, such as Filenet and LaserData, are also competing in this market.

Revenues are but one measure of the market for conversion products. Another is the actual volume of potential sources and the shift in storage types. Table 2 depicts some predicted trends in data sources by various media.

TABLE 1. DOCUMENT CONVERSION SYSTEMS: THE MARKET [1]

Year	Expenditures
1987	$100 million
1989	$ 2 billion
1990	$ 3 billion
1992*	$ 5 billion

** forecasted*

These figures indicate a significant shift from both paper-based and from archival microform storage systems to electronic imaging systems. A study conducted by Eastman Kodak estimates that about 21 trillion pages of information are stored in files, desk drawers, and archives. This tremendous volume, combined with the predicted shift toward electronic storage and retrieval systems, portends immense growth in the document conversion marketplace.

TABLE 2. TRENDS IN DATA SOURCES: PAPER, MICROFORM AND ELECTRONIC IMAGING [2]

Media	1989	1999
PAPER	95%	92%
MICROFORM	4%	3%
ELECTRONIC	1%	5%

INDUSTRY TRENDS

There are additional significant trends within the industry. One is a movement towards products assembled from components made by one or more other manufacturers. Traditionally, large computer and office automation companies have manufactured all the components used in an application such as an imaging system. Now these companies are assembling selected components from various sources into comprehensive and well-designed working systems. These "systems integrators" can offer multiple platforms and applications designed for a specific user by interchanging components and software programs across various lines. The result is a configured system designed especially for a given application environment.

A second trend involves the adherence to industry standards. These range from encoding standards, such as the ASCII encoding scheme, to connectivity standards, such as the Open Systems Interconnect (OSI) reference model.

A third trend relates to the increase in the incorporation of microcomputer-based systems for document image conversion, representation, and access. In some situations PC-based workstations are used to capture or convert images, with the workstation connected to a larger minicomputer or mainframe system. In other cases the entire application is based upon a hybrid personal computing system.

Buyers are also looking for complete "off-the-shelf" solutions, not just components they can acquire and graft on locally. Such systems typically include hardware, software, applications, and installation and support services. Products such as the Bell & Howell ImageSearch Plus system are offered as turnkey systems for conversion, representation, and retrieval of documents (text and image) stored as digitized images. Acting as a systems integrator, IBM incorporates Bell & Howell components into a bit-mapped "folder" application called Image Plus. [3] The system can run on various IBM hardware platforms, from the System/36 and the AS/400 all the way up to mainframe computers operating under MVS/ESA. Such applications environments offer high performance, digitizing up to one document page per second, while PC-based solutions typically support conversion rates of 30 to 60 seconds per page.

Nearly 80 percent of the marketed systems support text conversion to standard ASCII storage. [4] Text and image conversion remain a standard feature of most products. Some systems support document decomposition, separating the text from images and storing them as separate but, possibly, linked files. These distinctions between text and images are not always resolved by decomposition.

BIT-MAPPED AND OCR TECHNOLOGIES

Some systems address primarily office automation solutions and rely on what is referred to as "bit-mapped scanning" of document pages. Other offerings scan and convert text files (pages of documents) to standard encoding structures, primarily ASCII. The following examination of these two basic approaches to conversion can help to clarify available offerings.

Bit-mapped Scanning

Bit-mapped scanning is a first step in converting text or image to some digitized form. The bit map of a document page results in a digitized version of the original image capable of being stored electronically—magnetically or optically. Bit-mapped scanners can scan text, image, or both in combination. The quality of the resulting image depends upon a balance between resolution and a gray scale level.

Gray scale refers to the number of shades of gray expressed in representing the original image. The basic unit is the "spot," a cell of at least four dots. Each dot can be black or white, a combination that produces various shades of gray. Increasing the number of dots within the spot supports more gray levels, allowing a better representation of the original image. For example, eight dots support 64 gray shades and 16 dots per spot allow 256 shades or levels of shading.

Resolution is measured in the traditional dots per inch (dpi) and reflects clarity or sharpness of image, the same as it is used to describe TV picture quality. High resolution systems (e.g., 400 dpi) can cost $40,000 to $50,000. Images captured at 200 to 300 dpi can require up to one megabyte to store a single "page," which often necessitates a means to reduce storage requirements by employing compression algorithms.

Image compression algorithms can reduce by 30 to 50 percent the storage requirement for a single page by essentially "taking the white out." These redundant "white bits" can be reintroduced to replicate the original bit-mapped "page" upon retrieval.

One advantage of bit-mapped or digitized scanning is that such technologies are widely available across computing platforms ranging from PCs to mainframes. Bit-mapped scanners need not differentiate between text and images, as they store "pages" not the "content" of pages. Font preservation is invoked and the resulting output can be of archival quality. Resolution qualities can be very high and the resulting output can be stored on high density storage devices such as optical media.

Included among the disadvantages of bit-mapped scanning technologies are the huge storage requirements (in comparison to OCR): a low resolution, bit-mapped image of a single page can easily consume 100K bytes of uncompressed storage. Higher resolution can result in up to one megabyte of storage. Since a scanned document image becomes essentially a digitized replica of the original, page access is the primary means for retrieval. This result implies the creation or derivation of a document surrogate representing the original composition, because the bit-mapped representation of the contents of a "page" cannot be searched via full text access algorithms. The need for a surrogate can lead to additional storage requirements (indexes, abstracts, etc.), errors in representation (e.g., the selection of controlled vocabulary terms to represent the page or document), higher costs, and time delays. [5] A lack of standard access protocols for bit-mapped images is a major limitation of this conversion method. The requirements for bit-mapped scanning systems include the equipment for scanning, the technology for storage and retrieval, and a document surrogate for access.

OCR Scanning

Optical character recognition (OCR) involves a two-step process, resulting in both the mapping of text and its conversion to some standard encoding scheme, usually ASCII. Such conversion processes are only effective with pure text files, and images must be "decomposed," digitized, and stored by other means. Most OCR systems use a light source to illuminate the characters on a printed page—white reflects the illumination and black absorbs the light. A photosensor then translates the black and white segments into analog signals that a scanner processes into binary signals which can be stored electronically.

The key to this process lies within the scanning technology and software. Typical scanning processes involve the matching of digitized text against character patterns stored on disk or in memory. These patterns are mapped to the ASCII coding scheme and the resulting ASCII code is stored for later manipulation. Pattern recognition, the software component of an OCR conversion system, supports the extraction and analysis of features common to certain fonts used in the original documents. Several patented approaches to pattern recognition offer improved conversion effectiveness and efficiency.

Optical character recognition systems are successful only where images (graphs, charts, pictures, photographs, etc.) are not typically included within the document to be scanned. Some OCR solutions offer image decomposition as an option for situations that combine text with graphics or images.

OCR systems typically require lower storage capacities than bit-mapped scanners. A single page of text can be scanned and converted to ASCII storage consuming approximately 3K bytes of storage. The result is a standardized (ASCII) text file representation of the original document or text. This representation supports storage, transmission, and retrieval using full-text retrieval algorithms, such as key word searching, word proximity, and Boolean searching. This support allows many choices of a base technology, including PC-based systems, for user access.

OCR disadvantages include the aforementioned limitation to text-only conversion options. Some text editing may be required after scanning and conversion. OCR generally does not support font or image preservation. The requirements for an OCR system include a OCR scanning device, hardware for storage and retrieval and, possibly, full text access software.

THE MARKET TODAY

Most conversion systems that users have selected operate from minicomputer-based platforms. These document information processing systems can cost between $100,000 and $300,000 depending on the application and the resulting configuration. [6] While the need for high speed document conversion systems will most likely continue, such systems are relatively expensive for many of those smaller organizations that likewise have document information conversion and processing needs.

Developments in microcomputer technology, primarily involving OCR conversion software and hardware, have begun to infiltrate the marketplace. Priced in the $10,000 to $15,000 range, these systems can offer cost effective solutions for certain applications. They can easily be integrated with existing PC applications such as desktop publishing, facsimile transmission, and other general purpose applications. [7] In addition, hand-held scanners offer inexpensive conversion for the smallest applications. [8] Software products, such as WordScan Plus by Calera and OmniPage by Caere, [9] in conjunction with PC-based hardware are filling a market niche in document information processing, primarily for text file conversion applications. Developments will quite likely continue in both ends of the market, and future offerings will no doubt capitalize on the lessons learned by today's vendors and users.

NOTES

1. Independent studies for AIIM by Coopers & Lybrand and by Temple, Barker and Sloan.
2. ibid.
3. G.B. Anderson, "ImagePlus Workstation Program," *IBM Systems Journal*, v.29, no.3 (1990) p. 404.
4. Stanford Diehl and Howard Eglowstein, "Tame the Paper Tiger," *Byte*, (April 1991) pp. 220-238.
5. Christopher Locke, "The Dark Side of Document Information Processing," *Byte*, (April 1991) p. 194.
6. David Silver, "The Evolution of Document Information Processing," *Byte*, (April 1991) p. 188.
7. ibid.
8. Galen Gruman, "Scanning on a Budget," *Infoworld*, v.13, Issue 17 (April 1991) pp. 51-62.
9. Diehl and Eglowstein.

Dr. Thomas R. Kochtanek
Chair, Department of Information Science
School of Library and Informational Science
University of Missouri
Columbia, MO

CHAPTER
7

CREATING A LARGE-SCALE, STRUCTURED DOCUMENT IMAGE UTILITY

Pat Molholt and George Nagy

INTRODUCTION

For decades librarians have applied technology to the problem of harnessing information. Now they are challenged to bring vast numbers of printed documents into electronic form. While progress is being made in creating full text, on-line files, information stored as print-on-paper persists. This chapter discusses a methodology for integrating paper-based information into an electronic environment to improve information services through networked resource sharing.

The project was motivated by the convergence of several problems facing librarians and other information handlers. Foremost was concern over the need to integrate paper-based information into the electronic environment. Computer-based databases of index and abstract material, and CD-ROM corollaries, provide users with tools that point to vast amounts of paper-based information.

Unfortunately, only rarely—such as with the on-line public access catalog (OPAC)—do electronic databases become integrated with other information services. Even in the quasi-electronic OPAC environment, users must leave the workstation and go to the library's shelves or, in a growing number of cases, to the interlibrary loan desk to obtain the actual information. On the one hand, users are inconvenienced by having to move between electronic and paper versions; on the other hand, due to increased subscription costs and limited storage space, libraries are finding it increasingly difficult to maintain comprehensive paper-based journal collections. Having separate systems and, often, separate staffs for paper and electronic information is ineffective and inefficient for both the user and the library. The more closely we can integrate these environments the greater the benefit to all concerned, but doing so is expensive, despite technological advances.

A second need comes into play with this project—to provide improved access to print materials, especially the content, including graphs, charts, images, and other illustrations. With increased reliance on information resource sharing, users are best served in their quest for access to remote materials if they can ascertain that the item truly contains information relevant to their need, whether the item is stored a mile off-site, or 1,000 miles. In the case of journal articles, if users can browse the images of the article they should be able to learn quickly whether the article is indeed useful and worth retrieving. Early efforts at electronic document transmission include telefacsimile, but the need to physically locate, retrieve, copy, and transmit the item results in only a small savings; the resultant electronic image is incidental only to the delivery process and lost as soon as the fax is printed out. While it is true that some faxing is done into computer files, all the work at the front end of the process benefits only one requester. Should the same item be asked for a day later, the process must be repeated.

The third issue, preservation of paper-based information, has been with us for several decades and continues to threaten us—not only from the standpoint of the durability of the paper, but also the lack of shelf space. Building new libraries is costly and is becoming an increasingly rare alternative. Even storage facilities, if they are truly to preserve the material, not just warehouse it, can be expensive.

It is, then, the convergence of these needs and the options afforded by electronic processing, storage, and retrieval of information that led to this collaboration between the ongoing research in the DocLab at Rensselaer and Rensselaer's Libraries.

Alternative methods of delivery of computer-based information have been explored, some more successfully than others. The scanning and storing of full page images on CD-ROM is economical and the format of the material, including its graphics, is preserved. Such a resource, however, best serves only a single user. Although numerous instances of networked CDs exist, they are far from trouble free. Transmitting full page images at high resolution taxes even the fastest network. Another alternative has been the creation of ASCII files using optical character recognition (OCR). The accuracy of OCR is limited by the nature of the material, its quality, contrast, the page layout, and, in particular, the type font used in the document. A high rate of accuracy requires considerable post-editing. In addition, graphics in the form of illustrations, graphs, charts, formulas, and equations cannot be included. Given this range of problems, our project developed a compromise solution.

PROJECT OVERVIEW

This project builds on the work of the Document Imaging Group in the School of Engineering at Rensselaer. The collaboration with the library provided an application focus, and as we near the end of the two-year Higher Education Act, Title II-D Research and Demonstration grant, all involved agree that the exchange of perspectives and expertise has proved beneficial.

The work aims to digitize journal pages; automatically identify selected elements of each page such as the title, abstract, and captions beneath illustrations; convert the selected elements into ASCII for possible OPAC merge; and link the scanned document to the appropriate OPAC citation. In operation, the user should be able to search an

OPAC containing journal citations and, upon finding one of interest, move from the OPAC to the actual page image of the document selected. It is anticipated that the creation of the document image utility would be done on a cooperative basis, much like retrospective conversion of catalog records, and that the file would be shared by accessing a remote file server. Issues of copyright, access fees, and the like are not within the scope of this project.

METHODS AND TECHNIQUES

A variety of steps are needed to create the kind of document image our system calls for—movement from a paper-based journal article into the electronic medium of the computer requires exacting work at all stages of the process. The work can be divided into three general stages: pre-scanning preparation, scanning, and post-scanning analysis.

Preliminary to scanning even a single page of text, block grammars were written to match the title page, intermediate pages, and the last page of articles in two journals, the *IEEE Transactions on Pattern Analysis and Machine Intelligence (IEEE PAMI)* and the *IBM Journal of Research and Development.* These grammars contain rules that address the typical content of pages such as the presence of a full title on the first page or a running title on subsequent pages, and the location of references on the last page, including whole pages of references in the case of review articles. After these gross level determinations were made for each of the journals, sub-block grammars were written. Elements such as the title, abstract, authors' names, etc. are called blocks. Sub-block grammars define in detail how the authors' names are arranged, the size and type font used, and the physical location of the block relative to other blocks, such as the title and the abstract.

In addition, a single logical entity such as a paragraph of text may be found in many forms: a single column, a double column, split between pages, right justified, not justified, etc. To deal with these variations, "entity grammars" are written specific to each journal. Entity grammars deal with blocks that have the same label (e.g. title, author) but have a variant form from journal to journal. Further, some of the entity grammars were necessitated because of changes in printing conventions that occur over the years, changes that may not be noticed by humans—a slight alteration in the size or location of the title block, for example—but that wreak havoc with a computer program that expects something else.

The object of the grammars is to identify and demark the spatial structure of the document page and to label the elements or blocks of the document. These processes are sometimes referred to as segmentation and classification. Thirty-nine sub-block grammars were written for our set of twenty title and nontitle pages of *IEEE PAMI*.

After the grammars are written, journal pages are scanned on a black and white flatbed scanner at 300 dots per inch. In this project, with the publisher's permission, some pages were taken from a CD-ROM in digitized form. Adjustments for skew must be made to accomplish near perfect right angle alignment. If this is not done, the program that reads the pages pixel-by-pixel will not be effective. For example, if the page is not properly aligned, the parsing program will run into text (colored pixels) when it should find clear lines between text. Of the 20 pages scanned for this project, only one text page was rejected because of significant skew problems.

After a page is scanned and before it is analyzed, extraneous marks such as paper flaws and spots from a bad photocopy or bad printing have to be removed. This is done automatically and actually results in the removal of some punctuation and the dots on i's and j's, for example. For the parsing grammar these omissions are unimportant. All removed marks are replaced before the selected blocks of the document are seen by users or moved into the OCR stage.

Next, the page is partitioned by horizontal divisions into header, text, and footer sections. Each of these blocks is then further partitioned vertically. The process of successive horizontal and vertical division continues to the level of individual lines in a paragraph. Figure 1 illustrates the result of this process.

The basis for division is the examination of sequences of zeros and ones that correspond to blank and nonblank rows or columns of pixels. After the location of a partition in one direction is determined, the sequence of pixels in the other direction is extracted from each of the blocks resulting in the subdivision.

Four processing stages move the image from the pixel to the labeled block stage: atom generation, molecule generation, labeling, and merger. Stage one involves atom generation. In this stage a program written in C language counts the length of all the one and all the zero strings that have been read and assigns them to a class according to their length.

In stage two, groups of contiguous atoms, or sequences of ones and zeros, are assigned to larger units called molecules. In stage three these molecules are assigned candidate labels, such as a title or abstract. The assignment is made on the basis of the block and sub-block grammars. Rules, such as "only one title exists on a page and it is above any subtitles," help the system assign permanent labels.

By stage four, the labeling stage, strings have been segmented and labeled. Some blocks that belong together, such as text, may have been separated in the page layout by a wide white space that the system first reads as a new entity. This final stage merges contiguous entities or blocks that have the same label. Figure 2 shows a segmented and labeled page.

PERFORMANCE AND IMPROVEMENTS

With current methods and equipment the parsing or analysis of a single page of a document can take from two to four minutes. On a Sun workstation it is anticipated that the time could be reduced by recoding some of the routine instead of using parsing tools designed for general use and by using parallel parsing hardware. Other enhancements might include partial automation of the process of developing block grammars for new

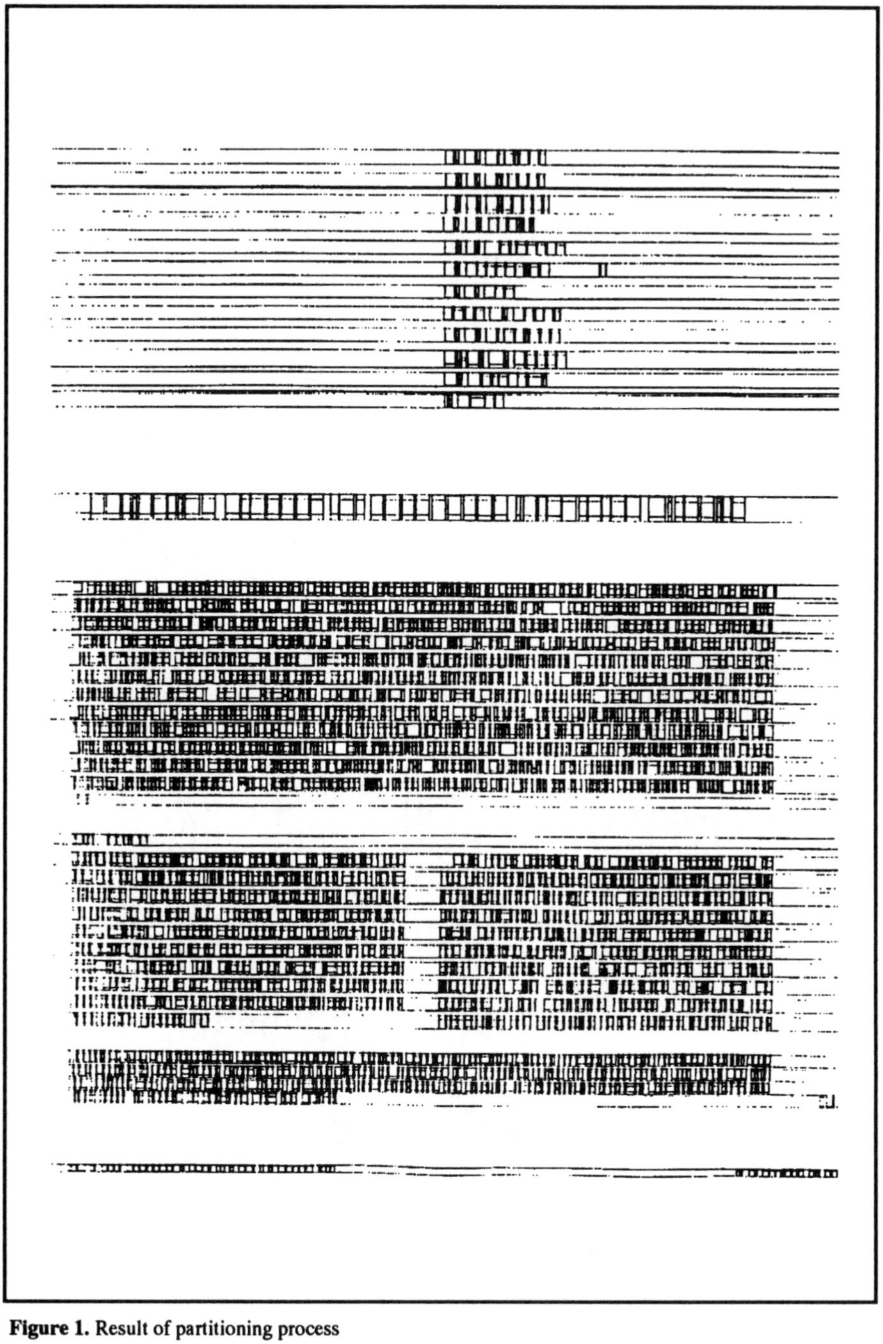

Figure 1. Result of partitioning process

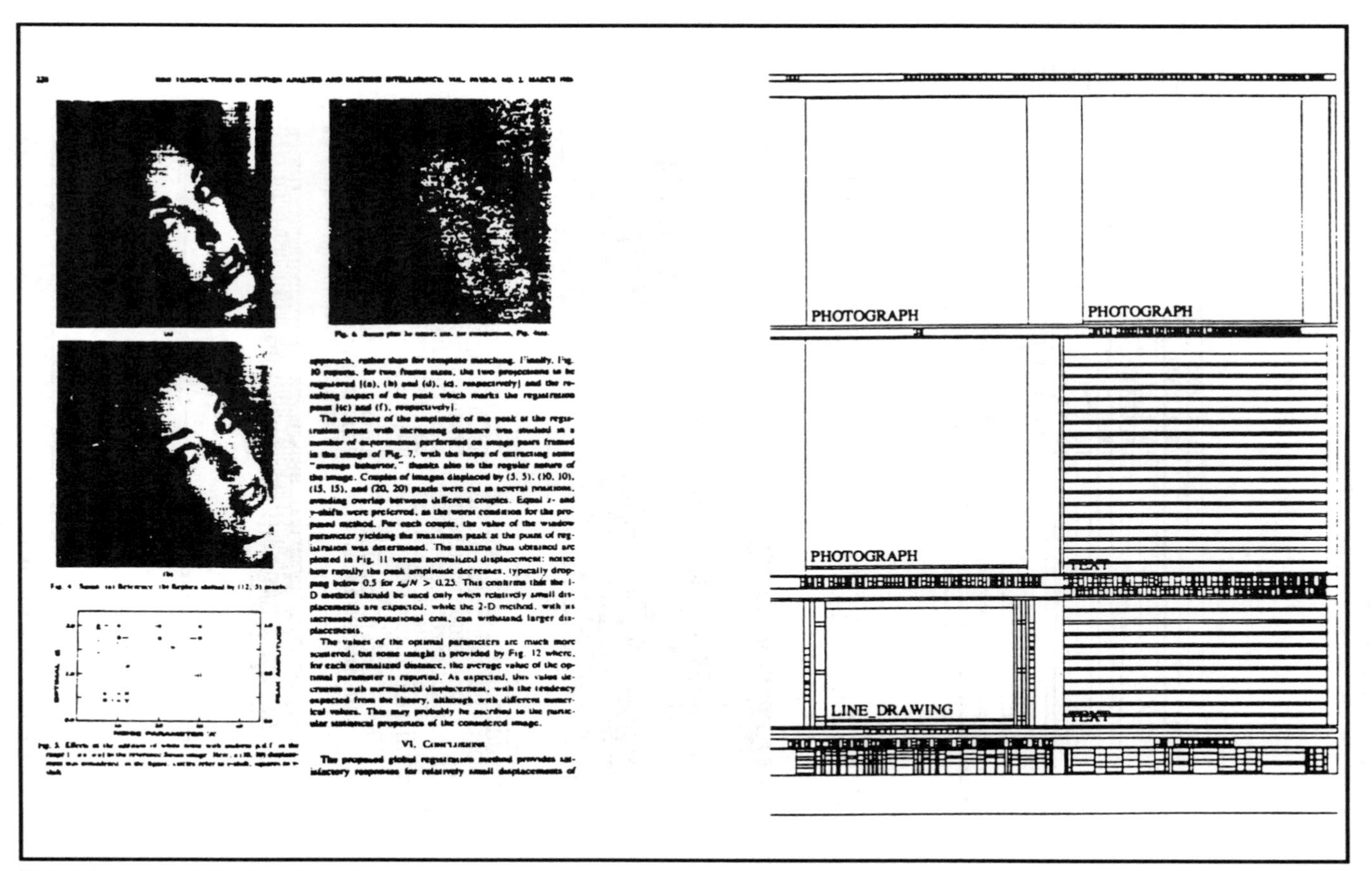

approach, rather than for template matching. Finally, Fig. 10 reports, for two frame sizes, the two projections to be registered [(a), (b) and (d), (e), respectively] and the resulting aspect of the peak which marks the registration point [(c) and (f), respectively].

The decrease of the amplitude of the peak at the registration point with increasing distance was studied in a number of experiments performed on image pairs framed in the image of Fig. 7, with the hope of extracting some "average behavior," thanks also to the regular nature of the image. Couples of images displaced by (5, 5), (10, 10), (15, 15), and (20, 20) pixels were cut in several positions, avoiding overlap between different couples. Equal x- and y-shifts were preferred, as the worst condition for the proposed method. For each couple, the value of the window parameter yielding the maximum peak at the point of registration was determined. The maxima thus obtained are plotted in Fig. 11 versus normalized displacement: notice how rapidly the peak amplitude decreases, typically dropping below 0.5 for $x_d/N > 0.25$. This confirms that the 1-D method should be used only when relatively small displacements are expected, while the 2-D method, with its increased computational cost, can withstand larger displacements.

The values of the optimal parameters are much more scattered, but some insight is provided by Fig. 12 where, for each normalized distance, the average value of the optimal parameter is reported. As expected, this value decreases with normalized displacement, with the tendency expected from the theory, although with different numerical values. This may probably be ascribed to the particular statistical properties of the considered image.

VI. Conclusions

The proposed global registration method provides satisfactory responses for relatively small displacements of

Figure 2. A segmented and partitioned page

journals, and introducing feedback from the OCR stage to improve the accuracy of the layout analysis.

SUMMARY

In addition to the library application discussed here, these techniques would serve to enhance information access and retrieval in several other areas. We often fail to recognize the amount of information conveyed by complex document layouts. Preserving layouts, as well as graphics, provides users of technical journals, reports, repair manuals, specifications, textbooks, and other layout-rich information with a more complete rendering of the resource. The techniques also can be used as a preprocessor for optical character recognition, in compression for transmission or storage of images, and digital reprographics. There is also the possibility to recover formatting codes, a kind of inverse formatting, from the block and sub-block information gathered in the parsing process.

This project has demonstrated, with a working model operational at Rensselaer, that the concepts are viable. Images can be scanned and analyzed, labeled, and linked to an OPAC. For such a project to be successful on a national, or even a regional basis, considerable effort must be applied to resolving issues of copyright as well as developing appropriate economic and access protocols.

NOTES

This project was funded in part by a two-year Higher Education Act, Title II-D grant awarded by the U.S. Department of Education, Office of Library Programs.

Pat Molholt
Associate Director of Institute Libraries
Rensselaer Polytechnic Institute
Troy, New York 12180-3590

George Nagy
Professor, Electrical, Computer and Systems Engineering
Rensselaer Polytechnic Institute
Troy, New York 12180-3590

CHAPTER

8

HYPERTEXT IMAGE RETRIEVAL: THE EVOLUTION OF AN APPLICATION

G. Louis Roberts

INTRODUCTION [1]

Begun in 1988 as a small, simple "proof-of-concept," this project has evolved into multiple production systems. The scope of interest and applicability of these systems have subsequently extended far beyond the designer's initial forecasts.

The project involved two organizations that needed to develop a responsive photograph retrieval system. The solution involved a proof-of-concept system, a pilot, and four phases of production implementation. Image, hypertext, and full text retrieval were the main technologies employed in the solution.

The project supports the business of the Boeing Commercial Airplane Group, specifically the efforts in Manufacturing Research and Development (MR&D) and the Quality Assurance Research and Development (QAR&D). The solution was developed internally by Applied Media Technologies, an organization within Boeing Computer Services. The images and data contained within the system are proprietary and intended only for internal company use. The phasing of the project is shown in Figure 1.

Customer

The customer is Boeing Commercial Airplanes Operations Technology, whose charter is to "Enable Boeing Commercial Airplane Group to be the industry leader in commercial transport airplanes by developing, implementing, and continuously improving manufacturing and quality assurance processes, and by assuring engineering design producibility."

Within Operations Technology, two client organizations use the image retrieval system described in this chapter. The business of MR&D is engineering design producibility. QAR&D exploits existing and emerging technologies to create improved quality assurance systems.

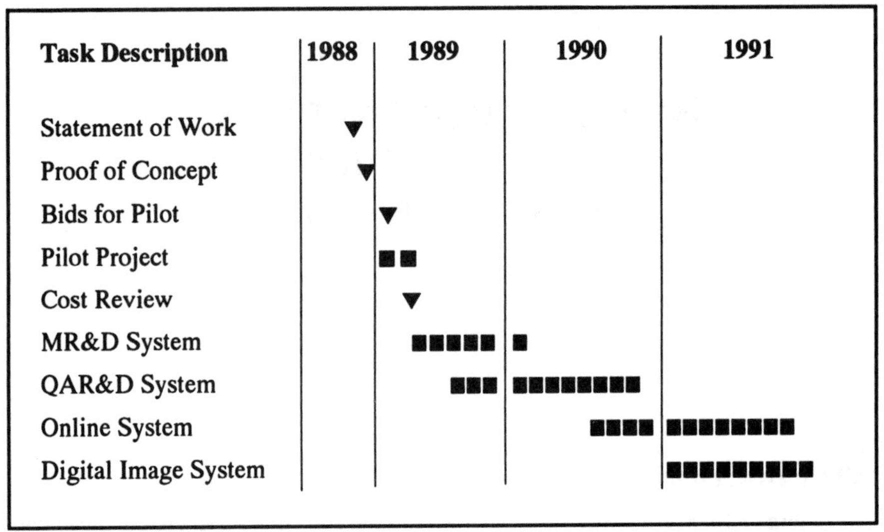

Figure 1. Project Schedule

Developer

The image retrieval system was developed by the Applied Media Technologies (AMT) organization, a part of Boeing Computer Services. AMT designs and implements business information retrieval solutions throughout the Boeing family of companies, specializing in the application of full text, hypertext, and imaging technologies.

Business Problem

Both organizations had accumulated a substantial inventory of pictures of machines, processes, procedures, and products, acquired over the 75-year history of the Boeing Company. Each client had been manually indexing and retrieving photographic images for that time.

Manufacturing Research & Development had over 40,000 photographs that users retrieved from a multidrawer "wall of files." The files were indexed in a three-inch index binder, which contained literally thousands of categories and subcategories of images. A copy of each image, together with an engineer's free-text description of the image contents, was kept on a 5-in. by 7-in. file card. See Figure 2.

Quality Assurance Research & Development's system used McBee *Keysort* cards. Seven major attributes of the photograph were coded numerically, each decimal code denoting a controlled vocabulary image attribute. In addition, the card contained an uncoded file number, program number, date, and engineer identity. See Figure 3.

Although different from one another, each system addressed similar needs: retrieval of photographs from a large archive. Both systems worked well only when they were

Category		Date	PHOTOGRAPH
Negative Number	*Both*		
	Color		
	Black & White		
REMARKS			

Figure 2. Manufacturing Research & Development Image Card

small. As the number of photographs increased, both had problems in the ability to locate specific photographs. For example, the engineering users who needed to retrieve only one or two images a month were unfamiliar with the filing system and found the system too cumbersome for their infrequent use; those retrieving several dozen images daily found the system lacked sufficient power.

Because of these problems, there was an increasing tendency not to use the manual system. Rather than searching the archives for a picture of a specific process, engineers instead called for a photographer. Newly photographed images were then categorized, indexed, and entered into the photo archives. This *worsened the retrievability problem* by increasing the archive size as well as adding to embedded costs.

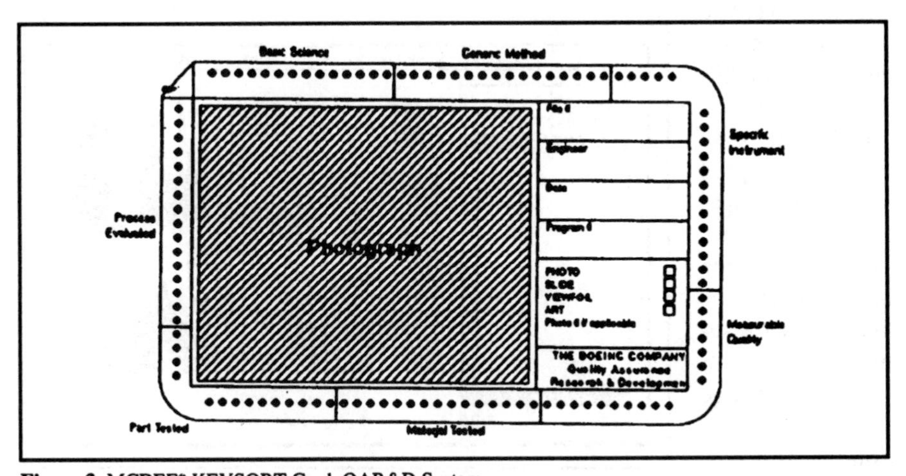

Figure 3. MCBEE* KEYSORT Card, QAR&D System

FUNCTION	ARCHITECTURE ELEMENT
Hardware Platform	Macintosh Plus
User Interface	HyperCard
Image Presentation	Mac screen, monochrome, 72 DPI
Indexing	HyperCard's "find" command
Network Environment	None (stand alone system)

Figure 4. Proof-of-Concept Architecture

PROOF-OF-CONCEPT

The initial proof-of-concept system was written in HyperCard, running on a Macintosh Plus computer. The user interface replicated the file card format that the MR&D engineers were familiar with (Figure 2), but substituted a scanned, black-and-white image for the color photograph. The architecture is as shown in Figure 4.

In the proof-of-concept, each text field was made sensitive to mouse clicks, so that users might navigate from topic to topic using point-and-click hypertext word retrieval, as well as simple card-by-card browsing through the use of "forward" and "back" navigation shown at the top of the card. See Figure 5.

The image shown in Figure 5 is of poor quality. Nonetheless, the engineers viewing the system for the first time were so pleased by the increased retrievability the system provided that they eagerly accepted poor quality images as "production." When told that the intent is to provide much higher resolution images, in full color, on a large screen, they became excited!

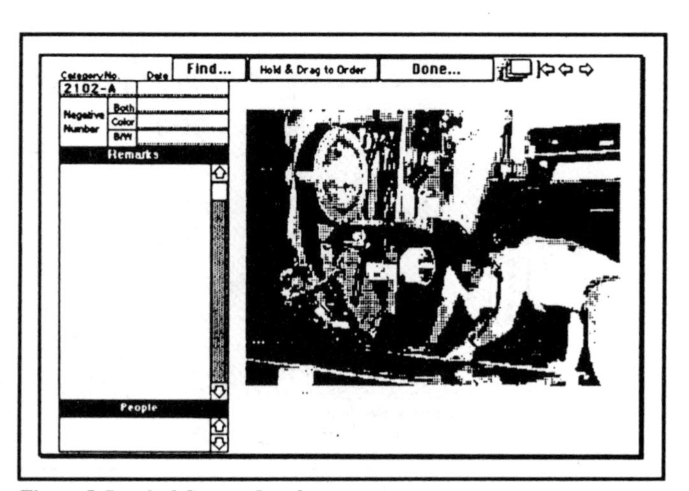

Figure 5. Proof-of-Concept Interface

FUNCTION	ARCHITECTURE ELEMENT
Hardware Platform	Macintosh Plus
User Interface	HyperCard
Image Presentation	Mac screen, monochrome, 72 DPI
Indexing	HyperCard's "find" command
Network Environment	Ethernet File Server (VAX)

Figure 6. Pilot Architecture

PILOT

The pilot system was similarly developed with HyperCard and a Macintosh Plus computer, using the architecture shown in Figure 6.

One thousand images were selected from MR&D's image archive. These images were photographed onto 35mm motion picture film using an animation camera. The resulting film was edited, transferred to videotape, and pressed onto a videodisc. See Figure 7. As each image was photographed, the data accompanying the image was typed into the various fields shown in Figure 2. All images were entered during a single photo session. [2]

The ability to control a Level 3 laserdisc player was added to the pilot application. [3] (Rather than using a commercial third-party set of laserdisc drivers, XCMDs [4] were used to directly control the Mac's serial port and to transmit any arbitrary byte string. Thus, the interface could cause the player to perform *any* function supported by its command set and not be limited to, or perhaps compromised by, functionality that a driver might provide.) Retrieved images were then viewed by connecting the laserdisc player to a conventional 9-inch color television monitor.

When the pilot laserdisc was returned from the pressing plant, engineering users and photo archivists participated in field trials so that client feedback could be incorporated into the interface. Management was presented a "live demo" of the prototype system and they authorized proceeding with production implementation.

PRODUCTION PHASE 1: MR&D

Because it had the largest number of images and the largest user community, MR&D was chosen as the initial production user group. Over a period of several weeks, 40,000 images were photographed and identified with a frame number. Over the next several months, the text data that accompanied each image was entered into the system data files.

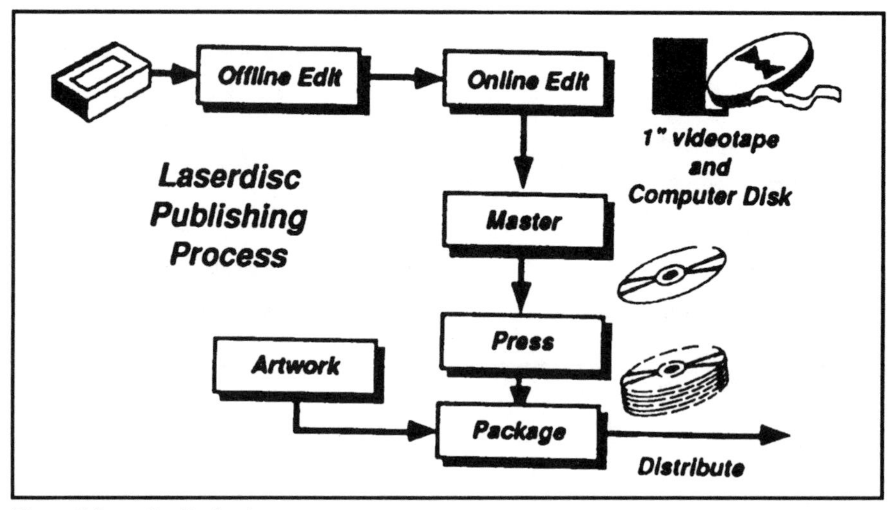

Figure 7. Laserdisc Production

Help screens were added, as well as screens to display MR&D's Organizational Policy and Procedure for image requests. Its entire three-inch binder of index categories and subcategories was ultimately placed on-line and made searchable with point-and-click retrieval functionality. Each category from the binder was linked to separate files containing descriptive details of each image. Figure 8 shows the architecture.

Functions

System functions are divided into separate files (HyperCard "Stacks") to make maintenance easier. HyperCard's "find" command makes retrieval easier. Each stack icon represents a file. The central drawing of 35mm slides represents the main photo archive:

FUNCTION	ARCHITECTURE ELEMENT
Hardware Platform	Macintosh Plus
User Interface	HyperCard
Image Presentation	TV Monitor, High resolution color
Indexing	HyperCard's "find" command
Network Environment	None (stand alone system)

Figure 8. Phase 1 Architecture

many stacks are required here. Each stack might contain data describing as many as 1500 photographs. The sole function of the Category Selector is to support navigation among the many files comprising the photo archive. See Figure 9, System Overview Interface.

Scenario: Use of Phase 1 System

The system is not (and was never intended to be) an image *delivery* system, but *is* an image *access* system, used to *view* images, so that they might be selected for ordering. It might be used as described in the following scenario.

An engineer wishes to illustrate a presentation by showing photographs of several steps in a manufacturing process. In the old, manual files system, several hours of searching might be needed. Instead, using a Photo Retrieval workstation, the engineer views an on-screen representation of Figure 9, which is the first screen of the retrieval application.

At point of first use, the "You are here" is flashing, located as shown. The engineer then clicks on the "Category Selector," enters criteria, and then retrieves a group of images relative to that category: "fastening" for example. At this point, more criteria are entered, to further refine the search: "riveting tools," for example. Images are displayed; and one or more is chosen. Stock numbers for the images are appended to an order list, for routing at a later time.

The user might then visit the Category Selector again, to choose a new category of images, which would in turn be added to the order form being built. Eventually, the user would print the order form, which would then be routed for any approval signatures needed, so that the original negatives might be retrieved from archives.

The system was designed from initial conception to function in Boeing's complex

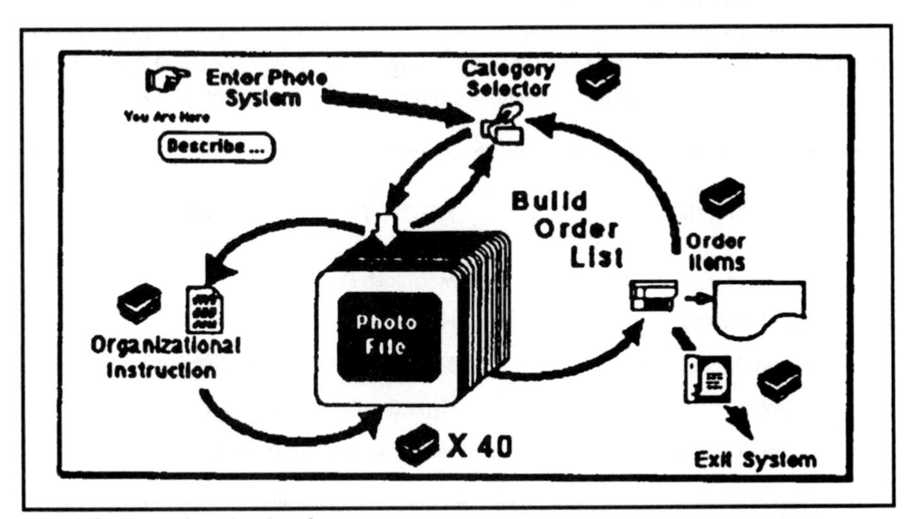

Figure 9. System Overview Interface

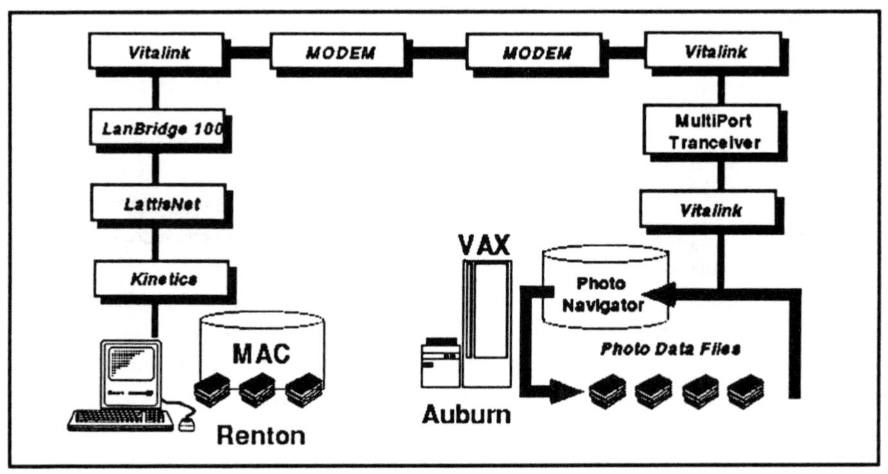

Figure 10. Proof-of-Concept Network Path

computing environment. Figure 10 shows the data files stored on a minicomputer file server and distributed via Ethernet. *Many* separate pieces of hardware were required to move images between the two plant sites in the Proof-of Concept.

PRODUCTION PHASE 2: QAR&D

Phase Two focused on Quality Assurance Research & Development. While users evaluated the first phase of production, capture began for the QAR&D's images. The architecture is shown in Figure 11.

Because this group had developed a controlled vocabulary, its use led to a very different user interface than the MR&D System. Figure 12 shows QAR&D's data being entered using a point-and-click mechanism, rather than by text entry on a keyboard.

FUNCTION	ARCHITECTURE ELEMENT
Hardware Platform	Macintosh Plus
User Interface	HyperCard
Image Presentation	TV Monitor, High resolution color
Indexing	HyperCard's "find" command
Network Environment	None (stand alone system)

Figure 11. Phase 2 Architecture

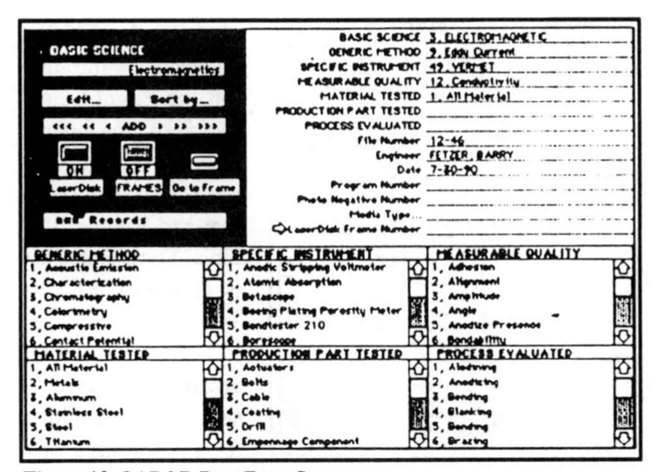

Figure 12. QAR&D Data Entry Screen

The QAR&D System uses multiple scrolling lists to select attributes of a specific image. The lower half of the screen provides six lists of selectable attributes. A record is built as list items are selected; the complete list is displayed in the upper right corner of the panel. The upper left corner of the panel contains control mechanisms: the basic science category is "Electromagnetics;" the number of records shows as "nnn." The interface includes control buttons to turn the laserdisc player on and off as well as to control the display of the physical frame numbers.

During index creation, the long, narrow "ADD" button lets archivists browse the laserdisc in several modes, including multispeed fast-forward or reverse, as well as frame-by-frame. When the image displayed on screen matches the image "in hand," an archivist clicks directly on the word ADD. The laserdisc is interrogated for frame number; that number is added to the record; and the completed data record is then appended to the file. Choosing the "Sort by..." pull-down menu arranges the data by any record category and moves a small arrow pointer icon to the newly sorted field.

"Stacks" store the seven major image categories; as shown in Figure 13 the "Basic Science" box functions as a pull-down menu to allow navigation between categories. The *eighth* choice allows the user to transfer to the Manufacturing Research & Development System.

PRODUCTION PHASE 3: ONLINE SYSTEM.

Based on abundant formal and informal feedback, the users were satisfied with their systems for about a week. Then their new capabilities led to an expansion of their requirements. "Wouldn't it be nice if we could..." began to be heard. In addition, both user communities recognized advantages provided by the "other group's" interface. The requirement for "global searching" across all image categories emerged, as well as the need for more powerful, Boolean information retrieval.

Architecture

A mainframe solution met the expanded retrieval requirements. It also gave all users within Boeing's wide-area network access to the descriptive text that accompanied the

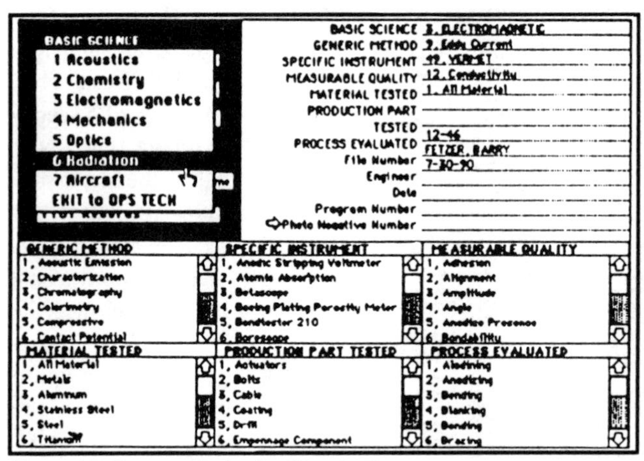

Figure 13. Category Navigation Menu In Use

photographs. This includes users throughout the Puget Sound region of Washington State; Wichita, Kansas; Huntsville, Alabama; and Vienna, Virginia. The architecture is as shown in Figure 14.

A client-server architecture was chosen. The application took advantage of a high level language application programming interface (HLLAPI) provided by the vendor of the 3270 terminal emulation hardware. See Figure 15.

HLLAPI allows the application to communicate over an SNA coaxial line without needing to "know about" the low level details of 3270 packet protocols. Another benefit is that all communications between host application and workstation interface can be thought of as occurring within an invisible, virtual "presentation space" between the two platforms. See Figure 16.

Platform

The Macintosh II hosted the interface. (The prototype and pilot work done on the Macintosh Plus transported easily and additional connectivity options, via NuBus cards,

FUNCTION	ARCHITECTURE ELEMENT
Hardware Platform	Macintosh Plus
User Interface	HyperCard
Image Presentation	Television Monitor
Indexing	BRS/SEARCH
Network Environment	SNA, 3270

Figure 14. Phase 3 Architecture

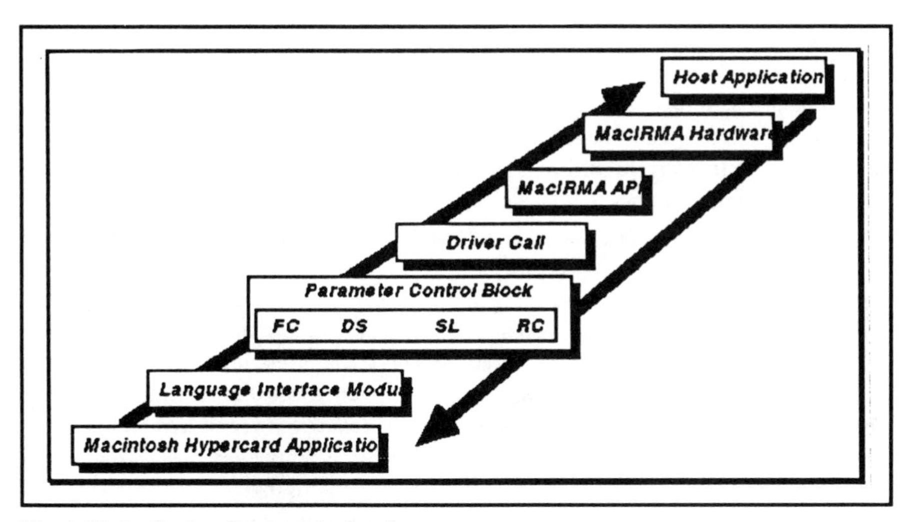

Figure 15. Applications Programming Interface

were available.) BRS SEARCH (running under MVS-CICS on an IBM 3090) provided the retrieval services and pointers to image frames stored on a laserdisc.

Features

With the photographs' text descriptions available on-line, anyone with access to the

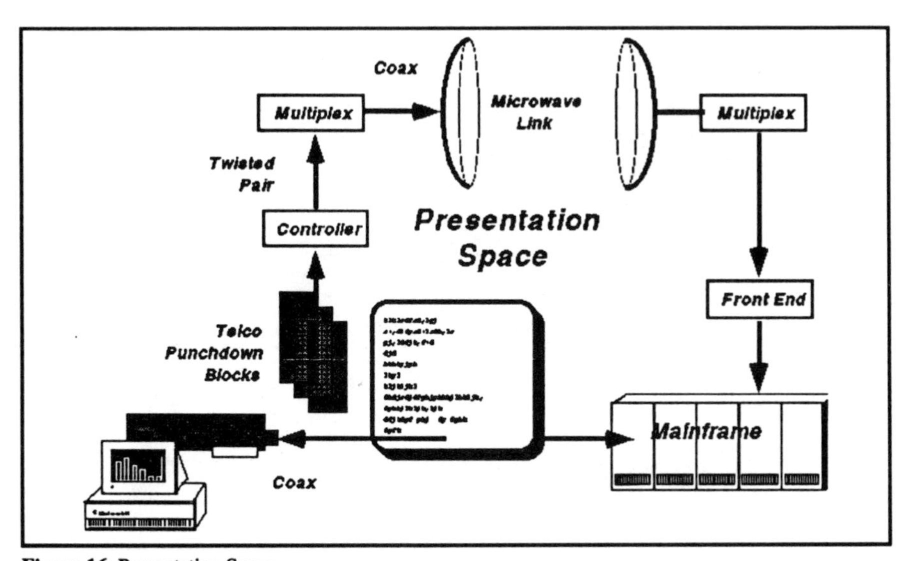

Figure 16. Presentation Space

network and appropriate permission can make *some* use of the system. Users with only "dumb terminal" access can use a mainframe-based MENTOR system of menus [5] to determine that an image of potential interest exists. Although they cannot view images, the user can still use the system for research and be provided with enough data to decide whether to investigate further. The system is therefore useful even to those users without the interface software, a laserdisc, or a Macintosh.

With only slight differences, the final interface echoes the appearance of the MR&D System. See Figure 17.

The multispeed laserdisc browsing button from QAR&D's interface is used, with a slight change in function: rather than "ADD" (invalid in a "read-only" environment) the central function is "???" If a user randomly spins the laserdisc to any particular frame, and is interested in the image, clicking on the "???" interrogates the mainframe database. The resulting information is then presented, thereby *telling the user which image is displayed*, and its associated details. Users *love* this feature! Immediately below, a button hides or shows the "native SEARCH" results. Although originally used for design and debugging purposes, it remains in the end user version because some users liked to "view the details."

Global Retrieval

The architecture of both systems supports retrieval *within* categories well: all images relevant to a particular type of instrument or process can be readily accessed with acceptable speed, using HyperCard's "find" command. Neither system, however, addresses retrieval *across* categories, since the "find" command only operates within a single HyperCard stack.

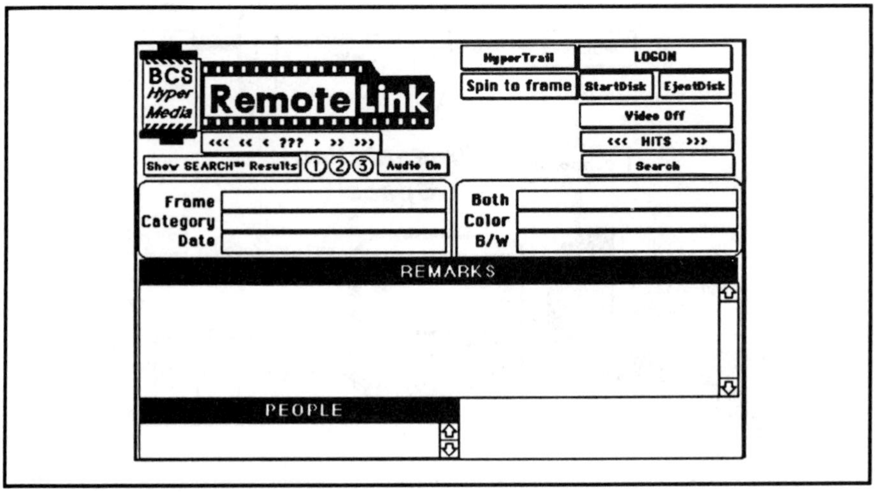

Figure 17. Network Interface

An example of an "across" query might be "locate all the images associated with a particular engineer." Depending on the length of the engineer's career, such a query might span dozens of categories or more. By combining all the data from both systems into a single online system, global retrieval is easily achieved. The single online system also facilitates control of the information's quality, using global search and replace editing on the input text files. The phases of information pooling are shown in Figure 18.

Video

The three round, numbered buttons (see Figure 17) control the laserdisc directly. Button One causes all MR&D documents to be displayed ("Chapter One" on the disc). Similarly, Button Two causes all QAR&D documents to be displayed ("Chapter 2"), and Button Three causes a full motion video to be shown that describes how to use the system.

Query Entry

Clicking on the "Search" button in the lower margin of the "control panel" displays Query Entry, shown in Figure 19. Using this panel, key words or phrases may be field-qualified so that their retrieval may be limited to particular fields. In this example, the word "GEMCOR" is being sought, limited to the data subset identified as the "Remarks" field.

Hypertext

Figure 20 shows a "HyperTrail" button in the upper right quadrant of the interface. At any time, on any screen (even the "native SEARCH" results screen, as shown) users may double-click on a word to simulate opening a hypertext link to a location elsewhere in the text. Behind the scenes, these links are implemented using BRS SEARCH results. The word representing the opening anchor point is picked off the screen based on the

Phase	Information Pooling	Result
Proof-of-Concept	None; one category only	1 stack
MR&D Pilot	37 separate categories entered	37 stacks
QAR&D System	7 additional categories	7 stacks
Online System	37 seperate categories merged	sibling database
	7 categories merged	sibling database
	37 + 7 categories merged	parent database

Figure 18. Information pooling phases

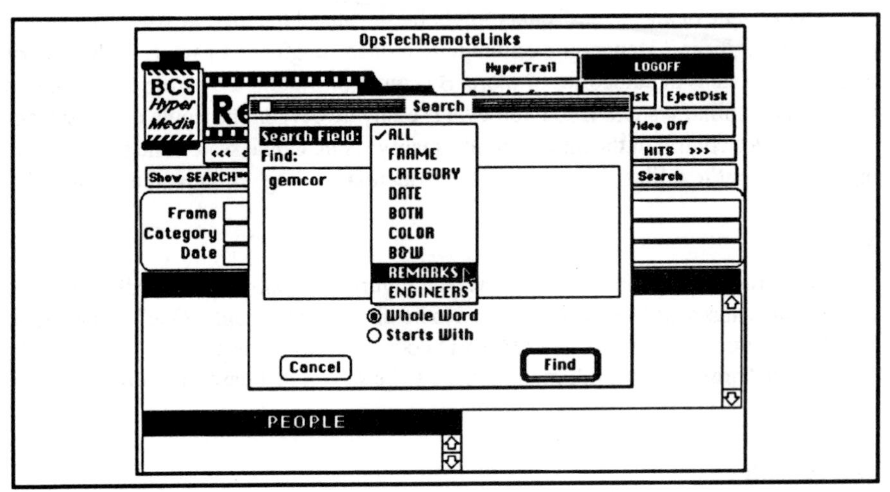

Figure 19. Query Entry

location of the user's mouseclick. HyperCard then builds this word into a query, which is then transmitted to SEARCH on the mainframe. Still invisible to the user, SEARCH accesses a database, gets a result set, and displays the first document of that result set within "presentation space." (As shown in Figure 16.) The interface retrieves these results and displays them, formatted for the user. Using the "HyperTrail" button displays a list of each link anchor point. Clicking within this list causes a return to the selected information node.

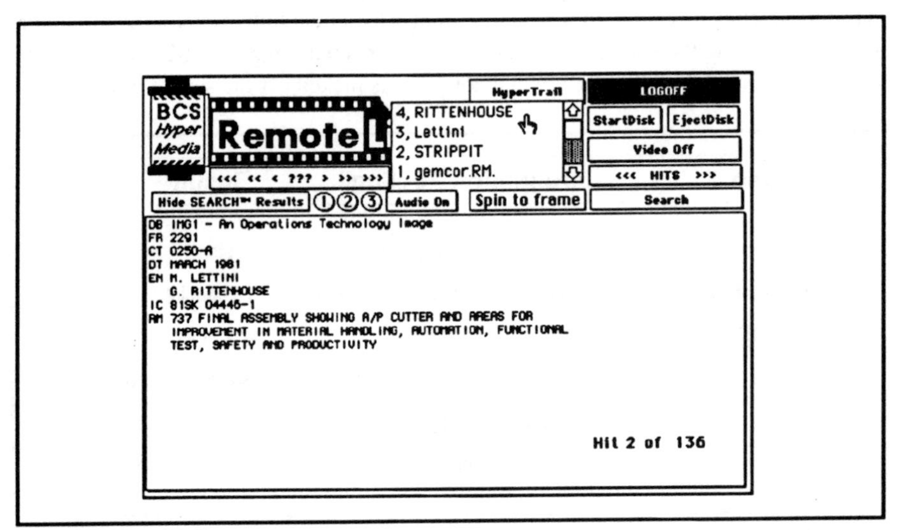

Figure 20. HyperTrail

FUNCTION	ARCHITECTURE ELEMENT
Hardware Platform	Macintosh II
User Interface	HyperCard
Image Presentation	Macintosh High res. color monitor
Indexing	BRS/SEARCH
Network Environment	Ethernet

Figure 21. Phase 4 Architecture

PRODUCTION PHASE 4: DIGITAL IMAGES

Work is currently underway to convert all of the images from their analog laserdisc format into digital images. Digital images will allow deploying a simpler hardware platform, i.e., a single-monitor system that does not include a laserdisc. It will allow single-point configuration control of both images and data, since both can be stored on a single network server. Network impact of image transmission and associated screen repaint time will be minimized by use of JPEG-compressed [6] image files. The tradeoff of smaller image size versus the advantages of better image configuration control and easier image update (no laserdisc need be pressed to update the digital system) is felt to be worth the associated costs. Figure 21 shows the architecture.

LESSONS LEARNED: PILOT SCALABILITY

As alluded to earlier, the Proof-of-Concept construction and data entry went very smoothly—so much so, in fact, that we went into Phase 1 production with some serious misconceptions. We discovered that capturing the data for 50,000 images is *not at all* the same as capturing 1000 images 50 times. Capturing the 1000 images for the Proof-of-Concept system was very clean: accomplished in a single session, on a single roll of film, by a single operator. This meant that during Proof-of-Concept, we did not confront change of film, change of frame counter, changes in lighting and exposure, or changes in operator technique, *all of which were significant* during the move to the production implementation.

LESSONS LEARNED: RETRIEVABILITY

The system design provides for Boolean retrieval as well as field-qualified retrieval, the advantages of which are apparent to information professionals. The system's *users*, however, tend to be satisfied with meager retrieval. Most retrievals seem to be of single words, or of simple phrases. In addition, there appears to be a learning curve associated with the use of hypertext links, which do not appear to be as intuitive as the designers expected for some users.

LESSONS LEARNED: INFORMATION QUALITY

A 75-year accumulation of data is bound to contain problems, and ours was certainly no exception. Inconsistent language in the "free text" MR&D System was the norm, brought about in part by changes in the vocabulary of the underlying engineering disciplines. Different abbreviations for the same term were encountered. Many different ways of entering dates were used. Missing data was encountered, for example, a date of "March" (of what year?) is of only limited use in retrieval from a 75-year historical database. Systems such as QAR&D require effort to design the controlled vocabulary, but its presence boosts confidence that adequate retrieval has been achieved.

FUTURE

Plans are in place to have "digital images" fully deployed by year-end 1991. We are considering using these digital images to distribute the retrieval systems on one or more CD-ROMs. It may also be feasible to deploy the system on a relatively new technology, LD-ROM, in which a large (12-inch) laserdisc is produced that contains 54,000 analog television image frames and an FM signal track of digital data. This system would allow rapid retrieval of large, high quality images, using a data retrieval system located on the same media.

NOTES

1. Nothing in this chapter should be construed as an endorsement by the Boeing Company of any specific product.

2. Rapid entry of all the images chosen for the pilot caused problems later on in the process. See "Lessons Learned" for a discussion.

3. Such devices are computer-controllable. They support direct selection of a specific frame or frames by receiving ASCII control codes via their serial port connected to a computer.

4. XCMDs (spoken "x commands") are extensions to HyperCard that enable additional functionality. XCMDs may be written in a high level language such as C or Pascal, or they may be written in assembly language. Many are available in the public domain.

5. MENTOR is the menu-building tool supplied with BRS/Search. The mainframe menuing system constructed using MENTOR is outside the scope of this discussion.

6. JPEG: Joint Photographic Expert Group, an industry task force dealing with standards for image compression systems.

G. Louis Roberts
Information Retrieval Technologies
Boeing Computer Services
MS 6C-98, P.O. Box 24346
Seattle, Washington 98124

Sound

CHAPTER

9

Access to Sound and Image Databases

Mary Kay Duggan

INTRODUCTION

Catalogs of information usually contain words and numbers that must represent images and sound. Users rely on the internalized visual and aural memory of their trained minds to recall mental images or sounds on command. For example, to locate a print of Leonardo da Vinci's Last Supper you enter the painter's name in a catalog to find a list of his prints, or collections of his works; if unsuccessful, you broaden your search to look, perhaps, for books on Italian painters of the sixteenth century and scan text and image pages. In order to relate a melody in your mind with a title, composer, or lyrics, you might hum the tune to a friend or music librarian in the hope of being supplied with a verbal cue from memory, or you might search through pages of music collections that cover specific decades, areas of the world, or types of music.

A number of projects are under way that combine images and sound with a catalog's traditional textual information. Multimedia catalogs have begun to revolutionize access by incorporating actual samples of—or complete—sounds and images for users to search and browse. This chapter's review of access to multimedia information focuses on newly released and developing databases, primarily in the humanities. Examples of innovative access techniques in purely textual databases are incorporated when they suggest new kinds of access to multimedia as well. Discussion of the importance of the definition of goals and objectives of a multimedia project and standards of quality of digital image and sound precede description of systems of access.

Two ambitious projects are described to help clarify the issues and problems of multimedia catalogs. These projects attempt to provide full access to multimedia information from the combined collections of libraries, archives, and museums. The first example covers the music and life of Edvard Grieg in images of manuscripts and printed material and sound from early recordings. The second covers manuscripts and early printed books in Old Spanish.

DEFINITION OF GOALS AND OBJECTIVES

The definition of goals and objectives of a multimedia project determines levels of quality, access, and interactivity. A limited vision of goals, together with weak hardware and software available at a project's inception, inhibits access from the start. Preservation may be a primary or secondary purpose in creating an archive of surrogates, in which case quality of data will be the dominant design feature. If the goal is improving access to the collection in a way that minimizes wear on materials and security risk, a compromise between quality and economy of storage size may be sought. If research is a goal, accurate and full descriptions of the data and authority control of access points are required. If access to the public for education and casual use is a primary or secondary goal, well-constructed end-user browsing and search techniques become high priorities. If transmission on a network is a goal, existing and proposed standards become crucial. If interactivity for educational or research purposes is important, the sophistication of the workstation and operating system platform move to the forefront.

Once goals of a project are specified, the individual image/sound object and corpus are defined. Examples of the kinds of considerations include:

- image reduction to size of monitor versus reduced image plus detailed images
- beginning of each sound (each CD? each band? each theme?) vs. complete sound
- 3D object, rotatable? still shots from 10 or 20 angles?
- moving images (reduced size? black and white?)
- color for definition of data, as in maps with color overlay
- alternate exposures of image, for increased legibility or for aesthetics
- image plus OCR/OMR text.

The project's goals and the definition of the object and corpus depend highly on the functional capabilities of hardware and software, access techniques, and interactivity, as well as on the necessity of integrating previously existing databases. Retaining flexibility with a file of scanned images or sound is important, just as it is for the traditional MARC records of books in library catalogs. By the time the multimedia database is completed, definitions of what is needed as well as standards for image and sound files and available hardware and software are likely to change.

The corpus of current multimedia databases range from local collections of historical photographs, an Apple Library of Tomorrow (ALOT) project at Fort Collins, Colorado, and oral histories in sound and transcription (Alaska), to national treasures such as France's Video Museum System's co-operative project to digitize all 20th-century works of art in public collections in France, [1] and to international projects such as the texts and images of Old Spanish literature, a project sponsored jointly by Spain and the United States. [2]

Edvard Grieg Project, Administered by MusikkFunn [3]

The manuscript music, notes, sketches, letters with transcriptions, and early sound recordings of Edvard Grieg that are deposited in the Bergen Public Library in Norway form the basis of a multimedia catalog that aims to have a completed product by 1993, the 150th anniversary of Grieg's birth. Primary goals of the project are to make the material more readily available to both researchers and the public and to preserve the collection from fatal accident or damage by the environment or wear. A secondary goal is to provide Grieg materials in a form that lends itself to the creation of digital multimedia publicity releases. The level of image quality must serve the preservation goals of the project, but that level must be kept to a minimum in order to keep the size of data files, and therefore the expense of storage, as small as possible.

The pilot project revealed that an acceptable level for the scanning of most documents is 300 dpi in black and white, but manuscript music and sketches require up to 800 dpi and 4 shades of gray to differentiate between the composer's writing in ink, the music staves, pencil corrections, and the paper. A significant problem turned out to be the size of paper accepted by the scanner (Agfa S800 GS2 A4); the standard paper size was too small for most of the material, so a new and larger scanner will have to be purchased for the full project. The project hopes for the rapid adoption of international image compression standards so that it can use computer software to further compress each image and resulting files while still allowing distribution of a published product that can be decompressed through inexpensive software. When sound digitization begins, preservation goals will also require high quality. In addition to pure sound files, a Musical Instrument Digital Interface (MIDI) will allow music documents to be input through a MIDI keyboard to create music notation coded files that can be indexed and searched for themes and harmonies through a MIDI keyboard plugged into the library computer.

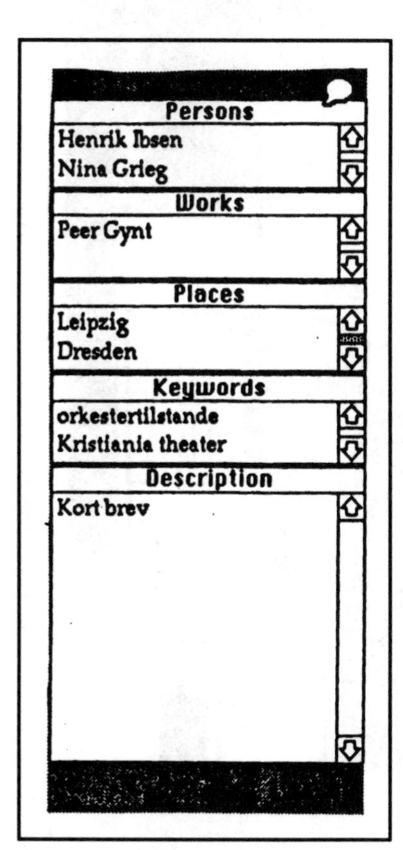

Figure 1. Indexes—Edvard Grieg Project

Descriptions of the multimedia documents in the Grieg database are in MARC format (NORMARC); all fields are searchable and Boolean operators can combine fields. Access

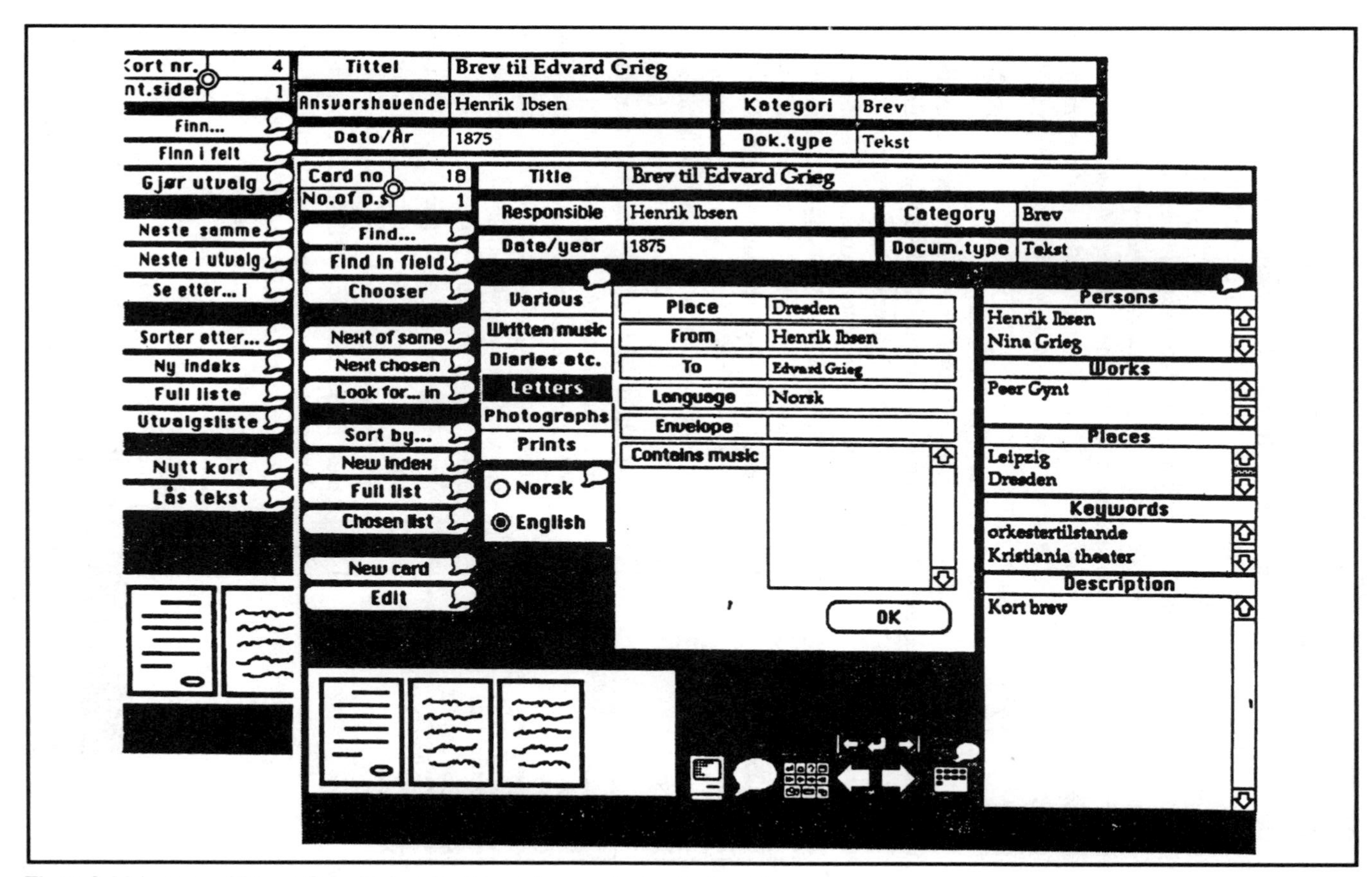

Figure 2. Main menu of Edvard Grieg Project: English window overlaid on the Finnish

to the database uses the concept of hypermedia as a means of relating textual, image, and sound components in a network of links and nodes. Currently available are four textual indexes: person, work, place, or keyword (see Figure 1). The interface, in Norwegian and English versions, allows access by single concepts in Boolean combinations. Figure 2 shows the selection in the English version of a letter from Ibsen to Grieg. Icons for manuscript images of the two-page letter and the single file of the transcription appear at the bottom of the screen. Figure 3 shows the beginning of the transcription in the Finnish version; buttons provide access to the manuscript images, the English version, or the search menu (Finn... or Find...). For the final product, a UNIX workstation will have the capability to display simultaneously image, full text, and music files in windows and through speakers.

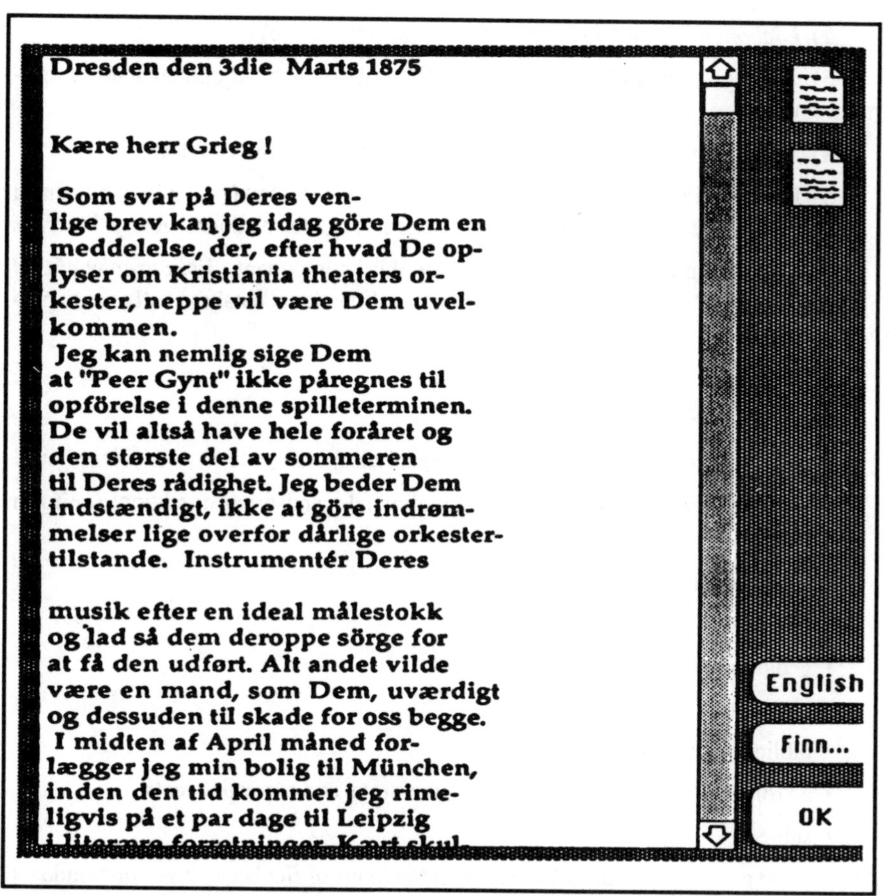

Dresden den 3die Marts 1875

Kære herr Grieg !

Som svar på Deres ven-
lige brev kan jeg idag göre Dem en
meddelelse, der, efter hvad De op-
lyser om Kristiania theaters or-
kester, neppe vil være Dem uvel-
kommen.
Jeg kan nemlig sige Dem
at "Peer Gynt" ikke påregnes til
opförelse i denne spilleterminen.
De vil altså have hele foråret og
den største del av sommeren
til Deres rådighet. Jeg beder Dem
indstændigt, ikke at göre indrøm-
melser lige overfor dårlige orkester-
tilstande. Instrumentér Deres

musik efter en ideal målestokk
og lad så dem deroppe sörge for
at få den udført. Alt andet vilde
være en mand, som Dem, uværdigt
og dessuden til skade for oss begge.
I midten af April måned for-
lægger jeg min bolig til München,
inden den tid kommer jeg rime-
ligvis på et par dage til Leipzig

Figure 3. The beginning of a transcribed letter, Edvard Grieg Project. Note icons which allow access to manuscript images of letter or to English transcription.

ADMYTE: Archivo Digital de Manuscritos y Textos Españoles [4]

The culmination of a series of pre-existing research projects, the Archive of Early Spanish Texts [5] has been funded by both Spanish and U.S. agencies and supported by IBM with a projected goal of an optical disk publication by 1992, the quincentennial of Columbus's first voyage. The goals of the project are: 1) the study of Spanish literature, language, and culture; 2) the creation of editions of texts; 3) the dissemination of bibliographical information and a locations list; and 4) the preservation of manuscripts and incunabula. The Archive has five parts; the first four are text files that completely index and support the images of the fifth:

1) Transcriptions of medieval Spanish language texts to the year 1600 (Hispanic Seminary of Medieval Studies, University of Wisconsin; OCR files by Biblioteca Nacional, Madrid)

2) *Dictionary of the Old Spanish Language* (interactive)

3) *Bibliography of Old Spanish Texts* (bio-bibliographical union catalog of primary sources)

4) A program to automate the creation of critical editions (UNITE)

5) Digitized images of selected manuscripts and incunabula (initially 225 Spanish printed texts before the year 1500, made available through the National Library, Madrid).

The following discussion focuses on the third component, *Bibliography of Old Spanish Texts* (BOOST), which uses a commercial relational database software to provide access to:

- citations of manuscripts and printed editions
- locations and descriptions of copies
- a guide to complete contents of each (analytics)
- citations of works, as separate from individual manuscripts or editions (uniform title)
- biographical information,
- institutions
- geography (with access by a map)
- libraries
- bibliography of secondary literature
- a "rolodex" of modern scholars, collaborators, and correspondents
- subject.

Access is to a single field or to Boolean combinations of fields displayed on windows with hypertext links to files.

Advanced Revelation is a commercial relational database system whose screens were designed for data entry. [6] They are too complex for end-user display or searching; the alternative menu system included in the release for user access is slow and clumsy. With little programming, however, the system allows development of tight authority control for a group of related files displayed in windows with relatively easy movement between files. Before publication, an end-user interface must be designed and addresses of image files entered in BOOST.

The full text of hundreds of Old Spanish works will be searchable with a hypertext link to the standard scholarly dictionary of Old Spanish, which includes spelling variants and etymology to assist in natural language processing.

An example of such a system without multimedia is *CDWORD*, the CD-ROM Bible database that combines the full text of the Bible in English and Greek, a well-constructed thesaurus, a scholarly dictionary, and commentaries with access through hypertext links. Overlaid windows move easily from a text word to the thesaurus to the dictionary. [7] The inadequacy of standard search strategies for full-text publications such as *CDWORD* is demonstrated by excessive retrieval on a word such as "love". [8] To increase search success, full-text (or full-media) databases may have to develop natural language processing techniques such as frequency of use of search term, use with other important words, use with other nouns or verbs, or use in a syntactically important sequence. [9]

Programming promises to take into account common spelling variants (u/v/b, nb/mb, i/j/y, f/h). UNITE, a program similar to the Apple shareware product Collate, [10] automates the creation of critical editions. Users can create their own version of a text from stored digital files of all known variants.

Digitized images of text versions can be displayed in windows adjacent to the transcribed text with links to other files. Plans now call for publishing BOOST on CD-ROM with an abbreviated version of Advanced Revelation; the complex hyperlinks require a 386 DOS computer for acceptable processing time. Publication format for the entire project has not been announced.

The Grieg and Old Spanish projects are examples of the new genre of full text/full image/full sound multimedia projects being undertaken by libraries and scholars to bring rare images and sounds to the personal workstation. Early software versions of hypermedia that enabled the designs, as well as scanners and personal computer workstations and windows, may limit the accomplishments. Both of these projects, as they move out of the pilot project phase to publication, will require access systems of greater sophistication and speed to relate their enormous files and search the files successfully.

IMAGE QUALITY

Because increasing image resolution and dynamic range create a geometric expansion of information per image, it is important to define the minimum level needed for the goals of databases like those with the notation and sounds of Grieg's music or the variant manuscripts of early Spanish texts. Michael Ester, Executive Director of the Getty Art History Information Program, performed an experiment with composite digital images of various levels of quality designed to identify the maximum perception of quality for the amount of stored data. [11] Fifty six art historians (curators, academic researchers, catalogers) viewed workstation images with resolution values in pixels (dimension of a digital image) of 250, 400, 800, 1000, 1500, 2000, and 3000. To give a sense of range, 400-resolution images are comparable to NTSC TV broadcast quality; 1500 images approach high-definition television (HDTV). [12]

Ester found that his well-educated user group perceived clearly the 800-resolution color image to be qualitatively better than other resolutions; the 1000-resolution was perceptively better for gray-scale (art historians are more forgiving for color images). That is to say, *most* could not recognize the better quality of resolution above those levels on a computer monitor able to display them. On the other hand nearly *all* viewers rated the 2000- and 3000-resolution images nearly equal, that is, they could not see the better quality of a 3000-resolution image, leading Ester to conclude that 2000 is "an appealing level for archival capture." For dynamic range, the study suggests a value for color not below 8 bits. Ester's findings, together with increasingly common 1000 pixel resolution monitors, may help to raise the quality of images stored in databases. When HDTV arrives in American homes, even children will be trained to expect 1000-resolution as a matter of course.

One goal of image databases is to provide prints to users. The Getty study showed that photographic positives produced from film output of a stored 1500-resolution image were perceived as better than photographs from slides or from duplicate transparencies of the museum archival transparency. High quality digital image catalogs can be expected to be used to produce photographs or slides for research and study.

In return for the benefits derived from the display and manipulation of a group of images on a single screen, users will allow considerable degradation of quality. The Berkeley Imaging System, licensed to Carlyle Systems for its UNIX-based public access catalog system, uses about 300-resolution quality for browsing several images at a time. After selection of a full-size image or a combination of images, software allows users to select images and scale windows to a size of their choice and move freely back and forth among window layers for study.

If an objective of an image database is the transfer of image files via broadband networks such as the projected NREN, access to reduced resolution level images for browsing may become very important to maximize transfer time and expense. The sequence in which software "paints" the image on a monitor could be designed to allow viewing in steps of resolution as requested by a viewer (for example, 300, 900, 1500), gradually filling in pixels if and when desired.

Access to blown-up details of a stored image is important for critical viewing and for interactive editing, enhancing, redesign, or blocking for "cut and paste," activities important for reuse of images. At 800 dpi resolution, a blown-up image is made up of the same dots spread over a larger area. Alteration of color and design becomes possible at the pixel level. Another kind of zoom function provides access not to a blown-up detail of an image but to an image at a much higher level of resolution. Entire images can be stored at 2000 dpi and zoomed in on any point or particular area normally displayed at 300 dpi. Details such as a face or a building could be stored at higher resolution.

Users can be made aware of zoom capability by: 1) a pull-down window with a verbal list of detail images available; 2) icons such as a magnifying glass; or 3) the word "zoom" in a box that highlights or shades those areas of the original image available in detail. The shaded areas are linked by buttons to the detailed images. The zoom icon can also lead directly to a browse screen displaying multiple details of images. Such techniques are most useful on systems that allow interactive multiple windows. In the Philips DVI catalog of Titian paintings, either a full image or details can be displayed only on separate screens, requiring the user to repeatedly move back and forth to understand the relationship.

MOVING IMAGES

Moving digital images require enormous storage space. One solution for handling the large size of files of moving images is to reduce the size of the screen and use black and white, the strategy of the 1990 CD-ROM of *Mammals: A Multimedia Encyclopedia* published by the National Geographic Society. [13] The display area on the screen shrinks to less than half size for the display of moving image sequences of mammals. Users often squint as the image area shrinks and their eyes adjust to the small area. The CD-ROM uses LinkWay software to combine color still images, sounds, moving images, maps, statistics, and text, in uncoordinated files chosen by the user. Such compromised access to motion is likely to be discarded as space and compression techniques improve. IBM's M-Motion software provides full-screen or user-defined window access for moving images that has been used for educational tools. The M-Motion computer card allows users to select a frame or sequence from a video or videodisk, size it, and save it for reuse. Within ten years, Intel expects to come out with its 80786 microprocessing chip with full-motion multimedia (DUI) technology built into the microprocessor itself. [14]

Surrogates have been the only answer for three-dimensional objects in catalogs today. Still shots from different angles of objects in the anthropology collection at the Lowie Museum at the University of California at Berkeley can be browsed on screens of 10 to 20 images via Carlyle's UNIX software. An image or group of images is selected for viewing on the full screen in sequence or on adjacent windows scaled as desired.

The electronic journal of organic chemistry, *Tetrahedron Computer Methodology*, is now published on disks for both Apple and DOS microcomputer systems. [15] A library could subscribe to and display the journal through its Internet connection and the online catalog, allowing users to view moving molecules as designed by contributors to the journal. Authors publish source code along with molecular theory, receive scholarly credit for both, and release it immediately into the public domain for reuse by other scholars and students.

A method of browsing databases of moving video sequences has been developed by Christodoulakis and Graham. [16] Major points in the video are described by a vertical row of icons on the right-hand side of the screen. The icons are divided by horizontal lines, much like the lines on a ruler, indicating time intervals between icons. Viewers can access either marked points on the ruler or icons.

SOUND QUALITY

The sound quality of bundled software and hardware has made the NeXT computer (44 kHz, stereo, MIDI interface) a favorite of music composers as compared to the Sun SPARCstation (8 kHz) and the Apple Mac with HyperCard (22 kHz, mono, MIDI interface) and no sound on DOS computers. To give a sense of range of quality, the telephone uses 8 kHz, the radio 22 kHz and the CD 44 kHz. The CD-ROM version of the *Electronic Whole Earth Catalog* [17] used up 340 megabytes of its 420 megabytes for 500 individual sound segments digitized at 22 kHz and a 4:1 sampling rate. Digitizing only a sample of the sound greatly reduces the file size: one minute of sound at 22 kHz uses 1200 kilobytes; but sampled at 4:1 it uses only 300 kilobytes, though the listener loses one-fourth of the information.

Compact discs, today's popular format for sound recordings, were the focus of three 1989-announced CD-ROM publications which would provide access to the CDs "in print," in a manner similar to coverage of text in *Books in Print*. The planned *Music Directory Plus* by Bowker and the digital *Schwann Catalog*—the latter to have had two access modes, one for record stores and one for library acquisition and cataloging—never appeared, apparent casualties of copyright battles. The editors of the magazine *CD Guide* did publish a CD-ROM, *CD Guide Optical Edition*; in addition to 40,000 titles and 5,000 reviews of CDs, it includes sound for selected CDs. Quality of sound is superb; the beginning of each track in 44 kHz, stereo, and color images of CD covers appear during listening. Sound publications intended to sell products require top quality digital data.

Pilot projects of sound segments in library catalogs of CDs [18] indicate that sound quality of 22 kHz with 4:1 sampling, mono, is adequate for browsing a library collection at a catalog workstation with earphones. If the purpose of a database is preservation or research, such irreversible sound sampling cannot be used. Today's software for compression often uses reversible sampling and, once standardized, such techniques will reduce storage of sound files to feasible size.

Optical Music Recognition (OMR) is in its infancy, only capable of recognizing melodies on single staves. [19] To enter music notation a database developer must choose a code for the information and type it in. No single standard has been adopted though talks are under way to choose one. [20] Once encoded by the developer or through a MIDI keyboard, music can be indexed for access by melodic pattern and harmony and displayed on the screen in notation, played through speakers or earphones, or downloaded for further play through a MIDI interface.

To enter sound, a database developer can directly copy existing digital material if there are no copyright restrictions, or use a MIDI keyboard to store the information for display as notation or sound production. MIDI keyboards are standard tools of composers, performers, music researchers and, increasingly, music librarians, and are a powerful tool for access to music.

ACCESS

Unusual media can be stored off site in isolated files. The College Library Access and Storage System (CLASS) by Cornell University and Xerox Corporation is a digitization project for deteriorating books. The image files will be annotated in the national utility MARC record as available for reprint from Xerox.

Within a database system, image or sound components are often isolated in separate files and must be summoned by one or more keystrokes. IBM's BookManager, a software application for storing and printing full text and graphics, notes in the text that a graphic exists; the reader calls it up by keystroke and it is drawn on the screen, the whole process taking many seconds. One wonders how authors would feel about the fact that readers must have extra motivation to call up illustrations and tables.

Much available software displays only one image at a time, in an on/off fashion. HyperCard is such a product used, for example, by the Fort Collins Public Library (grants from the American Society of Archivists and Apple Library of Tomorrow) for an image database of historic photographs and associated documents such as newspaper clippings. [21] The *Electronic Whole Earth Catalog* was an early HyperCard product that provided sound segments that could be listened to at any point in a stack, along with a choice of one of several screens of text, music notation of one of two screens, or a picture of the musician playing the music. The Library of Congress American Memory Project uses HyperCard and interactive videodiscs for access to photos, manuscripts, music, motion pictures, books and sound recordings.

A preferable mode of presentation is simultaneous access to multiple overlay images on a screen, preferably sized and overlaid by the user's preference. Such a mode has long been available on UNIX workstations such as NeXT or Sun. The Berkeley Imaging System on a Sun allows a search result of several images to be displayed on one screen. The user may choose one or more to present in full resolution in overlay windows, bringing any one to the fore with a click. The Emperor Project, begun on videodisk, is now being developed at MIT's Project Athena, on workstations with better resolution, multiple windows, and deeper description and access. [22] IBM's new M-Motion card can display overlaid frozen or live video images in multiple windows. An integrated file system allows a user to perform many tasks, freely moving about enormous quantities of data without closing files or moving up and down a hierarchy of directories, subdirectories, etc. Museum information systems include management, insurance, and exhibit information along with images and descriptions. The Berkeley Imaging System has an editing component that allows users to alter color and pixels, saving edited versions. Because the NeXT has sound-editing capabilities built in, it is a favorite of composers and music educators. Workstations in academic libraries will need sophisticated software to provide for the full use of materials by students. As unique multimedia research materials begin to be published in digital form, sometimes by the libraries themselves, public libraries, too, will need powerful hardware to provide access.

SEARCHING MULTIMEDIA: CONTROLLED VOCABULARY, FULL TEXT, NATURAL LANGUAGE PROCESSING

Multimedia databases have provided an impetus for the development of classification schemes (ICONCLASS), controlled vocabulary (Art and Architecture Thesaurus), and full text access to wordy hyperlinked files on media and associated names, places, dates, etc. (Lexicon Iconographicum Mytholigae Classicae [23]). Just as natural language processing is being developed for full text files, natural image or natural sound processing is likely to be necessary in the future for full media files.

ICONCLASS, a numerical classification code for images, has been adopted as an access tool for the Bildarchiv Foto Marburg in Germany, the Witt Library and Courtauld Institute in Great Britain, and the Harvard Fogg Museum and Princeton Index of Christian Art in the U.S. While the nine volumes of the code are very specific, different projects seem always to create further numbers, sometimes duplicating numbers with different subjects. Searchers cannot look for words, but must select a numerical code.

The Art and Architecture Thesaurus supported by the Getty Art History Information Program is a hierarchical listing of words with definitions and notes on usage that attempts to classify all artistic and architectural terms. Now available digitally, though only as words without the definitions and notes on usage, the thesaurus is available as a standardized vocabulary for access to images. In a recent article on "Subject Access to Visual Resources," Kevin Roddy identified several European efforts at standardization of access to iconography, principally through the International Documentation Committee, an arm of the International Council of Museums. [24]

Images and sounds are true international languages and any attempt to impose controlled vocabulary upon them carries with it the cultural bias of the language or languages selected for the index. Image databases now have no language searchable by the computer, nor any syntax that is readable as is ASCII text or encoded music notation. If the computer could be trained to recognize images, it could rank search results by criteria such as size (find all boats that occupy half of the screen), frequency (find all images that contain three or more columns), or proximity (find all horses with riders). One promising area of research would develop a thesaurus of standardized images for genres such as portraits and landscapes as well as particular features or styles, much as exists in black and white drawings in language dictionaries today for words such as *Ion-*

ic, *Doric*, and *Corinthian columns*, *frieze*, and *tympanum*. Such controlled images would be linked to the images of the database and could be used for browsing and searching without imposition of language bias.

Music can be encoded in a notational language that allows presentation on the screen in notation and searching for features such as melody or harmony, in isolated fragments or in proximity with other fragments. The full music file of the works of J. S. Bach being entered in Palo Alto at the Center for Computer Assisted Research in the Humanities was begun with the goal of searching the music notation to understand how the music works: what makes up the Bach style. Numerous projects for thematic catalogs are beginning to give us digital repertories of the themes of major composers and repertoires. [25] As a prelude to consideration of digital music publishing, Oxford University Press conducted a survey in 1990 of current digital research that indicated that encoded music projects in DOS, Apple, and UNIX environments were underway throughout the world. [26] One of the new projects is Case Western Reserve University's Musical Scores Project of the Library Collection Services Project. [27] It puts together digital musical scores, a searchable database/index about the works, links to commercial or university recordings, and graphics and text tools to allow the on-screen analysis of musical works, either as a "clear" overlay on the score image, or as a separate document. Structural analyses of music compositions appear in text and in music notation on screens with numbered references to points on the sound files, accessed by the conventional signs of commercial CD hardware: [28]

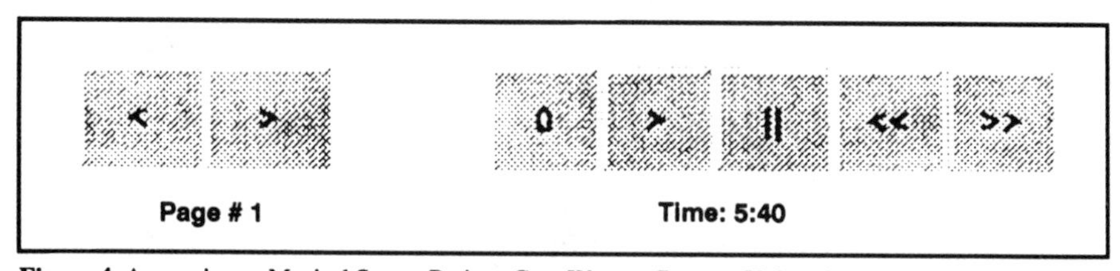

Figure 4. Access icons, Musical Scores Project, Case Western Reserve University.

All over the world individuals are doing research by creating multimedia databases that, as they reach completion, are forcing publishers to rethink their role. *Tetrahedron Computer Methodology*, the digital journal of organic chemistry, allows chemists to publish their software code along with their molecular research, claiming authorship immediately and then allowing the software to enter the public domain. The Oxford University Press survey last fall aimed to find out what kind of music databases were being created by researchers, what kind of platforms they were using, and whether they would be interested in publishing them digitally with Oxford. Dozens replied reporting a wide range of research and said they would prefer digital publication. Along with new research, the old repertoire of paintings and objects is being scanned, words of manuscripts scanned and input, and music notation encoded—and the medium of publication favored to preserve full research and access is becoming electronic.

If dissertations are multimedia (with data and evidence on videotapes, tape cassettes, photographs, and databases) publication and abstracts of dissertations should become multimedia. The giant retrospective projects that now require wholesale scanning and OCR work will be replaced by straightforward access to databases previously created. Such databases were digital from the design stage and were created because of their potential to provide access in new ways that stretch both the limits of technology and imagination and the way we think about information and problems and solutions. With the increase in digital information, the library catalog becomes not just a steppingstone or gateway to information, it is the information.

NOTES

1. P. Wentz, "Computerization in Museums: Databases to Image Bases," *Online Information '89*, Proceedings of the 13th International Meeting, London, 12-14 December 1989 (Oxford: Learned Information, 1989), p. 343.

2. Charles B. Faulhaber and Francisco Marcos-Marín, "ADMYTE: Archivo Digital de Manuscritos y Textos Españoles," *La Corónica* 182 (1989-1990), 131-145.

3. Contact person: Bård Uri Jensen, Western Norway Research Centre, Parkvegen 5, P.B. 142, 5801 Sogndal, Norway.

4. Contact persons: Charles B. Faulhaber, Dept. of Spanish and Portuguese, University of California at Berkeley; Francisco Marcos-Marín, Universidad Autonoma de Madrid.

5. Faulhaber and Marcos-Marín, "ADMYTE."

6. James Acquaviva and Jason Morgan, "Advanced Revelation: A Complete Application Development Environment," *Library Software Review* vol. 7:1 (1988), 46-52.

7. See Figure 1 in R.E. Anderson, P.J. Sallis, and W.K. Yeap, "Enhancing a Hypertext Application Using NLP Techniques," *Journal of Information Science* 17 (1991), 51.

8. See Table 1, Anderson et al, p. 52.

9. Anderson et al, pp. 53-55.

10. Collate 1.0, March 1991, Peter Robinson, Oxford University Computing Service, 13 Banbury Road, Oxford OXZ 6NN, England. E-Mail: PETER@UK.AC.OX.VAX. It can collate simultaneously up to 100 texts (prose and verse), permit the scholar to adjust the collation interactively, regularize spelling, and output in many formats, including marked-up text ready for processing by TEX.

11. Michael Ester, "Image Quality and Viewer Perception," *Leonardo* Supplemental Issue, "Digital Image—Digital Cinema" (June 1990), 51-63, Figure 1, grey-scale example of a composite frame, resolution levels from 250 to 3000.

12. "The relative information content of the resolution values can be derived from the image area, or the product of the linear dimension. A 2000-resolution image, for example, contains 4 million pixels (2000 x 2000), or 4 times as much information as a 1000 image. Similarly, a 250 image has about 6% of the information in a 1000 image." Ester, p. 55.

13. "IBM Multimedia: From Aardvark," *Multimedia Solutions* 5:2 (March/April 1991), 14-15.

14. Mark Magel, "Following the True (Big) Blue Path to Multimedia," *Multimedia Solutions* 5:2 (March/April 1991), 20-23; reprinted from *AV Video* 13:1 (January 1991).

15. Editor-in-Chief, W. Todd Wipke, University of California, Santa Cruz. (Oxford: Pergamon Press, vol. 1-1988).

16. Stauros Christodoulakis and Stephen Graham, "Browsing Within Time-Driven Multimedia Documents," *SIGOIS Bulletin* 9:2-3 (April/July 1988) 219-27.

17. Reviewed by Suzanne Stefanac in *Macworld* (Dec. 1989), 197. For a discussion with illustrations of music screens, see the author's "Multimedia Databases for Public Service in Music Libraries," *Fontes Artis Musicae* 38 (1991), 71-72.

18. See the author's "19th-Century Sheet Music," 4 Apple discs and a 10-page guide for a student assignment to design and create a HyperCard multimedia catalog.

19. Nicholas P. Carter and Richard A. Bacon. "Automatic Recognition of Printed Music," in *Structured Document Image Analysis*, ed. H. Bunke, H. Baird, and K. Yamamoto (Heidelberg: Springer Verlag, 1991). Bruce Pennycock, "Towards Advanced Optical Music Recognition," *Advanced Imaging* (April 1990), 54, 56-57; *Computing in Musicology, A Directory of Research 1990*, edited by Walter B. Hewlett and Eleanor Selfridge-Field (Menlo Park: Center for Computer Assisted Research in the Humanities, 1990), pp. 36-45.

20. Garrett H. Bowles, "ANSI X3V1.8M Work Group Report," *MLA Newsletter* (Music Library Association), no. 83 (Nov.-Dec. 1990), 12.

21. For information on "Making the Past Available for the Future: A Proposal for Graphically Indexing Photograph Collections," contact Karen McWilliams, Fort Collins Public Library, 201 Peterson Street, Fort Collins, CO 80524.

22. Ben Davis, Russell Sasnett and Matthew Hodges, "Educational Multimedia at M.I.T.," *Advanced Imaging* 4:7 (July 1989), 32-35.

23. Jocelyn Penny Small, "Retrieving Images Verbally: No More Key Words and Other Heresies," *Library Hi Tech* 9:1 (1991), 51-60.

24. Kevin Roddy, "Subject Access to Visual Resources: What the 90s Might Portend," *Library Hi Tech* 9:1 (1991), 46.

25. See for example the repertoire of 83,243 music incipits of the Répertoire International des Sources Musicales described by Joachim Schlichte, "Der automatische Vergleich von 83,243 Musikincipits aus der RISM-Datenbank: Ergebnisse—Nutzen—Perspektiven," *Fontes Artis Musicae* 37:1 (Jan.-Mar. 1990), 35-46.

26. Mary Kay Duggan, "The Future for Computerized Music Printing," paper given at the annual meeting of the Music Library Association, Feb. 13, 1991, Indianapolis, Indiana.

27. "IBM and Case Western Reserve: The Library of the Future," *Multimedia Solutions* 5:2 (March/April, 1991), 16-17.

28. Sample screens appear in a brochure available from Case Western Reserve University, Library Collections Services, Baker Building, Room 6, Cleveland, Ohio 44106. James Barker, Project Manager, (216) 368-5888, e-Mail: jab13@po.cwru.edu.

Mary Kay Duggan
School of Library and Information Studies
University of California, Berkeley
Berkeley, California 94720

CHAPTER

10

EXPLORING MULTIMEDIA: AUDIO OBJECTS, OPERATORS, MANAGEMENT

Fredric Gey and Lai Shi Vera Choi

WHAT IS MULTIMEDIA?

Multimedia is the next generation of information to be stored, retrieved, and interactively manipulated on the computer. Multimedia generally extends computer use from the mere processing of text and numbers, to the additional senses of vision (i.e. images) and hearing (i.e. digitized speech and music). [1] The next step beyond images, sound, and music will be the integration of these to animated motion. Animation can consist of freeze-frame recording of images in real-time, such as might be displayed in high-speed video photography, or video camcorder recordings of natural environments. It might also mean their simulation using techniques of three-dimensional reconstruction and ray-tracing and the dynamical equations of motion to create an entirely new simulated reality.

This chapter examines particular elements and examples of the new multimedia technology and discusses some of the database and representation problems in developing multimedia applications. One of the fundamental problems found with multimedia is storage capacity. To quote Fox, [2] "The space not only consumes valuable disk capacity (an entire CD-ROM would normally be required to handle 30 seconds of directly stored motion video) but also places severe demands on computer and I/O bandwidth (it would normally take over an hour to play back the 30 seconds of video from the CD-ROM)." One solution to this problem, of course, is to use some form of data compression for digitized images and speech. Compressed images are sent across communications channels as well as stored in archival mechanisms for later retrieval. The speed of the interactive processor is utilized to decompress the images in real time.

Images

Multimedia images are digitized representations of two–dimensional pictures. These may be input with a digital scanner such as a page scanner (similar to a copier) or a video camera with attached hardware to convert the analog signal to digital form. The unit of information storage is the pixel (one picture dot on the display). Pixels have intensity levels (known as gray levels) that identify the degree of intensity of the image at that point.

For black and white recording, a standard 8-bits per pixel will register 256 gray levels. Color is represented by the degree of intensity at each pixel of the three primary colors: red, green, blue. Using 8-bit intensity levels for each color results in 24 bits (3 bytes) of storage per pixel.

The storage required for digitized images of high quality is then determined by the resolution of the display monitor. A high-resolution 1024 by 1024 screen (such as might be used for CAD applications) requires 3 megabytes per color image and 1 megabyte per black and white image before applying any compression technique.

Sound and Music

The sound component of multimedia is a digitized representation of sound wave motion over time. Sound digitizers take a snapshot (sample) of the amplitude of the pressure wave generated by the sound in the atmosphere as shown in Figure 1. [3] The sample rate (in the thousands per second) is central to the accurate representation (fidelity) of the original sound. Human hearing can receive and detect frequencies from 20 to 20,000 cycles per second (Hz).

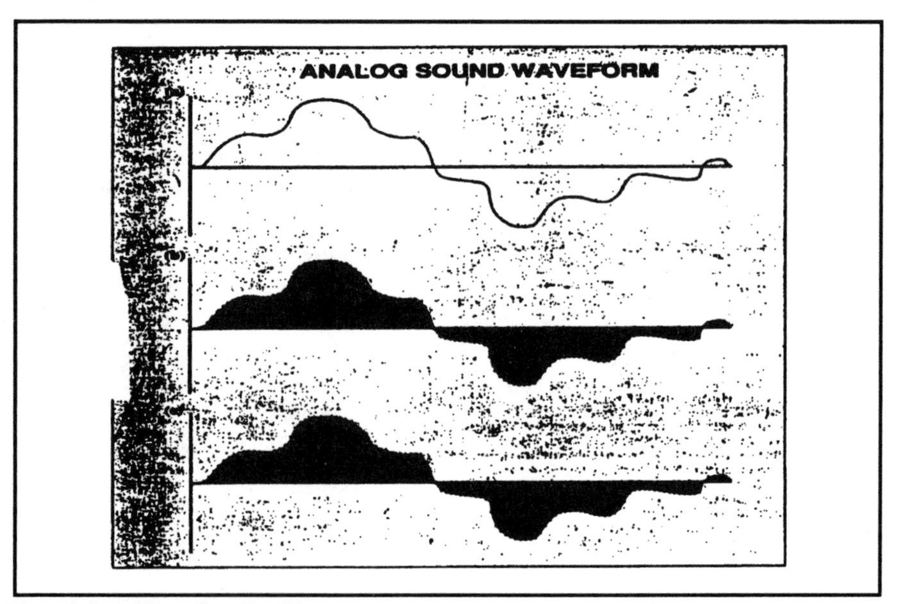

Figure 1. Sound Wave Sampling [3]

Commercial sound digitizers such as the Farallon corporation MacRecorder can sample at rates of 8,000 to 22,000 numbers per second. [4] Each sound is an 8-bit number (one byte). Thus, without compression, each second of sound (at highest sampling rate) is 22K bytes, or 1.32 megabytes per minute. Even this rate is considerably below the accuracy and sample rate of a typical audio CD, which uses 16-bit (2-byte) resolution and 44.1kHz—more than double the upper limit of human hearing.

The *Electronic Whole Earth Catalog* (described below) used over 500 sounds each of one minute duration. Had full 22,000/second sampling been used, the sounds would have occupied more than the capacity (650 megabytes) of a single CD-ROM. By cutting sampling in half, only half the CD was used for sound.

A MULTIMEDIA EXAMPLE: *ELECTRONIC WHOLE EARTH CATALOG*

The *Electronic Whole Earth Catalog,* [5] produced by Point Foundation and Broderbund Software, with assistance from Apple Corporation, is the electronic analog to the *Whole Earth Catalog*, a book-length catalog of tools and ideas published in the 1970's. This computer version on CD-ROM incorporates the navigational capability of Apple's HyperCard and segments of digitized sound to create a multimedia presentation. The *Electronic Whole Earth Catalog* runs on Apple Macintosh hardware with one megabyte of memory via HyperCard and requires the Apple CD-ROM drive.

Components of the Catalog

The catalog consists of:

- HyperCard—10,000 cards were created to structure, represent, and navigate the catalog's information
- Images—4000 graphic images were digitized and incorporated into cards, providing visual representations of information (as in the original published book)
- Sounds—500 sound resources of approximately one minute each were incorporated into the catalog's music and bird image sections
- Word index search—text entries were processed and an inverted index created for word searching of the catalog's contents.

Advantages and Disadvantages

The electronic version exhibits major advantages over the published book. The advantages include the incorporation of sounds, content linkages available using the HyperCard interface, and the ability to look up by word in the index. Major disadvantages over the published book were the constraints of the display environment, in particular a single font (Geneva) for written text; display size limitations on images (to fit the Mac screen); and the diminution of sound quality caused by less than optimal sampling (the

Figure 2. Professor Longhair [5]

creators claimed that most high-frequency sound, i.e., >5000kHz, was lost in the creation process). In addition, the current version of HyperCard does not utilize color, so the images are all in black and white. Finally, cost is a major drawback, since even a minimum system requires about $3,000 worth of Apple's computer gear to run, coupled with the $150 cost of the CD-ROM that contains the catalog.

A Sample Entry—Professor Longhair

Figure 2 is an image extracted from the blues music section of the catalog, particularly from the article describing artists from Alligator Records of Chicago. The artist on display, Professor Longhair, was a rock and roll pioneer of the unique New Orleans sound. Clicking of the button showing two 1/8 notes plays a minute of the song "In the Wee Wee Hours" from the album *Crawfish Fiesta.*

EXPLORING MULTIMEDIA

To gain experience with multimedia, the authors decided to enhance an existing image database management system by adding audio objects and an audio management interface. The University of California, Berkeley's *ImageQuery* system provided the basis for the development. Because of its file-driven open architecture, it seemed relatively easy to incorporate audio objects using a storage structure similar to that available for images. The hardware chosen was the Sun Microsystems SPARCstation, which has a speaker and a sound chip that provides telephone quality audio output through the speaker. The speaker is addressed as a symbolic device to which appropriately formatted digitized sound waves may be directed.

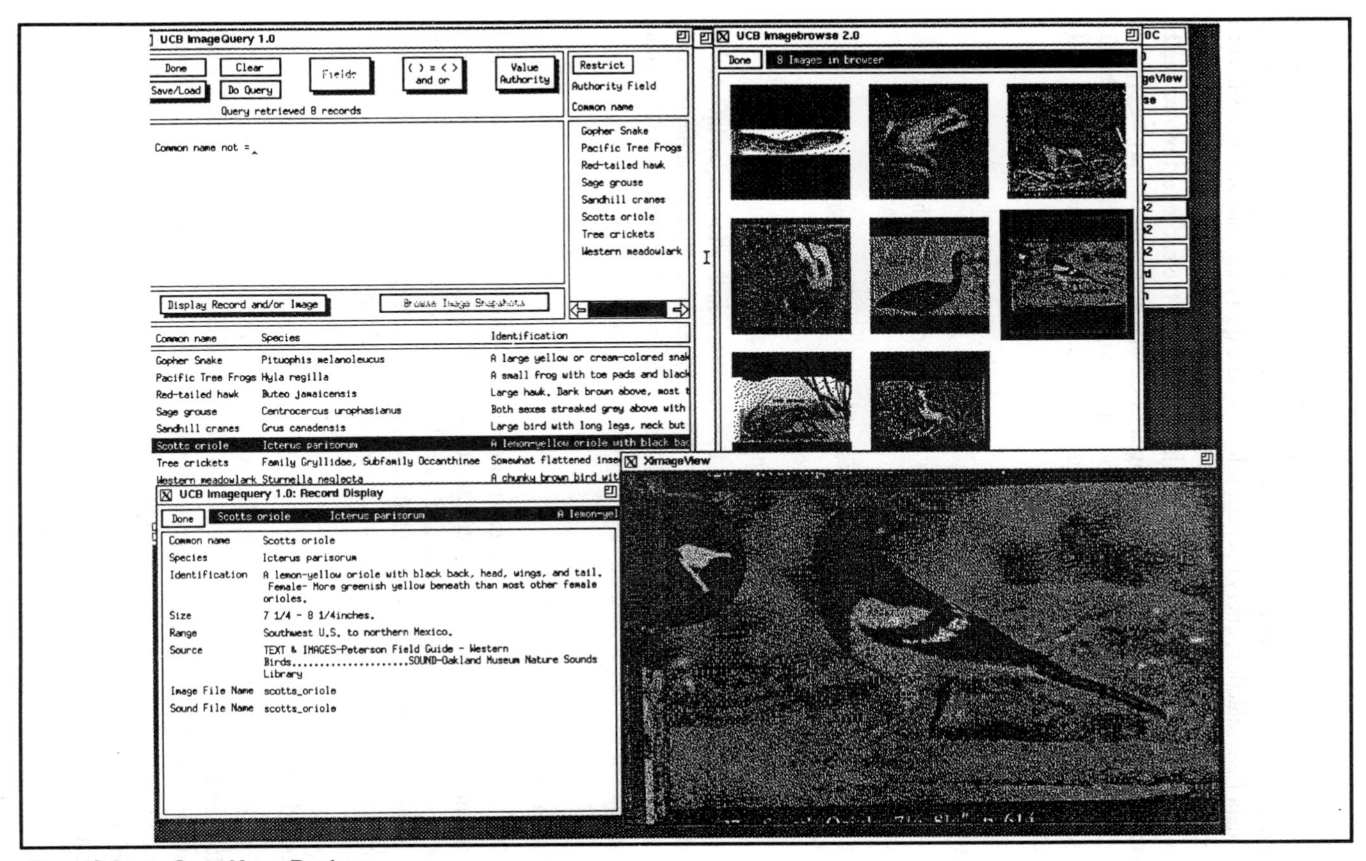

Figure 3. Image-Query Nature Database

Berkeley *ImageQuery*

The *ImageQuery* image database system [6] is often used for geographic mapping databases. [7] As shown in Figure 3, it has a main control panel window with buttons for data field selection, query operator selection, and query execution. The results of a particular query are displayed in a scrollable window below the control panel. Since the window is horizontally scrollable (as well as vertically), the entire text record can be displayed on the screen. In addition, images associated with records may be browsed for further selection and display. For a chosen record, an associated image can be displayed to a desired location on the monitor screen (the image for Scott's Oriole is in the figure).

Audio Interface

The computer management of audio depends upon the availability of the following facilities:

- Storage for digitized sound samples
- A sound chip for digital to analog conversion
- An audio play mechanism (i.e. a speaker or headphone jack).

The Sun SPARCstation stores audio in u-law companding format, an international standard for digital telephony. An AMD 79c30 digital subscriber controller chip converts the audio output to the speaker. This design provides for telephone quality audio input/output with a standard 8K sampling rate and 8-bit samples.

Components of AudioPhile

Creation of the audio interface, AudioPhile, was done within the X-Window environment using the audio device (/dev/audio) as a STREAMS device. As shown in Figure 4, controls for pause/resume and output volume levels were implemented using athena wigits and custom icons built for the play device. The Sun Microsystems sound library was called for actual play and for the display of the sound wave.

Sound and Image Sources

The eight audio sound samples for the nature database were supplied in MacRecorder format by the nature sounds librarian of the Oakland (California) Museum [8] from the museum's collection of over 10,000 nature sound recordings. Images associated with the sounds were digitized using a MicroTek color digitizer from the University of California geography department computing facility and came from a variety of sources, primarily the Peterson [9] and the Audubon [10] field guides.

Since Sun's u-law companding format is different from the MacRecorder format, a utility was used to convert from the former to the latter. Conversion had to take into

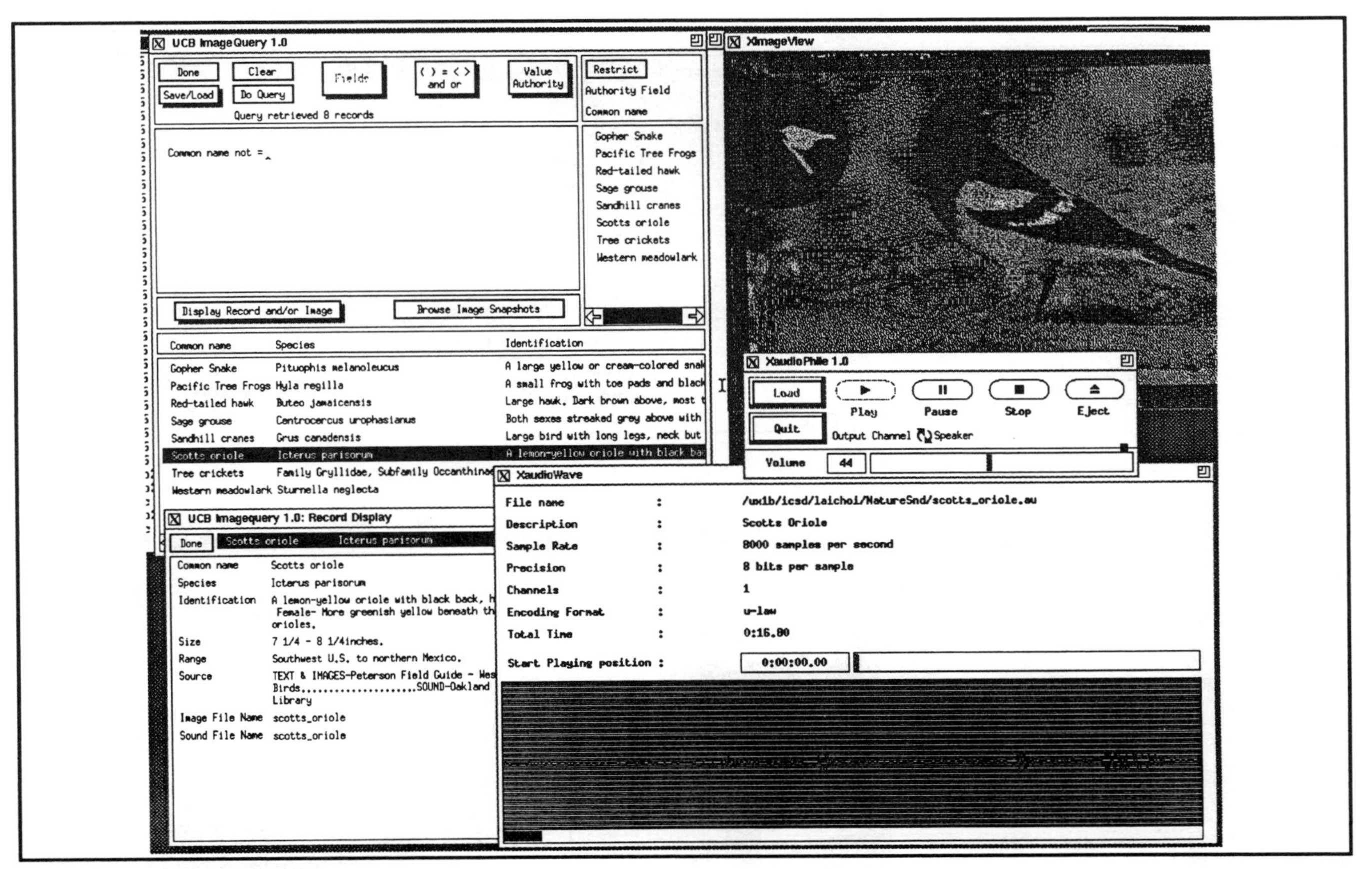

Figure 4. AudioPhile and AudioWave

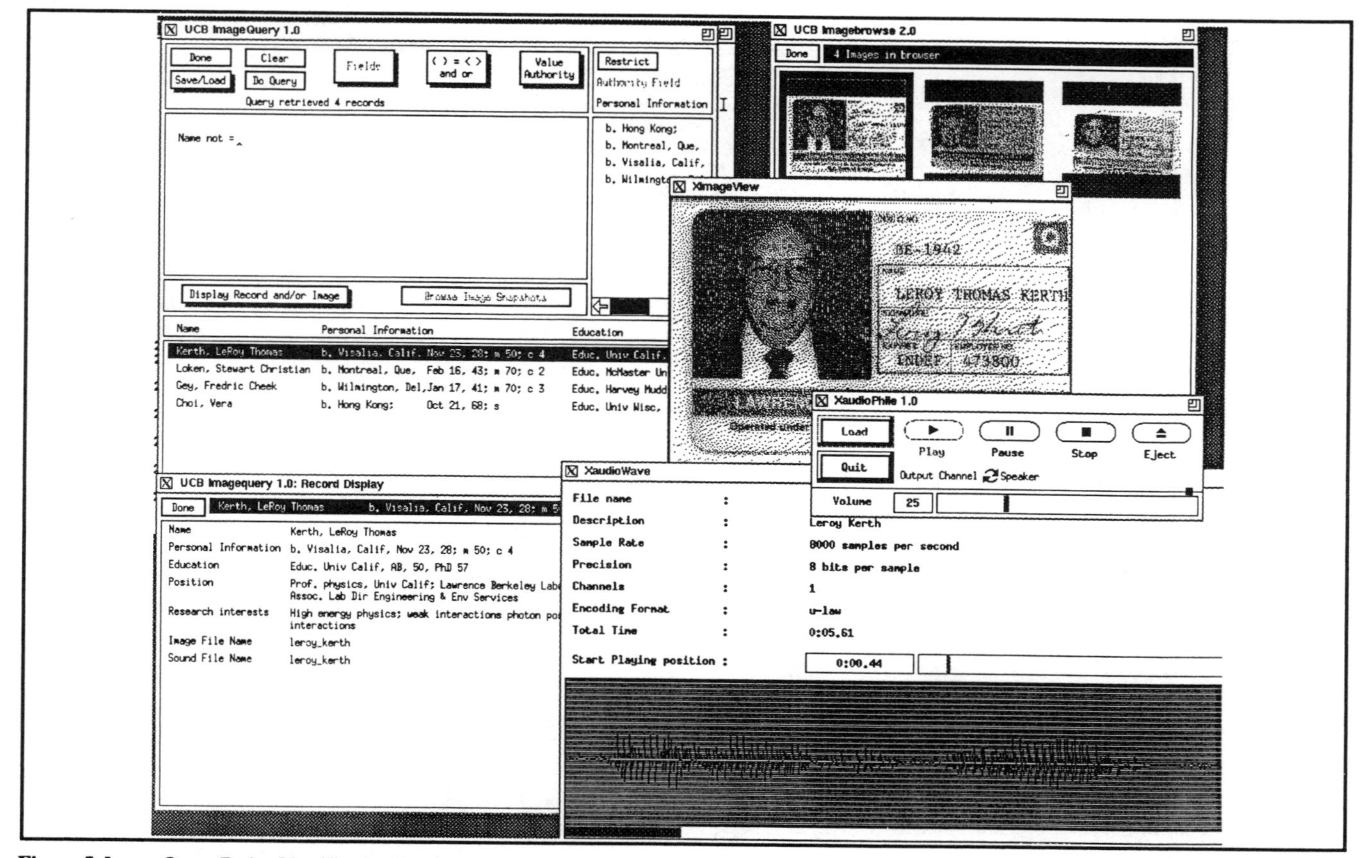

Figure 5. Image-Query Badge Identification Database

account that the Oakland Museum samples had been recorded at 22,000 samples per second, while the Sun expected 8,000 samples per second.

A second database (Figure 5) was created by digitizing official identification badges of several individuals, including the two authors. Information on the other individuals was extracted from *American Men and Women of Science,* [11] while voice samples were recorded with a dictating recorder and digitized using the MacRecorder. The combination of audio and images with text enables new levels of precision in interactive security (identification of individuals), and one can imagine the development of on-line, on-demand biographies.

A GENERAL DISCUSSION OF AUDIO IN MULTIMEDIA

Once a project such as this one has been successfully demonstrated, attention should be turned to what general characteristics should be available in a multimedia system that incorporates digitized audio. Just as a text management system incorporates document editing facilities, similar facilities should be added to audio management.

Audio Management and Operators

A successful audio management suite of operations would include those in two major areas: *editing* and *analysis*. In editing digitized audio objects, the following operations should be included:

- time slicing to edit particular time ranges of sound
- cut/paste operations to extract audio subsegments
- high/low pass filtering to smooth spikes or noise
- pitch manipulation for audio perception shifting
- mixing of multiple sounds to produce new sounds.

In the analysis of sound objects, *sonograms* and *spectrograms* are standard facilities in the repertoire of audio engineers.

Audio Compression

A major factor in multimedia applications is the storage space necessary to contain the digitized audio sample points. As mentioned above, the commercial development of the *Electronic Whole Earth Catalog* required sampling at 8,000 samples per second instead of the 22,000/second available from the digitizing device. This meant that frequencies higher than 5.5kHz were lost to the listener.

In our application some analysis indicated that many of the sample points lay in the small digit range of possible samples, thus indicating that the application of standard compression techniques would be successful. The audio wave of Figure 5, which originally had 87,873 bytes was compressed using the UNIX "compress" utility, which utilizes a standard Zif-Lempl compression encoding algorithm. The resulting compressed file of 27,648 bytes shows a better than 3-to-1 compression ratio. More sophisticated techniques that take advantage of the distribution characteristics of audio sampling might achieve even better compression.

SUMMARY

This chapter barely scratches the surface of multimedia audio operations in research and production today. A more comprehensive review would include the integration of speech processing programs to synthesize voice from written text, speech recognition efforts to allow computer systems to be audio command-driven, sound editors, music composition systems, and the control of electronic musical instruments through the MIDI (musical instrument display interface) data transmission protocol. We attempted here only to give some flavor of the components of multimedia and the state of commercial multimedia products, as well as describe the components of research and development that go into the development of audio components of multimedia.

NOTES

1. Stavros Christodoulakis and Christos Faloutsos, "Design and Performance Considerations for an Optical Disk-based, Multi-media Object Server," *IEEE Computer*, V. 19, No. 12, December 1986, pp. 45-56.

2. Edward A.Fox, "The Coming Revolution in Interactive Digital Video," *Communications of the ACM*, V. 32, No. 7, July 1989, pp. 794-801.

3. Gene Smarte, "Sounds," *BYTE*, December, 1989, pp. 245-248.

4. Farallon Corp., *MacRecorder Reference Manual*, 1989, Emeryville, CA.

5. Whole Earth Catalog, *The Electronic Whole Earth Catalog*, CD-ROM machine-readable product and product literature, Broderbund Software, 1990. Oral presentation at the Hypermedia Group offices Emeryville, California April 4, 1990.

6. Barbara Morgan and Steve Jacobson, "Berkeley Image/Query System," System documentation available from Advanced Technology Planning, Information Systems and Technology, University of California, Berkeley, CA 94720, 1990.

7. Daniel Holmes, "Multimedia Geographic Information to Support Scientific Research: ImageQuery," 1991 ASIS Midyear Meeting. Santa Clara, CA, April 26, 1991.

8. Paul Matzner, Oakland Museum, Oakland, California, 1990 (private communication).

9. Robert Stebbins, *Peterson Field Guide to Western Reptiles & Amphibians*, Houghton-Mifflin, Boston, 1985.

10. Miklos Uduardy, *Audubon Society Field Guide to North American Birds*, Alfred Knopf, New York, 1977.

11. *American Men & Women of Science*, 17th edition, 1989-90, Bowker Company, New York.

Fredric Gey
School of Library and
Information Studies
University of California
Berkeley, CA

Lai Shi Vera Choi
Information and Computer
Science Division
Lawrence Berkeley Laboratory
University of California, Berkeley, CA

CHAPTER

11

PROJECT JUKEBOX: GOALS, STATUS, RESULTS AND FUTURE PLANS

Peter J. Knoke

INTRODUCTION

Notable among the University of Alaska Fairbanks (UAF) Rasmuson Library's holdings is the Alaska and Polar Regions (APR) Oral History collection. The collection comprises about 6000 audio tapes containing first person accounts of Alaska history by pioneers, Native Elders, and Alaska statesmen. The tapes constitute a rich, diversified, and unique store of information for anthropologists, folklorists, historians, and other social scientists. The program's success has drawn statewide attention, and Rasmuson Library has become Alaska's major repository for Oral Histories. In the past, historical organizations, government agencies, and cultural groups have generously donated their recordings to the program for safekeeping, and they continue to do so. In addition, Rasmuson continues to add materials to the collection as a result of specific funded projects.

The Oral History collection has been building since 1974. It's 6000 tapes have a length of about one to one and one-half hours each. Although the tapes are now manually indexed and accessed, the Oral History index data is being added to the Western Libraries Network (WLN) to allow automated searches.

The contents of the tapes range from eyewitness accounts of earthquakes and floods to Native Elders recounting traditions rich in local history. Pioneer miners, journalists, fishermen, trappers, and educators share their stories and provide a sense of life on the frontier. The interviews focus on such matters as the development of environmental policy, the research of Alaskan scientists, and the early days of mail delivery by dog team.

A typical example of an interview tape is a discussion with a relative of the man, Felix Pedro, who discovered gold in the Fairbanks, Alaska area in 1902. The narrator tells about Pedro's skill as an outdoorsman, his Italian family, and his relatives who settled in Tacoma, Washington. He provides personal and valuable perspectives in the 1-1/2 hour tape on the man who significantly influenced the development of Fairbanks, Alaska's second largest city.

PROJECT JUKEBOX GOALS

Project Jukebox has three main goals relative to the Oral History collection. They are to be achieved by the use of emerging computer technology, specifically the so-called multimedia system technology. The three goals are:

- control operational costs
- preserve collection
- improve access.

As the Oral History collection has grown, the Oral History program challenge has been to find ways to process new acquisitions in a timely fashion, to access them with precision, and to ensure their physical preservation. The latter task includes the copying of deteriorating tapes in the existing collection. Each year the challenge becomes greater while the personnel resources available to meet it remain the same. The program has turned to computer technology and automation as a way to meet its goals.

The present manual system is characterized by several problems. A major one is high personnel costs, which continue to rise as the collection grows (at about 10% per year). These costs relate to both the required number of workers and to their required skill levels. The staff requires some highly trained individuals in order to deal effectively with the nuances of the present manual system. Moreover, the training costs are high in a university environment with its inevitable rapid personnel turnover in student-clerical jobs. An automated system such as that envisioned by Project Jukebox would help to solve this problem of ever-rising personnel costs by allowing present Oral History staffing levels to remain approximately constant as the collection grows.

Collection maintenance costs can be reduced by rebasing the tape collection onto a (relatively) deterioration-free medium. This helps with the preservation goal. Finally, changing the present access scheme to fully electronic "user friendly" access is expected to improve system access greatly with regard to ease of use, speed, and increase in the number of potential users.

Significant front-end costs are anticipated in getting the Project Jukebox system developed and operational. Furthermore, after the system is fully operational, workers will need to index and digitize new tape acquisitions. In a few years, however, the system will allow staffing levels considerably lower than would have been possible without the system. Collection preservation and access enhancements are significant additional system benefits.

PROJECT HISTORY

Project Jukebox began in January 1990 when Engineering Management student Felix Vogt selected the Oral History problem as the subject for his Master of Science project. His report, entitled "Project Jukebox: Using Modern Technology to Preserve Endangered Recordings—A Feasibility Study," was completed in April 1990. Thereafter,

Felix and William Schneider (Curator of the Oral History Collection at UAF's Rasmuson Library) and David Hales (Head of the Rasmuson Alaska and Polar Regions Department) collaborated in a grant proposal to the Apple Library of Tomorrow (ALOT) program. This proposal was based on the Vogt project, and it requested assistance with a Project Jukebox prototype development. The proposal was well-received, and in May 1990 Apple Computer Company gave Rasmuson a MacIIx, a Mac SE30, a scanner, a laser writer, an EO drive, a CD-ROM drive, and other hardware and software needed to build the prototype. Also in May, a team of Apple experts (Steve Cisler, Sam Dicker, and Monica Ertel) visited Fairbanks to view the Project Jukebox site and to discuss key technical problems. This visit helped to establish initial project directions.

The Project Jukebox development began immediately and in the following year a prototype was developed and partially tested. This chapter reports on some particulars of the prototype design, some lessons learned, some major challenges remaining and plans for the project.

DESIGN APPROACH

The project name was chosen because we envision a jukebox-like automated storage and retrieval system to host the Oral History collection. The name "jukebox" originally referred to a device for providing convenient access to recorded music; in today's computer jargon, it refers to similar devices that hold optical storage discs, such as CD-ROM. If the Oral History tapes were rendered on CD-ROM discs with an automated access mechanism and suitably indexed, then the jukebox approach would meet the project's access goals. If the Oral History records were rendered on deterioration-resistant media, then the goal of reduced maintenance costs could also be met. If the Oral History jukebox were viewed as a workstation or server embedded in a communications network and therefore accessible from remote terminals, it would help to meet the goal of increased accessibility. Furthermore, this system can be designed for operation by library patrons and staff members who don't require the experience and training now needed to work with the Oral History collection. It would therefore have the widely sought ease of use feature for both patrons and administrative users.

Thus the developmental system was initially conceived as an Oral History jukebox attached to a computer workstation. The latter acts as a server for both local and remote terminals in a communications network.

The jukebox plus workstation system has three main parts, namely a front end, a back end, and a human-machine interface. The functions of each of these parts are:

Front End (FE): Stores the WLN-compatible index cards, and provides the means for their automated search.

Back End (BE): Stores the Oral Histories and associated records (transcripts, photos, maps etc.) and provides for automated search and navigation within multimedia objects. (In the current computer vernacular, these Oral Histories plus associated records are referred to as "multimedia objects").

Human-Machine Interface (HMI): Provides ease of use for both library patrons and Oral History collection administrators.

Given the continuing rapid advances in computer and communications technologies, there's no doubt that our design concept is technically feasible. Compact Disks (CDs) have been rapidly replacing phonograph records in recent years, and the digital CDs provide both longer life and better sound quality than their predecessors. Long-lived and low cost CD-ROMs (Compact Disc—Read-Only Memory) are specialized versions of CDs for optical storage of computer databases and are increasingly used for many purposes, including supplementing or replacing textual, graphical, and image materials in libraries. Erasable Optical Memories are now common, as are WORM (Write Once, Read Many) optical drives. Multimedia technologies are evolving rapidly. Computer communications networks of ever-increasing bandwidths (data rates) are evident everywhere. Many other technologies needed to implement the Project Jukebox paradigm are similarly approaching maturity. Again, technical feasibility is not in question.

Nonetheless, it is no small task to develop an optimal implementation of this design concept. Some technical design goals present formidable challenges, such as achieving a certain system response time (e.g., 15 seconds) with a single CD-ROM jukebox that attempts to serve many local and remote users concurrently.

Although technical feasibility is not in question, other concerns remain. Issues include whether Project Jukebox development and implementation costs are reasonable, whether the system benefits justify those costs, whether the basic system technologies are sufficiently stable to avoid premature obsolescence, and whether system maintenance, staffing, and other operational costs will be reasonable. One of the purposes of the prototype development is to provide answers to such questions.

DEVELOPMENT APPROACH

Vogt's initial Project Jukebox feasibility study concluded that a jukebox-based system using any one of a number of available optical storage systems could be both technically and economically feasible, and that such a system could satisfy Oral History collection preservation and access goals.

For a next step he recommended that a Project Jukebox prototype be developed. He suggested the following four-stage, seven-year system development plan:

STAGE	ACTIVITIES	TIME FRAME
1	Develop prototype workstation	1 year
2	Field test workstation, develop remote access	6 months
3	Integrate workstation with mass storage device (jukebox)	6 months
4	Load complete Oral History collection onto jukebox, and test complete system	5 years

So far this plan and schedule have been followed. Stage 1 involves mainly software development using an approach called "rapid prototyping." This method comprises reiterations of short implement-test-redesign cycles until functional requirements are satisfied, followed by a system redesign to improve efficiency. Software design tools that provide high productivity for the programmer speed up the cycles, often at the cost of implementation efficiency.

Although Stage 1 of the plan and schedule was followed closely, Stages 2, 3, and 4 will not be pursued exactly as originally proposed, due to both technical and financial reasons. The impediments include the current unavailability in Alaska of high-bandwidth, low-cost telecommunications and of very high capacity, low cost CD-ROM-based jukeboxes. In addition, the prospects are dim for the near-future funding of the digitizing and processing of the more than 6000 hours of Oral History tapes.

Current plans for the future of Project Jukebox are discussed later in this chapter.

DESIGN CONSIDERATIONS

Some of the main design issues for the Project Jukebox multimedia system are briefly discussed below.

Digital Sound Representation/Compression Scheme

Project Jukebox is a pioneering effort with some unique aspects. Many multimedia systems are now in development, but most of them add sound to multimedia objects consisting of text, images, and video. Project Jukebox, however, adds text, graphics, and images to objects in the form of sound recordings, which occupy most of its database. The amount of space needed to store the recordings is very great and the exact storage requirement depends on the scheme used for representing digital sound.

Thus, an important design consideration is the choice of a digital sound representation scheme (we assume use of a digital rather than an analog scheme for many reasons, among them preservation, quality, and possible record requirements). An important related consideration is the choice of a digital sound compression scheme. Without an effective compression scheme, the economic feasibility of Project Jukebox becomes doubtful because of very high data storage costs. For example, to store 6000 hours of Oral History tapes using the scheme now used for compact disks (with music) would require about 2 terabytes (trillion bytes) of storage.

Data Communications Scheme

The full-blown Project Jukebox system consists of an Oral History jukebox/workstation combination serving remote terminal users via a data communications network. As international teleconferencing on commercial TV proves, no technical feasibility problem exists for such a high bandwidth network. Alaskans, however, face specific problems related to cost and response time.

For example, the distance between the Rasmuson Library and some likely remote terminal sites equals 500 miles or more. Also, the current telephone network that serves many of those sites supports data rates of only 1200 bits per second. If we suppose that an Oral History file desired for remote use contains 100 megabytes of data (a very possible size), to transfer that file to the remote terminal at 1200 bits per second (150 bytes per second) requires 667,000 seconds, or about 7.7 days. At current Alaska long distance rates ($0.48/minute during daytime, with evening and night discounts) the file transfer would cost about $4000. Clearly some creativity is needed to solve this problem.

Archival Store vs. On-Line Store

In an optimal Project Jukebox design, the archival storage medium and representation scheme will probably differ from the on-line storage scheme. The best archival storage medium, for example, might be Digital Audio Tape (DAT) with a representation scheme of 22K samples per second and 16 bits per sample, while the best storage medium for on-line storage might be CD-ROM with a representation scheme of 11K samples per second and 8 bits per sample. The optimal data compression schemes are likewise likely to differ.

Emerging Technical Standards

Multimedia technical standards, such as for CD-ROM, are still emerging in areas important for Project Jukebox. It is important to pick a viable CD-ROM recording scheme initially; otherwise we might have to re-cut a lot of CD-ROM disks prematurely or face excessive restrictions in the future choices of CD- ROM drives or jukeboxes.

Usage Conditions and Agreements

Some speakers have granted Oral History interviews only on the basis of certain conditions guaranteed by the interviewer, and some Oral History collection donors have specified that certain kinds of uses will not be allowed. These conditions may restrict who may access the history (applicable at some archives but not at Rasmuson Library), or how or for what the history may be used (e.g., radio or TV broadcast might not be authorized).

Speakers' concerns can be legitimate. For example, an unscrupulous person with access to the digital recorded words of another person could easily synthesize a new tape and make the speaker say whatever the user wants said, because digital records of any kind are easily so edited. Even easier is the use of spoken words taken out of context. These possibilities imply the need for Project Jukebox design security features.

The manual Oral History system already faces some of these security issues and concerns. Under this system, a patron borrows a copy of a recording to review. The possibility of having patrons sign a letter of intent at the time of loan has been discussed, but this policy has not yet been implemented. Such a letter could demonstrate, for library record purposes, that the borrower had read and had agreed to abide by the stated usage restrictions. A similar feature has been incorporated into the human-machine interface portion of the Project Jukebox prototype design.

STATUS

At this writing (early May 1991), the Project Jukebox summary status is as follows:

- initial prototype development and testing completed
- successful prototype "marketing" completed
- prototype redesign in progress.

Further discussion of these items is provided in the following sections.

PROTOTYPE DESCRIPTION

As was noted earlier, the Project Jukebox prototype design has been divided into 3 parts, the front end, the back end, and the human-machine interface.

The initial Project Jukebox prototype has been scaled down from the full system—it stores and manages only 50 Oral History tapes instead of 6000. The digitized tapes and corollary information are stored on EO disks (capacity, about 660 megabytes per 2-sided disk; drive manufacturer, Pinnacle Micro Model REO 650; cost, about $200 per blank disk).

Front End (FE)

This part of the system was intended to store 50 Oral History index cards and to provide the means for their user friendly automatic search. The Oral History index cards use a format which is upward compatible with Western Library Network (WLN) index card standards.

FE was designed, implemented, and tested as a 15-week project by a 4-person team of UAF computer science seniors. The main implementation language was HyperCard, and about 2600 lines of script were required. FE was implemented on a Mac SE30 using the ORACLE relational database package. ORACLE was chosen partly because it is a mature and widely used system that is also available for Apple Macintosh computers, and partly because it includes an interface to HyperCard. The HyperCard interface is important because we used the same language to implement the prototype back end with which FE had to connect.

Ease of use was provided because FE screens were typical HyperCard screens with labeled buttons, and because the FE also provided a context-sensitive help. FE tests revealed adequate functionality and interfacing to BE, but a slow response time. Reasons for the latter weren't fully explored. Problems with ORACLE included undesirable string length restrictions and undesirable file export restrictions. The latter interfered with a desired capability to export WLN-compatible Oral History index cards from the Mac/Oracle database to another WLN card database hosted on a different computer. This capability was important to avoid double entry of WLN index cards. The library staff was not pleased with the relatively high price of ORACLE for the Macintosh and, because of this and other problems, ORACLE will not be used in the redesigned Project Jukebox prototype. HyperCard gave no problems except that its lack of recursion capabilities complicated some of the code design.

Back End (BE)

BE was designed and implemented by a single programmer over a 1-year period. For the first 6 months the programmer worked on a half-time basis, but on a full-time basis for the last 6 months. Fifty Oral History tapes were selected, digitized, and enhanced with pictures and transcripts to serve as the multimedia objects for prototype test purposes.

The main tools used to implement BE were HyperCard (Version 2.0) and Digidesign's Audiomedia package (Version 1.2). Other software used include the Mac operating system (Version 6.0.5) and Finder (Version 6.1.5). In the Audiomedia package, a separate standalone application allows digitizing of the audio tapes, and a set of Xcmnds allows the use of the digitized sound. The Audiomedia package includes a hardware card with an embedded DSP (Digital Signal Processor), which plugs into the MacIIx. The DSP is supported by software in the Audiomedia package.

After some discussion, the Rasmuson Library staff decided to digitize the Oral History tapes using 22k samples per second and 16 bits per sample. This digital sound representation scheme can be compared with that now used for music stored on compact disks, namely 44K samples per second and 16 bits per sample. Note that the former scheme requires about 160 megabytes of storage per hour of sound, while the latter requires about 320 megabytes of storage per hour of sound. For 6000 hours of Oral History recordings, the latter scheme translates into a requirement for nearly 2 terabytes of digital storage capacity.

The digital storage capacity requirements for Project Jukebox could be greatly reduced if the "true" digital sound quality requirements were determined. Some efforts were made to determine those requirements for digital storage of the Oral History tapes. Simple, non-rigorous experiments using Farallon's MacRecorder indicated that lower sampling rates and a smaller number of bits per sample (e.g. 11K samples/second and 8 bits/sample) might yield adequate sound quality. Such a sound representation scheme requires "only" 40 megabytes per hour of taped sound.

An important prototype development goal, however, was to build a functionally complete working prototype in one year. But that target was unreachable if the project stalled on the digital sound representation quality issue. Therefore the 22K/16 bits representation was chosen for the time being, and the project was continued.

Tests conducted since the initial sound representation decision tests indicate that the highest frequencies in the 50 selected Oral Histories are 6K cycles per second. Theory (Nyquist's Theorem) indicates that those frequencies require a 12K samples/second rate to capture all the information in the analog Oral History tapes. Thus it appears that the sound representation scheme for the prototype errs on the conservative side.

It is noteworthy that during the development of the BE prototype the programmer worked closely with the Oral History Curator, Will Schneider. This close collaboration, taken together with the use of rapid prototyping tools, has resulted in a BE design that meets all known requirements including a number that were never formally stated initially. In other words, the rapid prototyping approach has worked as it is supposed to.

Human-Machine Interface (HMI)

The Project Jukebox prototype has four main types of HMI, namely:

- Patron User/FE
- Administrative User/FE
- Patron User/BE
- Administrative User/BE.

For both the FE and the BE, the HMI development emphasis was placed mainly on the Patron User, and the main goal was to achieve ease of use.

PROTOTYPE MARKETING

The Project Jukebox prototype generated much interest at Rasmuson Library. Several demonstrations were given, including one for National Park Service personnel (NPS). As a result, the NPS appears likely to fund the development of one standalone Jukebox-like station for field use on the Yukon River in Eagle, Alaska. The envisioned host computer for the Eagle station is a Mac SE30 with a few CD-ROM disks. The CD-ROM disks are expected to store about 200 hours of Oral Histories and associated data (pictures, etc.)

Other interest has derived from the Project Jukebox prototype demos. For example, recent interest was shown in 4000 hours of Oral History tapes covering the Alaska Constitutional Convention, which took place in the late 1950s (Alaska entered the union January 3, 1959).

PROTOTYPE REDESIGN

The initial prototype is being redesigned as a result of initial tests and because of new requirements derived from the National Park Service's application. The NPS requirements were reduced from the original 6000 hours to 200 hours, thereby generating much less concern about enormous data storage requirements. Furthermore, a much simpler FE design seems adequate because of the greatly reduced number of index cards.

Renewed and intensified interest has developed in the important (but, so far, neglected) subject of data compression. Sam Dicker of Apple's Advanced Technologies Group has developed a "virtually lossless" data compression scheme, which achieves about 4:1 compression without requiring excessive computer power. Apple appears willing to share this algorithm with Rasmuson, and Rasmuson is very much interested. The compression scheme could reduce data storage requirements from the present 160 megabytes per hour to 40 megabytes per hour, and it could be used immediately in the NPS Eagle, Alaska application.

For larger databases, some kind of existing database management package might be appropriate for FE implementation. The UAF student team based the initial FE design on ORACLE. The team later became interested in another candidate database package—*HyperHit* by Software International. This package looks promising and its applicability is now being examined.

LESSONS LEARNED

The Project Jukebox team never doubted the system's technical feasibility. Nevertheless, a multimedia system such as Project Jukebox requires the creative handling of many tradeoffs to achieve a balanced design that approaches optimal performance. The prototyping exercise shed light on how to handle some of these tradeoffs.

The rapid prototyping exercise conducted in the library revealed many requirements that otherwise might not have surfaced until much later. For example, it indicated a new requirement for the inclusion of the transcript as part of the multimedia object, and many of the current HMI features emerged as part of a trial-and-error process. Thus the prototyping effort helped greatly in determining Project Jukebox requirements.

The prototyping effort was also helpful in clarifying Project Jukebox benefits. Although one can imagine the affect of combining Oral History records with speaker photos, area maps, transcripts, and area photos, one must experience the real impact of the combination to fully appreciate it. The prototype provided that experience.

Will Schneider believes that Project Jukebox is revolutionary for two kinds of researchers. The first kind, which he calls the "patron researcher," can access multimedia sources all at once instead of separately as before. The second kind, which he calls the "collector researcher," can now collect both the basic data and its context at the same time. For example, as an Oral History collector/researcher, Will must now try to collect pictures, maps, and other items along with his oral records, because they all become part of the same multimedia object.

The value of some development tools and hardware and the weaknesses of others were revealed as a result of the prototyping effort. The EO disk was new to the library staff and it proved acceptable for its data storage and retrieval function. Anomalies were discovered, however, such as the asymmetry of read and write (slow write, fast read).

As a result, it was necessary to digitize the data from analog tapes onto hard disk first, and transfer it to the EO disk later, because the EO disk does not write fast enough to keep up with the generated number stream in real time.

The contact with Apple's various ALOT groups continues to be helpful as the Project Jukebox design evolves.

Some insight on data compression algorithms for digitized sound was developed, as was insight regarding appropriate digital audio representation schemes. Considerably more needs to be learned in these areas.

PROJECT JUKEBOX FUTURE PLANS

Because of probable funding from the National Parks Service and possible funding for such projects as the Alaska Constitutional Convention audio tapes, it appears that further development of Project Jukebox is assured for the next few years. These projects can be described as ad hoc applications of the Project Jukebox-derived technology.

What about the original problem of the more than 6000 deteriorating tapes, and the ever-rising personnel costs? Present plans call for the incremental conversion of the collection by digitizing new acquisitions as they arrive and digitizing old holdings when they are needed for one of the ad hoc projects. Will Schneider refers to this collection management and maintenance concept as "batching." Although rooted in financial expediency, the plan has a number of attractive features.

What about the remote access to the centralized Project Jukebox collection via computer network? Plans for this capability are now delayed pending favorable developments on the Alaska telecommunications scene. Prototype design continues to be such as to permit remote access in the future. For the short term, however, remote patrons with suitable workstations are best served by the physical distribution of CD-ROM disks.

SUMMARY

Project Jukebox is an ongoing project at the UAF Rasmuson Library to control operational costs and to preserve and improve access to a growing collection of Oral History tapes that now number more than 6000. The system design assumes the use of a CD-ROM jukebox connected to a computer workstation that provides both local and remote access to the collection. The project name is derived from this concept.

The initial prototype has been developed and tested over the last year at the Rasmuson Library. The necessary hardware was supplied by Apple in May 1990 under its ALOT (Apple Library of Tomorrow) program. This was done in response to a grant proposal from Rasmuson. The project staffing is funded in part by Rasmuson and in part from grant support.

Lessons learned include increased knowledge of which development tools, hardware items, and techniques work well and which do not for this application. Knowledge of digital data representation schemes and associated compression schemes has increased, but more needs to be learned in order to optimize the Project Jukebox design.

Prototype redesign is now in progress to better meet the specific requirements of a standalone, scaled down Jukebox system for a National Park Service application in Eagle, Alaska.

Future funding prospects are bright, partly as a result of interest generated by prototype demonstrations. Besides showing technical feasibility, those demonstrations show how the Project Jukebox multimedia technology can be revolutionary for researchers. Plans for the originally envisioned large scale system using a central server and multiple remote terminals await forthcoming technological developments.

Peter J. Knoke
Department of Mathematical Science
University of Alaska at Fairbanks
Fairbanks, Alaska 99708

Museums and Archives

CHAPTER
12

INTERACTIVE MULTIMEDIA IN MUSEUMS

David Bearman

INTRODUCTION

Typically, when I speak or write about interactive multimedia in museums, I am addressing either museum professionals interested in applying the technology or interactive media developers interested in serving museum requirements. In this chapter, I attempt to address both perspectives by first discussing the history and present applications of interactive multimedia in museums, and then the nature of museum requirements and how designers could better satisfy them. Finally, I reflect on the prospects for interactive multimedia in museums.

HISTORICAL FRAMEWORK

By their very nature museums have always been multimedia experiences; i.e., opportunities for patrons to interact with artifacts, specimens, and realia accompanied usually by text and often by image and/or sound. Since the early 20th century museums have strived to interact more assertively with visitors. In the 1920's at the Deutches Museum in Munich and the Palais des Decouvertes in Paris, American museologists were impressed by cranks and handles that enabled visitors to interact with machine models. By the late 1930's interactive exhibits in museums had some multimedia attributes: at least one I encountered in a 1939 photograph of the Buhl Science Center consisted of recorded sound and image selectively played back under user control. A museum technician stood behind the exhibit and placed the needle on one of several record players based on a selection made by a visitor on the public side of the wall!

Except for the technology it employed, this 1939 exhibit was interactive multimedia in the sense we tend to use it today. But the dominant model for interactive multimedia in museums until recently was a very different kind of exhibit characterized by the Exploratorium in San Francisco. Exhibits in this magical museum all encourage interaction, whether requiring visitors to build bridges so they can walk across them, move backgrounds to illustrate how certain fish try to hide in their environments, or pump bellows to explore the harmonics of sound. One favorite installation, the "Ames Room," reveals the mental constructs surrounding vision when visitors to an oddly distorted room are viewed as being of abnormal size in a strictly rectangular space. But these exhibits are not responding with multimedia output to visitor selection from a menu, they are themselves multimedia: tangible, three dimensional experiences. [1]

A new paradigm of multimedia appeared with the earliest computer-based interactive multimedia (which probably dates from 1976, before videodiscs and personal computers), when Myron Krueger a computer artist, installed "Videoplace" at the Connecticut Museum of Natural History. At Videoplace visitors created a multimedia environment by feedback from their movements. An even more recent paradigm is hypermedia, which is 30 years old as an idea, but not much more than 5 years old in a platform that museums could implement.

When the first museums entered the world of interactive multimedia, the hardware costs were much greater. Platform vendors needed interesting content to show off their latest technology and museums could not afford to take on projects without their support, so a symbiotic relationship developed in which museums participated in projects initiated by the vendors of new distribution media who saw museum content as a means of promoting their technology. Examples of these projects include:

- Philips' sponsorship of the "Van Gogh" videodisc, completed about 1985
- Intel's sponsorship of the "Palenque" Digital Video Interactive (DVI), completed about 1988 and being released commercially in Spring, 1991
- Philips' sponsorship of the "Golf" Compact Disk Interactive (CDI) completed with the Golf Museum of the U.K. in 1989, and of the Smithsonian Interactive disk in 1991.

Similar projects can be expected from each new medium vendor. The risks to the participating institutions are, of course, that the medium they choose may not win the ultimate battle for consumer acceptance and the product will become obsolete. In the interim, the institutions will have gained experience and the projects promoted by the medium vendor.

More recently, as costs have fallen, most of the world's large museums have experimented with interactive multimedia without direct sponsorship of the distribution media vendors. Products of these experimental efforts in the U.S. that have produced commercially available products include [2]:

- The National Gallery of Art videodisc, which has 1600 stills, gallery tours, and a documentary history of the museum dating from about 1985
- The J. Paul Getty Trust "Greek Vases" videodisc
- Several videodiscs from the National Air and Space Museum (Smithsonian Institution) photo-archives

- The Library of Congress videodiscs of WPA photos and more recent CD-ROMs from the "American Memories" series
- The Metropolitan Museum of Art tour.

Internationally, museum projects that have led to videodiscs now available in the U.S. include those from the Louvre, the Museé D'Orsay and the Museé Albert Kahn in France. Other major museums internationally that have developed an interactive multimedia product that I have seen include Canada's Museum of Caricature and the Canadian Heritage Information Program, the National Museum of Ethnology in Japan, the Tate Gallery and National Museum of Art in England, and the National Museums of Denmark, Germany, the Netherlands, and Sweden.

A surprisingly large number of smaller museums, with visionaries and computer programmers on their staffs, have also created interactive multimedia products. The first museum disc I saw in the early 1980's was of the Helen L. Allen Textile Museum in Wisconsin. Why they decided to put 12,000 images of textiles and costumes on a disc I still don't know, but the product has been commercially available for years. Probably the impetus was an individual, as it was in the case of the Eadweard Muybridge disc developed by Jim Sheldon to accompany an exhibit at the Addison Gallery of American Art at Phillips Academy, a boys' preparatory school in Andover, Massachusetts. Overall, my resource lists now include projects from more than 200 museums worldwide, of which, unfortunately, only a few are commercially available.

Lately a number of important interactive multimedia programs have been produced by consortia of museums. The Interactive Video Science Consortium, an organization that has over a dozen Science Centers in its membership, was organized in 1988 and now makes about three or four new programs a year. [3] The Museum Education Consortium, a collective representing six art museums organized in 1989, is creating a generic hypermedium for discovery-based learning in the arts. [4]

Over the past decade a number of publications, conferences, and special events have contributed to museums' growing interest in interactive multimedia. In 1982 the National Air and Space Museum at the Smithsonian established an experimental facility to produce videodiscs of its photographic archives in order to reduce the wear and tear on historical prints caused by constant retrieval of images from its vast collections. In 1985, the Smithsonian established the "National Demonstration Laboratory for Interactive Technology" under the direction of Glen Hoptman to collect and display work that was being done in museums worldwide. In the same year, Joan Cash, until recently executive director of the Multimedia Industry Association, wrote an article in *Museum News* that excited broader interest. [5]

Work got underway rapidly. Theoretical examination of the potential of image/databases was launched in 1986-88 by the Getty Trust and Brown University. [6] Videodisc projects were undertaken by enough museums to lead me in 1987 to write "Optical Media: Their Implications for Archives & Museums". [7] The appendix of that report listed 88 museum projects, and many more discs, installed and in the making. In 1988 Roberta Binder published "Videodiscs in Museums: A Project and Resource Directory," which described these same projects in greater detail. [8] The following year, Isobel Pring organized IMAGE '89 in London, an invitational conference attended by about 60 museologists from around the world at which a dozen major projects were shown and discussed. [9] In 1990, the Library of Congress announced its "American Memory" project, which is intended to make its multimedia collections publicly available on CD-ROM. The International Council on Museums formed AVICOM, a new committee which held its inaugural meeting in June 1991 in Paris at which it reviewed interactive multimedia projects from throughout France.

Interest in interactive multimedia in museums is very high. The American Association of Museums conference in 1991 had eight full sessions on interactive media. The International Conference on Hypermedia and Interactivity in Museums (ICHIM '91) in October 1991 scheduled over 30 sessions and received requests to present additional projects from around the world at least weekly. [10]

The reasons for the interest are two-fold. First, (although it shouldn't be a prime motivator, it is), the technology is available, sufficiently inexpensive, and capable enough to be attractive. [11] What we now think of as the interactive multimedia platform (which includes a microcomputer with several megabytes of RAM, a high resolution color monitor, and a videodisc, CD drive, optical memory device or high capacity magnetic memory device) is a relatively new kind of system for "standard" desktop use. Startup costs for such a basic computing system, whether IBM or Macintosh, begin at about $3500, plus a videodisc player and editing tools at about $1000, a CD drive and editing tools at less than $1000, and a 19-inch multiscan or 27-inch, 600-line monitor at $650. In other words, the entire hardware platform can now be obtained for about $6500. Image quality is now adequate and authoring tools are relatively easy to use. The general public is becoming more comfortable with computer use and patrons like interactive programs when they encounter them in museums.

Second, the nature of the museum is changing in response to changes in research and in the "edu-tainment" industry. A 1988 study by the Research Libraries Group, entitled "Information Needs in the Humanities: An Assessment," documented the increasing reliance of humanities scholarship on unpublished evidence, whether from material culture, or archives, or museum artifacts. [12] Museum professionals can only be encouraged by these findings and excited by the recently announced intention of RLG, following its PRIMA report recommendations (other reports were subsequently prepared for social sciences and sciences whose findings were in keeping with those in the humanities [13]), to develop a museum information network. We can also be excited by the potential of interactive multimedia in education, not just higher education, as a vehicle for self-directed learning. But we recognize that some of the appeal of the medium is that it provides a way to compete with entertainment on its own terms, and we must wonder whether "infor-tainment" and "edu-tainment" will be able to hold their own.

APPLICATIONS OF INTERACTIVE MULTIMEDIA IN MUSEUMS

Museums have used interactive multimedia in a variety of ways. The program for the International Conference on Hypermedia and Interactivity in Museums reflects almost a dozen different applications of multimedia programming. It is useful to examine these applications in more detail because they differ from each other considerably, and demand very different technological solutions.

Directories, Orientations, and Tours

Interactive guides to museums were among the first applications of multimedia, but they are far from the simplest. They must be accessible to a wide range of users, so they must pay special attention to matters of user interface design. They need to accommodate virtually any initial query, so they often need an elaborate thesaurus. And they are most effective when linked to graphics of floor plans, enabling users to "plan a visit," which usually requires that they enable users to print out what they locate. Some very elaborate systems have been designed to enable users to reserve tours or purchase event tickets after deciding on their program for the day.

The appeal of interactive orientation kiosks seems to be that they are "up front" in the museum, where everyone will encounter them, but the drawbacks to date seem to outweigh the benefits. Precisely because they are up front requires that a large number of them be available to accommodate the flow of visitors. If the program really takes advantage of interactive multimedia, users may spend several minutes with it, which demands even more kiosks. If the program is simple, a traditional brochure with floor plan may work better.

Collections Information Data/Imagebases

The simplest multimedia application in museums is probably both the most cost effective and the least common: simply build a multimedia database of collection documentation. The database is so cost effective because it requires no educational programming overhead, and yet it can serve as the source of images and data for a wide array of future programs. Except for certain items in museum collections that would otherwise be extremely difficult or impossible to display (such as the video created by Andy Warhol that is now the property of the Warhol Museum in Pittsburgh, or the documentation of the Holocaust collected by the U.S. Holocaust Memorial) few museums have been drawn to multimedia collections documentation. The exceptions are museums with large photographic archives.

This lack of data/imagebases that could serve as resources for future interactive multimedia programming is unfortunate both for the individual museums and for the community of museums. The ultimate benefits of interactive multimedia systems will be difficult to achieve unless the cultural heritage community creates reusable multimedia resources. Otherwise, the costs of creating every interactive multimedia program from scratch, including acquiring the necessary illustrative materials, documenting them and acquiring an image, are too great. Large-scale, multi-institutional, ventures may be required to make such multimedia libraries. One example of such an undertaking is the Perseus Project launched by Harvard University classicists in 1988. The project now engages classicists around the country who are adding to its corpus of literary texts, its images of classical art and architecture, its CAD drawings of temples, and its dictionaries and lexicons. Its sponsors are creating a resource that they and all their graduate students can use to access information required for the understanding of classical Greek and Roman culture. [14]

In-Depth Study

During the past decade, numerous interactive multimedia programs created for museums were intended to allow visitors and students to study items displayed in exhibits or held by the museum. Such study originates with the object itself to illuminate aspects of the culture that created it, the artistic community in which it was created, or the uses to which it was put. An extraordinary example of the potential of interactive multimedia to encourage study is the Museum Education Consortium "Impressionism" prototype, [15] which allows users to examine multiple aspects of the life, work, and technique of impressionist painters. A similar product is installed in the National Gallery in London and plans are in place for in-depth study applications at New York City's Metropolitan Museum of Art and elsewhere.

The main advantage of these applications is that much material routinely researched in museums can be brought together under the control of a common interface. On the other hand, such a program suggests to users that similar information will be available for all items; but because background research materials are uneven, such is not the case—preparing an interactive program for even a small part of a collection becomes a massive research project of its own. Of course it is cumulative and could have a long life if planned with careful attention to portability standards.

Interactive Installations

The most commonly recognized interactive multimedia in museums are usually installed in kiosks within exhibits where visitors can examine still images, role-play games, or explore unexhibited materials. Interactive exhibits are typically menu driven from a keyboard, mouse, or track ball. Some employ touch screens and light pens, and many other kinds of interfaces are being explored. Virtual realities, which would enable visitors to touch and move within other worlds, are potentially the most comprehensive form of such interactive installations (see Chapter 21).

Since the logic of an interactive application is that it responds to a single will, most interactive installations are limited to one person using the system at a time. But some installations are even exploring group interaction, where an entire audience equipped with interaction pads on each armrest in an auditorium acts as a single will. Such an installation is being planned for the "interactive planetarium" shows at the new Carnegie Science Center.

Museums without Walls

Traditionally, the location or the layout of the museum has impeded access because visitors could not get to the exhibits or could not experience them fully when there. Traveling exhibits have been used to bring museum experiences to remote places, but they do not eliminate the barriers experienced by the physically handicapped, linguistically different, or intellectually impaired. Interactive multimedia, however, can present materials at different levels of complexity or in a variety of languages; they can provide braille interfaces for blind persons or printed text in place of voice for persons having impaired hearing; and they can be developed with specialized interface devices to enable severely handicapped persons to interact. In addition, the entire package can easily be brought to remote places—even into individual homes. The full potential of interactive multimedia to provide mobile museums has barely been explored, but we can hope more will be done when playback systems and specialized interface devices become more common.

Participatory Experiences

In 1976, Myron Krueger created a gigantic interactive visitor participatory installation, entitled "Videoplace," at the Connecticut Museum of Natural History. By walking through Videoplace, a visitor creates sound and light patterns whose sole purpose is to make interactive art. Programs installed in the mid-1980's at the Exploratorium in San Francisco used interaction with the sun ("Sun Painting"), between lasers and the human body ("Shadow Box"), and between people in pitch black spaces and textured surfaces ("Tactile Dome") to provide visitors with a heightened experience of reality. "Fluxbase," a "virtual exhibit environment" created at the University of Iowa, is an artist's authoring and documenting toolset on a computer-based interactive multimedia system for self-expression. [16]

Public Spaces

Several years ago traffic stopped on the sidewalk in front of the IBM Gallery of Science in New York. People turned towards the windows of the street level gallery and used their bodies and pointers on a virtual touch screen occupying the plane of the windows. Recently a team at Apple Computer's Multimedia Laboratory has been recreating experiences of the Globe Theatre for a public space interactive exhibit.

Tools

Interactive multimedia can be a tool in the hands of museum professionals as well as a vehicle for enhancing visitor experiences. One such tool is the visual thesaurus, which enables users to employ graphics and images to find specialist terminology that is not part of their working vocabulary. Another tool is Computer-Aided Design (CAD) software linked to an image database used to plan exhibit layouts in three dimensions.

One of the most difficult tasks confronting any museum curator is the construction of a meaningful explanation of reality from archaeological data points; i.e. the "visualization" of a complex, data rich, universe. Before computers were put to work plotting data from digs on CAD representations of a three-dimensional space, the completion of an archaeological excavation and the first presentation of its results usually took many years. Interactive multimedia with CAD tools is not simply a method of interpreting archaeological holdings to the public, but a primary analysis tool of researchers.

Imaging technology is also used in damage and condition reporting, most notably in the monitoring system set up to observe the "Charters of Freedom" (more commonly known as the Declaration of Independence and the Constitution) at the National Archives and Records Administration. These systems involve interaction by a trained conservator as does the three-dimensional measurement research at Canadian National Research Council and work underway at the MIT Archaeological Materials Laboratory that uses a number of different wave lengths of light to provide evidence for understanding the materials working techniques of traditional cultures. Recently an IBM research laboratory employed such systems to reconstruct the exterior and interior of an ancient human skull from digitized x-ray photographs in a way that enabled researchers to examine the skull from every possible angle and to measure its capacity and any linear distances automatically. Such study tools are becoming more common in the marriage between computers and conservation science.

Publications and Products

Interactive multimedia are products that can be created by museums for other museums and for consumers. Like exhibition catalogs and videotapes, interactive multimedia products can be sold in museum shops (a specialized section of the museum shop at the Canadian Museum of Civilization sells nothing else), through museum catalogs, or to other museums in lieu of or in addition to traveling exhibits.

The full potential of interactive multimedia as museum products is barely visible because virtually no consumer market yet exists for CD-ROM or videodisc multimedia products. But the situation will change in this decade—those institutions with content to sell will be avidly wooed by content publishers and distributors hungry for new titles (and eager to show that the medium has a value beyond the distribution of pornography). The potential of this market is hinted by the appearance of such vast content owners as National Geographic, Time-Life, ABC News and the Smithsonian in the Ztek and Voyager catalogs.

Networking

Until quite recently the concept of networking interactive multimedia was unthinkable due to the immense storage requirements of images and the bandwidths required for their transmission. Recently the head of Photographic Services at the Smithsonian Institution put some images on a public data network to test general interest and was amazed to see how many users downloaded them to their own computers. Several firms in the U.S. are considering mounting databases of museum images and providing access to them by telecommunications, and one firm is providing online access to images and data from art auction catalogs as an alternative to printed catalogs. [17] In Europe an experiment dubbed the "European Museum Network" has been underway for several years. Its sponsors hope to unveil a real-time motion video link between the exhibits in half a dozen major European museums in 1992. We may yet see costs of communications plummet sufficiently to make at least some applications of networking attractive.

ISSUES FACING MUSEUMS IN USE OF INTERACTIVE MULTIMEDIA

In spite of more than a decade of experimentation and an impressive array of real and potential applications, interactive multimedia computing has yet to have a major impact on museums. A wide range of underlying reasons for this failure present issues that must be addressed in order to realize the full potential of interactive multimedia.

The Market—Audiences, Evaluation, Products

The first set of issues are associated with the absence of an identifiable market, within or outside the museum, for interactive multimedia products.

Museums have, to date, viewed interactive multimedia as though it were equally suited to all audiences, overlooking its particular appropriateness for some of the constituencies they serve and thus failing to develop programs accordingly. It is no secret that our culture has yet to fully integrate interactive multimedia, which means that few adults will have experienced it. Children, on the other hand, are experiencing using the technology, if only in the video arcade or at home with Nintendo. Adult members of the general public may have little incentive to use interactive multimedia systems, but if the product can explain the museum in an adult's native tongue, or enable handicapped visitors to experience museum exhibits previously hidden to them, then the incentive may overcome the lack of computer experience. The ability to present an interface tuned to the visitors' needs is the strength of computer interactive multimedia; when museum professionals design and implement systems that exploit that strength, the results are often exciting.

Museums have likewise been slow to recognize the potential of computer interactive multimedia for evaluation of the museum experiences of visitors and to use the results to implement changes in exhibits. Evaluation has historically been a troubling and imprecise area of museum studies; interactive multimedia computing systems provide a way of providing detailed feedback about what visitors do in the galleries, what interests them, how the size of labels affects the time spent reading them, and many other aspects of the exhibit as a communicative experience. Potentially they could alter the ways in which we receive and process feedback, and they provide a means whereby changes can be made to exhibits to test hypotheses derived from evaluation of visitor activities.

Museums have dramatically expanded their output of commercial products in the last decade. Exhibits now almost always have published catalogs. Many museums manage mail order houses, selling not just the traditional notecards and calendars, or even the more recent historical reproductions, but a vast array of products associated with the museum holdings or illustrative of its function. Increasingly we find sound recordings and videotapes in the museum shops, so surely, we imagine, interactive multimedia products cannot be far behind (indeed, some such products have been created and sold in the museums, and the National Gallery and the Smithsonian, at least, have turned a profit doing so). Other products made by museums are being sold through commercial multimedia catalogs.

But nothing museums have done or are doing changes the fact that no consumer market yet exists for interactive multimedia. Museums and other holders of large quantities of interesting materials are advised to invest in making multimedia products ("software" or "content") now, so that they will have the products to offer when the consumer market arrives (always just over the horizon). These entreaties have resulted in the production of at least some interesting products designed to meet both consumer market and museum requirements; they have also led to some unattractive compromises. Doubtless such compromises will become more frequent and their effects more widespread if the consumer market does develop; on the other hand museums may soon be abler to afford to develop a great deal more interactive multimedia products if the market reaches the size many expect.

Impact on Museum Programs

Several possible impacts of multimedia on museums are still controversial. Advocates of "museums without walls" and "virtual museums" see interactive multimedia as a deliverance, not just a delivery vehicle. But not everyone is convinced. The benefits of museums reaching a large part of the population that lacks the financial resources to visit museums and those afflicted by infirmity or physical disability are universally acknowledged. The concept of creating simulation environments that contain representations of holdings which could be in museums, however, remains an area of dispute. Some see simulation as interpreting more realistically what museums traditionally tried to achieve through dioramas or through life size installations that visitors strolled within; others see the virtual experience as ersatz.

The museum is also transformed by having to compete with experiences dominated by mass media—a familiar problem. But the demand placed upon interactive multimedia production by the quality of television programming or the nature of the interaction supported by Disney World or Busch Gardens, is exacting. And high quality television production is very expensive.

One consequence of the cost of quality has been extremely positive—museums have formed consortia to support the development of interactive multimedia programming. Through pooling of resources, member institutions of the Interactive Video Science Consortium have developed a modest library of titles to which several are being added annually. The Museum Education Consortium is testing an interactive multimedia tool that provides a standard interface through which art museums can provide opportunities for self-directed learning by visitors and students.

If more museums were to invest in building the infrastructural information resources of multimedia (the image and sound bases that represent the raw content of such programs), the costs of developing high quality programming might plummet. In Europe, national undertakings with precisely this strategic objective are far advanced in Denmark, well underway in France, and planned in other countries.

Copyright

If they do invest in capturing images and sounds, however, museums confront another of the unresolved issues that may impede the widespread availability of interactive multimedia: copyright. The beauty of interactive multimedia is that by weaving new pathways through images, sounds, texts, and sequences of motion images, designers can easily "author" new products. But what museum curators can do with their own information can be done equally by others with museum information. And, by and large, we rejoice when such creative uses are made of materials developed by museums.

Indeed, all would be well except that we wish to control the use of images and sounds from our collections because we earn royalties from the licensing of our copyrights in such items. Copyright law clearly protects the individual images from being copied for commercial uses, regardless of the form of storage, but the law remains vague about protecting our rights in the compilation of such images by another "author" in a different interactive multimedia product.

In addition, copyright law in the U.S. today provides an exemption to the prohibition on copying for "fair use," a category that covers a variety of private and educational purposes. Unfortunately, the networks that must provide access to digital data and image bases cannot recognize a "fair use" from a prohibited use. Copying to a local computer involves the same technical methods regardless of the subsequent use, even if only to "view" the program. Eventually these problems will be worked out. Already professional photographers in the U.S. are cooperating to protect their digital image copyrights; museums may do the same or join with the photographers in due course. And the law will no doubt be altered to cover the new technical and cultural circumstances surrounding multimedia.

Value of Repurposing

Although copyright law erects a barrier that impedes new program creation, it is a boon to at least one museum application. Like other users, museums can author new and original multimedia materials from components provided by others. This method of making interactive multimedia programs is called "repurposing," an inexpensive and much respected approach. Numerous discs of still and motion images have been compiled by others and are available from commercial disc catalogs at modest cost. A museum could easily purchase discs of space photographs from the NASA Voyager expedition, the National Geographic's multimedia mammals disc, or the videodisc of Works Projects Administration photographs issued by the Library of Congress, and author an interesting interactive program customized to its audience and its collections. Authoring tools for such repurposing efforts can be acquired for as little as $200 and their use can be easily mastered by any curator in a matter of days.

Managing Installations

Of course making an interactive program is only one step in museum use of interactive multimedia. The real challenge of interactive multimedia is to install it intelligently. From the first stages of planning and designing a product, its intended use—integrated into an exhibit, in a study center, or available as a reference tool for the museum's research library—must be taken into account. But even when so planned and designed, the problems of maintaining an interactive multimedia product are not solved.

Interactive multimedia products are, by definition, an experience available to a single user at a time. If only one workstation is provided, most visitors will not use the product at all. If many are provided, the costs will escalate along with the problems of keeping the hardware operating at all times; and if the hardware breaks down, the system actually detracts from the rest of the exhibit or study center experience.

As alluded to earlier, different visitors will have different experiences and abilities to use the interactive product. Interface instruments (such as keyboards, mice, trackballs, etc.) and interface presentation (the way the screens are laid out and the functions are selected) make a considerable difference. Special approaches are required when young children, the visually impaired, the physically handicapped, or the elderly are the intended users.

Museum directors may disagree whether cost overruns, visitor bottlenecks, or downtime most threaten the effectiveness of interactive multimedia. But whenever they talk about the subject, it is clear that maintenance of installations is a serious matter.

Design Challenges

In my view, the most important long-term issues for museums relate to design problems. As with all other aspects of the museum, the interactive multimedia experience will communicate something; the trick is a design that communicates what was intended, in a manner that makes visitors want to return.

Museums generally employ an instructional approach called "discovery-based learning," which they combine with a variety of free form creativity experiences to offer both education and enjoyment. Interactive multimedia are well suited both to the delivery of discovery-based learning opportunities and free form creativity experiences, but much of the history of interactive multimedia design is more directive, with more explicit pedagogical aims. The dominant interactive multimedia design strategy is "self-paced" rather that "self-directed" learning, and much of what has been written about interactive multimedia design is based on delivering instructional materials with concrete learning objectives. Even the game-playing, simulation interactions that are such an effective interactive multimedia application are typically designed to teach, as opposed to providing an opportunity to learn. Museums will need to adjust the design of multimedia systems to fit their objectives and methods if computer-based interactive multimedia is to become a vital component of their services.

Equally important, museums need to integrate multimedia computing into their current methods of providing experiences for visitors. Too often the multimedia kiosk seems glued to the edge of the exhibit, relating to little outside itself and using methods so different from those employed elsewhere in the museum that it reinforces its distinctness.

I especially hope that museums address these design issues and develop interactive multimedia programs, because their experience in the design of exhibits is especially relevant to other multimedia designers. Although the terminology varies, museums have always had to address the question of making exhibits work for different levels of age, experience, education, and interest. They have long had to contend with the ability of the individual visitor to construct a personal path through the exhibit, traveling from any given item or area to any other, and reading or not reading any given label. And they have experience in designing the individual "nodes," such as exhibit cases or brief motion picture or sound sequences, so that, in the terminology of the multimedia designers, they are of similar "granularity," or convey the same amount of information and demand roughly the same amount of time.

But these same design principles, which govern both exhibits and interactive multimedia programs, present a challenge to the integration of multimedia into museum exhibits. After all, how can the visitor spend the same amount of time or have the same amount of information conveyed at an exhibit case as at an interactive multimedia kiosk? Solutions need to be found, and these may well include structuring multimedia systems so that they are dispersed throughout an exhibit to be experienced in relatively small doses, or incorporating noncomputer-based interactive experiences that occupy equal amounts of time and convey equally complex information.

Ultimately, however, the design challenges that museum interactive multimedia designers will need to solve are the same that confront their counterparts elsewhere:

- Identify means by which users can access images other than by text
- Find methods of retrieving relevant information from sound bases

- Provide language-independent, image-based, hypermedia interfaces and develop a language of interacting with such systems that is universal within our culture
- Explore the potential of visual thesauri to lead us from the image to the word as a means ultimately of searching text databases for information about things whose names we do not know.

Of course, museum professionals will not have to solve these problems alone, but taking part in their solution, which lie at the boundary of technology, will provide many of them great personal and professional rewards.

TECHNOLOGICAL CHALLENGES AND BARRIERS

Just across those boundaries, in the realm of the technological, we can find additional reasons why interactive multimedia computing has yet to have the impact that it might. Unresolved problems related to data capture, data storage, data processing, and dissemination standards remain, but it is important for museums to see that many of these are close to solution.

Standards and Capture/Display Quality

Image capture and interchange standards have been captives of specific niche applications until recently. Facsimile standards were of little use for photography and photography standards of little use for cartography. An international joint standards committee, JPEG, has recently made a major breakthrough for still images, however, and probably paved the way for motion image standards as well.

Until the advent of the CD-Audio standard, sound capture was at least as arbitrary. But now that the high end of the human hearing range has been defined, it is easier to plan for sound capture.

There have been few developments of note recently in the area of raster-to-vector conversion, or optical character recognition (OCR), so capturing the meaning of text and images for subsequent processing is still beyond our reach. But the costs of large scale textual data capture in rasters has fallen to $0.15/page or so at resolutions that will support OCR in the future. Thus, large scale projects for full text capture are currently underway.

Storage

Virtually no standards exist for optical Write-Once-Read-Many (WORM) memories, but standards for the various compact disc formats are evolving to cover most areas of concern for interoperability and interchangeability (in spite of the differences in boards and software required to run CDI, DVI, and CD-ROM). For those who do not need rapid access to images, magnetic tape technologies, including digital audio tape, and the use of videotape for digital data storage show great promise in holding large volumes of data inexpensively.

Production Environments

Few large scale multimedia database systems exist, and none of those can be construed as a "production" environment for interactive multimedia. As a consequence, standards for such an environment are only just beginning to be considered and it will be many years before they arrive. Probably they will have their origin in dynamic documents in office systems, thereby emphasizing functionality and presentation over interface commonality or interactive use.

Unfortunately, there is a near absence of any kind of production environment capability for hypermedia. Large scale hypermedia environments, whether defined by numbers of users, quantities of data, or numbers of links and nodes, are nonexistent. Hypermedia can be an interface to a very large database, but it remains a method of managing only small sets of data.

Dissemination

There still exists no standard for CD distribution of images that is acceptable or has widespread market penetration. The CD-ROM (and XA) are restricted to hackers, the CDI and DVI formats are not commercially available, and the PhotoCD approach of being compatible with CD Audio standards and players of the next CD Audio generation has yet to be demonstrated. Obviously CD product dissemination has far to go.

Videodiscs based on broadcast standards are still stable, although all three major television broadcast standards (NTSC, PAL, and SECAM) are threatened by analog and digital HDTV. It is anyone's guess the direction these standards will take. And, despite recent efforts by Kodak to declare a de facto color display standard, display characteristics are likely to vary for a considerable time, rendering whatever is captured different from monitor to monitor.

Higher speeds of transmissions than currently available T1 speeds (to say nothing of modem speeds) are critical even if greater compression can be achieved. Useful schemes exist such as the GTE ImageSpan progressive transmission programs or the Kodak PhotoCD approach that uses thumbnails which are unaltered abstracts of richer (VGA) images that are, in turn, derivatives of an even richer (HDTV and beyond) image. But these schemes cannot substitute for generally available, very high speed transmission.

Imagining Technological Futures

The past 20 years has witnessed a near constant vision of a future information environment that contains all the knowledge of mankind in digital form and that not only enables but actively assists individuals to explore and analyze this universe. Even in the face of adverse experience, the predictions that the envisioned day would arrive within the next five years have been unchanged—the 5-year target merely moves blithely ahead.

Hypertext and hypermedia methods cited as enabling such intellectual travels have been stable in their popular explication for the same 20 years. We have therefore had ample opportunity to address how widespread societal use of computer interactive multimedia would affect museums and other cultural repositories. Interestingly, the museum profession has little to show for its speculations; to understand the impact of interactivity on museums we are still best served by studying San Francisco's Exploratorium, an institution that until recently provided its vast array of interactive multimedia experiences without computers.

CONCLUSIONS

So where does this leave us? Computer interactive multimedia has great promise for museums, but there is little "transformation" to show. Disappointment is greatest where the fanfare was most intense, as in the Canadian Museum of Civilization that, despite its brave pronouncements of five years ago, still contains only a few, very modest, and unintegrated, examples of computer interactive multimedia. [18] Science Centers have, by and large, done best in integrating the technology; it works quite well beside other forms of interactive multimedia now at the Exploratorium in San Francisco and fits neatly with other high technology at the Franklin Institute in Philadelphia and at La Villette in Paris.

More disturbing to me is that multimedia computing in museums still results from one-off projects, rather than as a component of a long-term strategic plan. Museums need to recognize that the methods of information processing and delivery in the next century will be digital, and they should begin now to build digital image and knowledge bases reflecting their holdings and the contexts of the creation, discovery, use, and meaning. It is especially disappointing to me that where imagebases have existed for some time, as in the major national museums, they are not being put to use by these museums.

In the U.S., some national inventory projects are proceeding as though the digital image revolution and multimedia computing had not yet occurred. We see no changes yet in the Index of American Paintings, the Index of American Sculpture, or the Catalog of American Portraits, but other databases such as the Avery Art Index and several commercial databases of auction catalogs are demonstrating that large imagebases of museum holdings are on the way. At least one commercial firm, Interactive Home Systems, is actively bidding for museum images to construct a multimedia image and knowledge base.

As the technology improves and the expense continues to drop, we can expect to see more activity. The future of interactive multimedia in museums, however, is ultimately tied to the future of interactive multimedia as a consumer product. Until the consumer market develops, neither the push nor the pull for widespread adoption will be felt.

We need pay more attention to the museum-specific issues, which until recently have barely been discussed. And we need more serious, critical evaluation of the dozens (still not 100's or 1000's) of discs produced by museums in the past decade. To me, the need to share ideas is paramount: I look forward to the first International Conference on Hypermedia and Interactivity in Museums (ICHIM '91) and its planned biennial successors to provide the opportunity for such exchange. [19]

NOTES

1. Hilde Hein, The Exploratorium (Washington DC, The Smithsonian Institution Press, 1990)

2. Many commercially available museum discs are listed in the catalogs issued by the Voyager Company, 1351 Pacific Coast Highway, Santa Monica CA 90401, 213-451-1383

3. The Interactive Video Science Consortium, c/o Association of Science-Technology Centers, 1413 K St. NW, 10th fl., Washington DC 20005

4. The Museum Education Consortium, c/o Museum of Modern Art, 11 West 53rd St., New York, NY 10019

5. Joan Cash, "Spinning Toward the Future: The Museum on Laser Videodisc," *Museum News* (August 1985), p. 19-35

6. Marilyn Schmitt, general editor, "Object, Image, Inquiry: The Art Historian at Work," report on a collaborative study by the Getty Art History Information Program and the Institute for Research in Information and Scholarship, Brown University (Santa Monica, Getty Art History Information Program, 1988)

7. David Bearman, "Optical Media: Their Implications for Archives and Museums", Archives and Museum Informatics Technical Report # 1 (Pittsburgh, PA, Archives & Museum Informatics, 1987)

8. Roberta Binder, "Videodiscs in Museums: A Project and Resource Directory" (Falls Church VA, Future Systems, 1988)

9. Isobel Pring, editor, Image '89: "The International Meeting on Museums and Art Galleries Image Databases: Proceedings of the IMAGE Meeting 18-20 May, 1989" (London, IMAGE, 1990)

10. David Bearman, editor, "Proceedings of the International Conference on Hypermedia and Interactivity in Museums" (Pittsburgh PA, Archives & Museum Informatics, 1991)

11. The technology was not as ready or capable even two years ago; see David Bearman, "Implication of Interactive Digital Media for Visual Collections," *Visual Resources*, vol. 5, 1989, p. 311-323

12. Constance Gould, "Information Needs in the Humanities: An Assessment" (Stanford CA, Research Libraries Group Inc., 1988)

13. Constance C. Gould and Mark Handler, "Information Needs in the Social Sciences: An Assessment" (Mountain View CA, Research Libraries Group, 1989); and Constance C. Gould and Karla Pearce," Information Needs in the Sciences: An Assessment" (Mountain View CA, Research Libraries Group, 1991)

14. For a popular account of Project Perseus, see Elli Mylonas and Sebastian Heath, "The Perseus Project," *Instruction Delivery Systems*, vol. 4(6), Nov/Dec 1990, p. 12-13

15. David Bearman, "Unveiling the Products of Cooperation: IVSC and MEC," "Archives and Museum Informatics", vol. 4(2), p. 7-8

16. Joan S. Huntley and Michael Partridge, "Fluxbase: A Virtual Exhibit," in Sandra K. Helsel and Judith Roth eds., "Virtual Reality: Theory, Practice and Promise" (Westport CT., Meckler, 1991), p. 75-91

17. David Bearman, "More Art Auction Imagebases," *Archives and Museum Informatics*, vol. 5(1), page 18 discusses products by Artifacts Inc., Centrox, and Astor House

18. Frederick Granger and Stephen Alsford, "The Canadian Museum of Civilization Optical Disc Project" (Ottawa, National Museums of Canada, 1988)

19. The Second International Conference on Hypermedia and Interactivity in Museums (ICHIM'93) is scheduled to be held in Cambridge, England, September 20-24, 1993.

David Bearman, President
Archives & Museum Informatics
5501 Walnut Street, Suite 203
Pittsburgh, Pennsylvania 15232

CHAPTER

13

Designing Multimedia Systems for Museum Objects and Their Documentation

Judi Moline

INTRODUCTION [1]

Previous investigation indicates that the resources needed by museum professionals parallel those of humanities scholars. Although a museum's records management component goes beyond the normal requirements of an individual researcher, many of the data fields are pertinent for both research and administration functions. In reality, the parallel is so great that we should accelerate the rate at which resources are made available in an online computer environment, thereby facilitating the work of both curators and researchers.

This chapter illustrates how hypertext and multimedia can be applied in museums to facilitate humanities research. It presents a model of museum professionals' information needs and shows how these needs can be met. The solution is based on the Open System Environment (OSE) and the necessary data interchange standards.

THE MUSEUM'S ROLE

In order to understand the scope of a multimedia system for museum objects and their documentation, we must first understand a museum's purpose in terms of physical demands and services provided.

The Physical Components of a Museum

A museum is defined in the Museum Services Act, 20 U.S.C. Section 968(4), as "a public or private nonprofit agency or institution organized on a permanent basis for essentially educational or esthetic purposes which, utilizing a professional staff, owns or utilizes tangible objects, cares for them, and exhibits them to the public on a regular basis". [2] The objects usually have been accessioned, the formal process used to accept

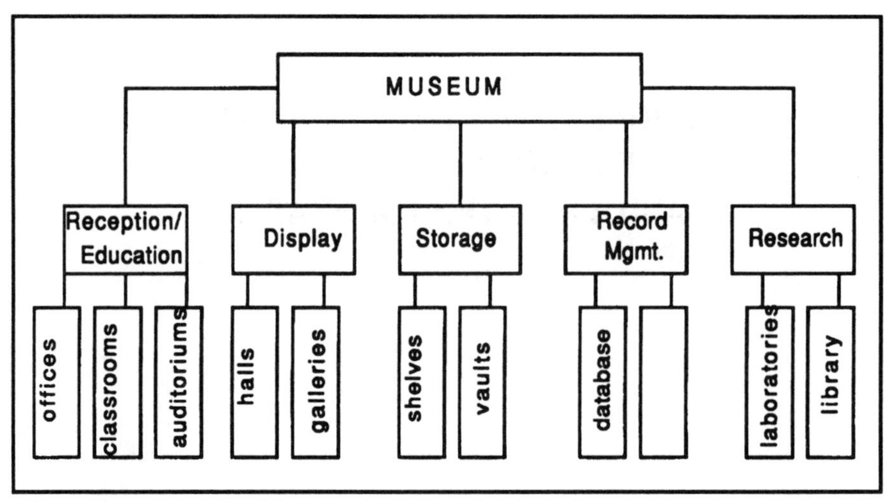

Figure 1. The Museum's Physical Space

and record an item. Deaccessioning is the formal process used to remove an object from the collection. [3] Thus, a museum has physical requirements, as well as procedures. There must be adequate space for storage, display, educational programs, and staff requirements (see Figure 1).

The Services Provided by a Museum

The tasks performed by museum staff (see Figure 2) result from the collection management policy, which explains why a museum is in operation and how it conducts its business. Further, the policy articulates the museum's professional standards, serves as a guide for the staff, and provides information for the public. A good collection management policy covers a range of topics: the purpose of the museum and its collection goals; the method of accessioning objects for the collections; the method of deaccessioning objects from the collections; loan policies; the handling of objects loaned to the museum; the care and control of collection objects; access to collection objects; insurance procedures relating to collection objects; and the records that are to be kept of collection activities, when these records are to be made, and where they are to be maintained. [4]

A View of the Museum Professional as an Art Historian

Museum professionals' research is based on extensive collections of artifacts that represent museums' reason for existence. Much of the work of the museum profession centers on those objects. When a unique object is accessioned, the following steps, often occurring over an extended period of time, are required:

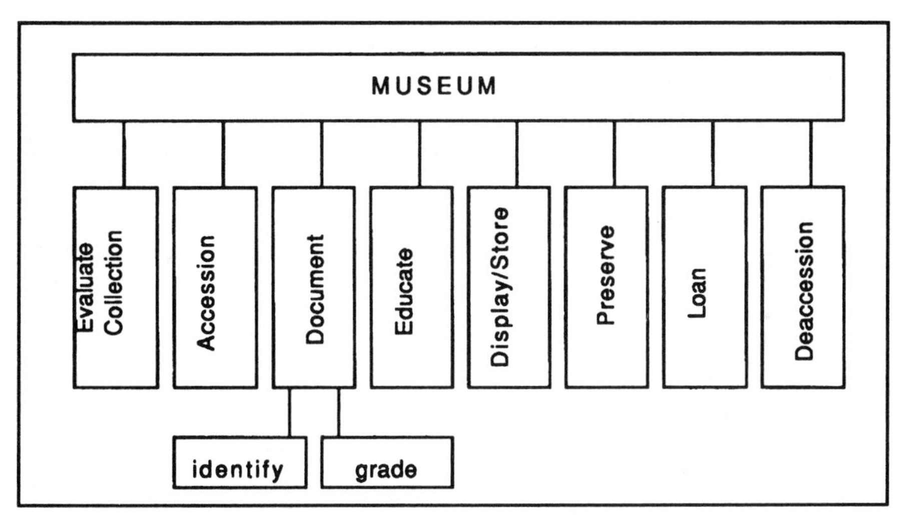

Figure 2. The Tasks Required of Museum Staff

• **The object is thoroughly described**, usually by filling in fields in a database. These fields include descriptive data, as well as management data.

• **The object is analyzed** concurrently with the description and usually extending beyond the database entry. This research seeks to generate a complete dossier on the object, placing it in its historical setting. Scientific analysis may be made of the material. Documentation will include photographs and drawings and any information available as to when and where the object was found and a record of where it has been since its discovery.

• **The object is fitted into the museum collection, both physically and conceptually**. Based on this analysis, the "conceptual fitting" may cause major changes in historical thinking if the object presents new and/or unexpected evidence. Collection catalogs might require revision and it would be important to publish the new material evidence to open the area for further research.

Parallel to the example given for the museum professional is the work of the art historian. Tasks of the art historian include classifying an object and interpreting it. In order to achieve these goals the researcher needs a large database of models against which the object in question can be compared. As details are compared, the significant ones are noted while the unimportant, as determined by a heuristic based on experience, are ignored. This comparative analysis includes aspects of style, composition, motif, iconography, etc. and results in the object's classification. The second goal, that of interpretation, assumes that the classification has been made. At this point the researcher uses bibliographic references and explains the object in terms of causes, effects, and circumstances. [5]

THE INFORMATIONAL NEEDS OF ART HISTORIANS AND MUSEUM PROFESSIONALS

A preliminary analysis of the tasks performed by museum professionals provides a list of the resources and tools needed to perform the task. For example, to accession an object, the object must be available along with a database and some set of measurement instruments. Although it is difficult to make a clear demarcation between accession and documentation, Figure 3 draws some arbitrary lines. Therefore, for documenting an object, the resources and tools might be as shown. The schema is not the important issue here and there is no clear-cut separation between resources and tools.

Analysis of the tasks performed by museum personnel and art historians and analysis of the tools needed to perform those tasks form the basis for a model hypertext, multimedia system that should be generic enough to meet the needs of many small museums. It is possible to sketch a computer-mediated multimedia system that would facilitate the work of museum professionals by providing needed resources and operations (Figure 4).

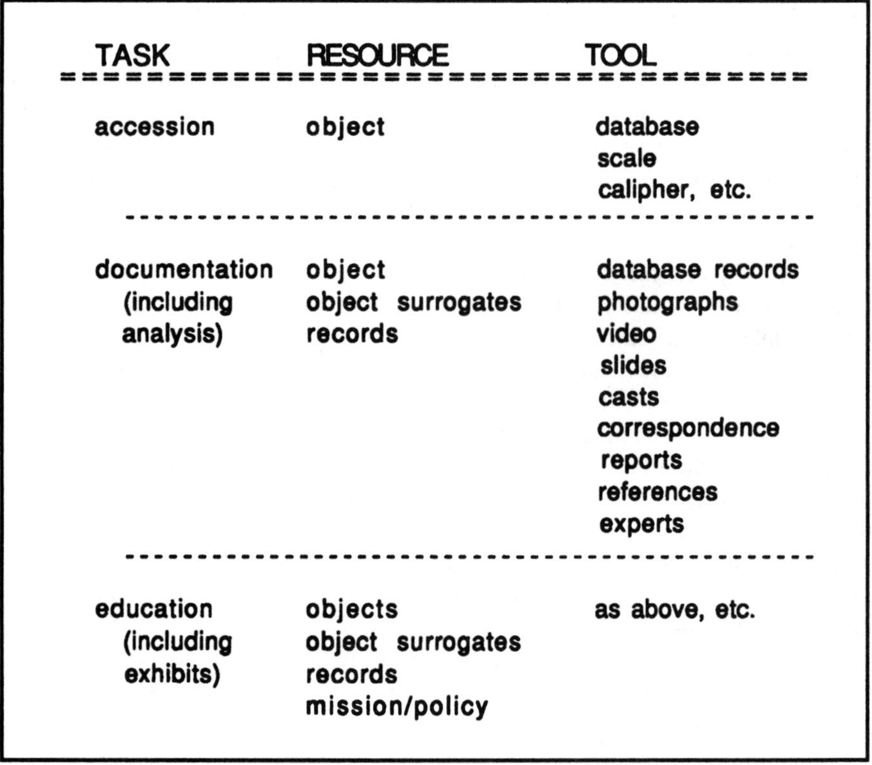

TASK	RESOURCE	TOOL
accession	object	database scale calipher, etc.
documentation (including analysis)	object object surrogates records	database records photographs video slides casts correspondence reports references experts
education (including exhibits)	objects object surrogates records mission/policy	as above, etc.

Figure 3. Tasks, Resources, and Tools

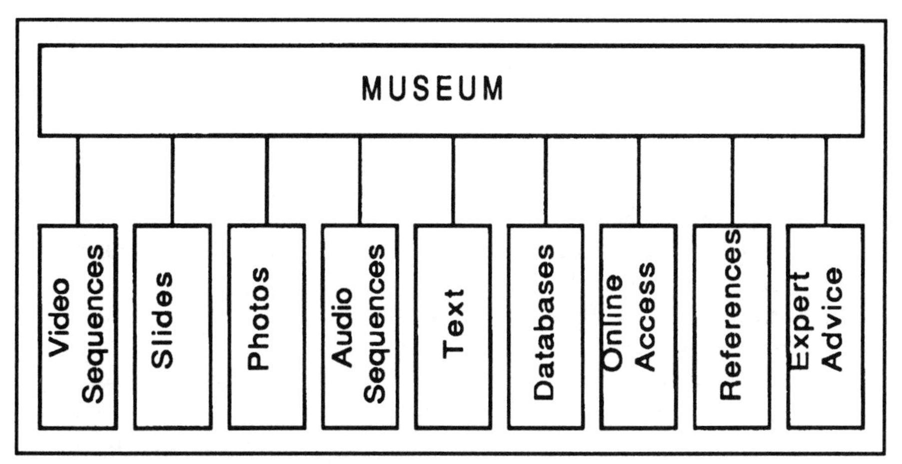

Figure 4. A Computer-Mediated Multimedia "Museum" Resources and Operations

The Informational Needs Model

The informational needs model presents a broad-based computer system with a variety of input/output devices and software (see Figure 4), which must be tailored to the users' requirements. All information about each object held by the museum would be available online in easily searched databases accessible from terminals all over the world. Each museum's system could be tied in with those of other museums, universities, libraries, and collectors. Further, books, encyclopedias, journals, catalogs, etc. could be made available. Such "libraries" now exist on CD-ROM (see Appendix A for a list of acronyms).

Other aspects of this vision of future museums are in place today. For example, electronic library catalogs are readily available over networks; standards have been developed to facilitate data interchange; and some software has been developed to run on multiple platforms. Nonetheless, many issues remain to be addressed. One important issue: "Do we really want such a system for museums?" This question is for others to resolve. The goal here only concerns determining technical feasibility. The outstanding issues are being addressed by industry consortia and various national and international standards bodies. Some of these efforts will be mentioned later.

Resources Needed to Resolve Administrative Concerns

In addition to the more obvious tasks identified in Figure 2, other issues could be facilitated with computer assistance. Some of the administrative concerns that fit in this category are statistics, preservation, and status. For example, the following statistical concerns could be programmed into the system: relative value of each object from an historical perspective, the frequency of "use" of any object whether locally or for loan purposes, and the relative cost of upkeep for any group or type of item. Preservation schedules could be put online to assure their completion on time (e.g., time line and requirements for maintenance). Status issues might include priorities for deaccession or exchange and policies for loan, exhibition, and research.

Resources for the Researcher

A survey of numismatists, whose tasks are similar to those of other museum researchers, identified the resources they use: the objects (i.e., coins and medals), file cards, spreadsheets, bulletins, fellow collectors and experts (e.g., dealers), and bibliographic resources. The latter includes coin books, coin catalogs, auction catalogs, journals, specialized newspapers, genealogies, and histories. [6]

Besides the traditional database access, and other paper- oriented resources, a multimedia approach could be taken. The researcher could be provided with a video sequence showing the object from various angles, an audio sequence made by the archaeologist who found the object, artificial intelligence in the form of expert systems, etc. To facilitate searching where links among the various types of resources might be appropriate and to allow for browsing, a hypertext interface might be made available.

THE OPEN SYSTEM ENVIRONMENT

The Open System Environment (OSE) is a conceptual framework that provides a context for user requirements and standards specification. It is shown in Figure 5 in its

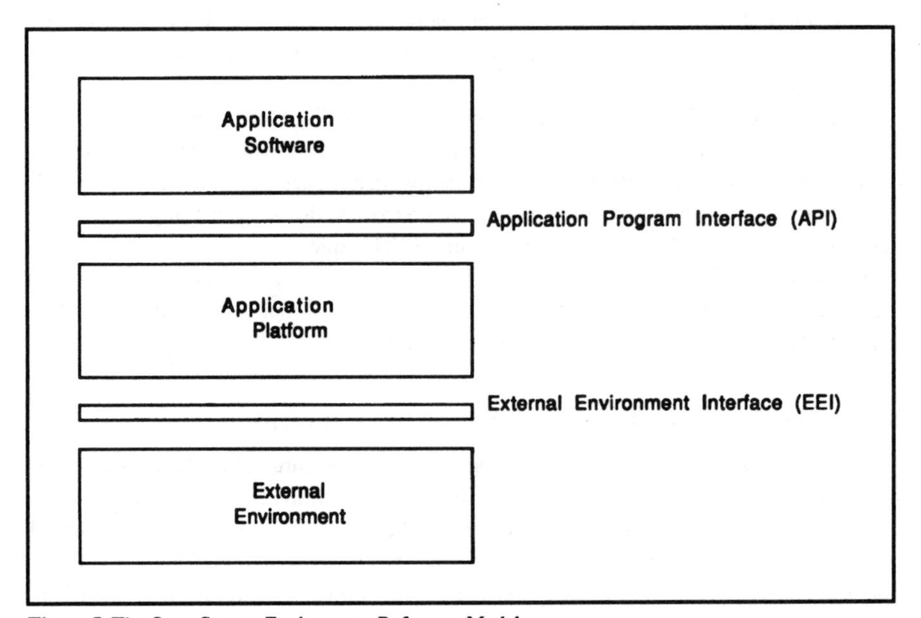

Figure 5. The Open System Environment Reference Model

simplest form. [7] Within the Reference Model, standards address interfaces between entities and between services and supporting formats across those interfaces. The Reference Model is not a layered model; the application platform provides services to users across both platform interfaces. [8]

The preliminary needs model presented in the previous section identifies a few of the services that a computer-mediated "museum" might offer its clients and other researchers. This model will be further developed here in the framework of the Open System Environment. [9] The examples in the following discussion are given to facilitate the development of a concrete model for the reader. They are not intended to represent the design of an actual Open System Environment implementation.

Application Software

Once the user requirements or needs are specified, the application software can be selected. Sample categories of this software are included in Figure 6. Each application should be capable of communicating and synchronizing with other applications when necessary using communication mechanisms. [10] It is important that the software packages selected use standard interfaces such as those specified in the section on the Application Program Interface.

Application Program Interface

The Application Program Interface (API) "is a combination of a number of standards-based interfaces. It can be thought of as a bookshelf containing several standards-based APIs, with each API a separate book on the bookshelf. . . . An API is required to provide access to services associated with each of the external environment entities. An additional API is required to provide access to services associated with the application

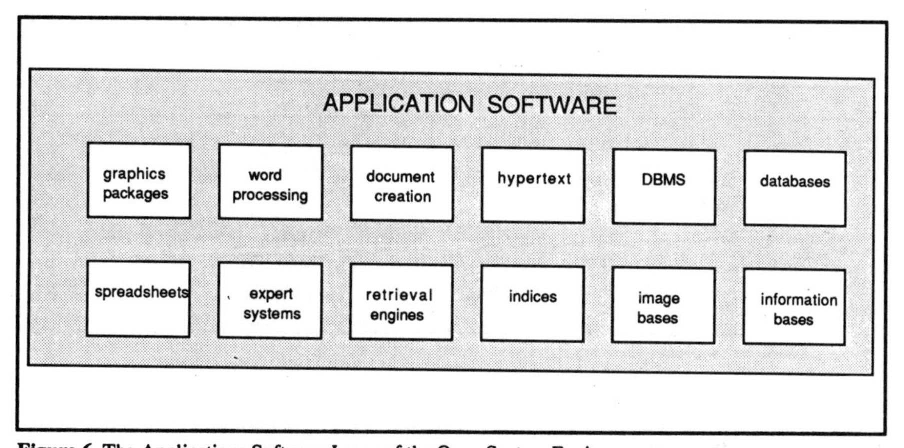

Figure 6. The Applications Software Layer of the Open System Environment

platform internal resources". [11]

The API allows for portability by providing a standard interface between the services of the application platform and the needs of the application software. Portability is the ability to use application software on heterogeneous hardware/software platforms. Figure 7 specifies sample available standards for each of the services provided by the Application Platform: POSIX relates to operating system services; X-Windows to user interface services; SQL to data management services; SGML, ODA, and CGM to data interchange services; ECMA/PCTE to programming services; and PHIGS to graphics services. GOSIP is the Federal Government's profile of standard data communication protocols for network services. (See Appendix A for acronyms.)

Application Platform

The Application Platform is well-defined in the Open System Environment Reference Model. [12] The components are shown in Figure 8. [13] Features needed for each particular application or system would be selected and implemented; not every application platform would provide all features. [14]

Operating system services include kernel operations, commands and utilities, system management, and security. User interface services include client-server operations and a virtual toolkit. Data management services include the data dictionary/directory component for accessing and modifying data about data (metadata), the database management system component for accessing and modifying structured data, and the distributed data component for accessing and modifying data from a remote database. Data interchange services establish data formats for interchange of documents, graphics data, and product description data. Programming languages and language bindings, and computer-aided software engineering (CASE) environments and tools are included as components of programming services. Until there is a standard, the ECMA/PCTE (Portable

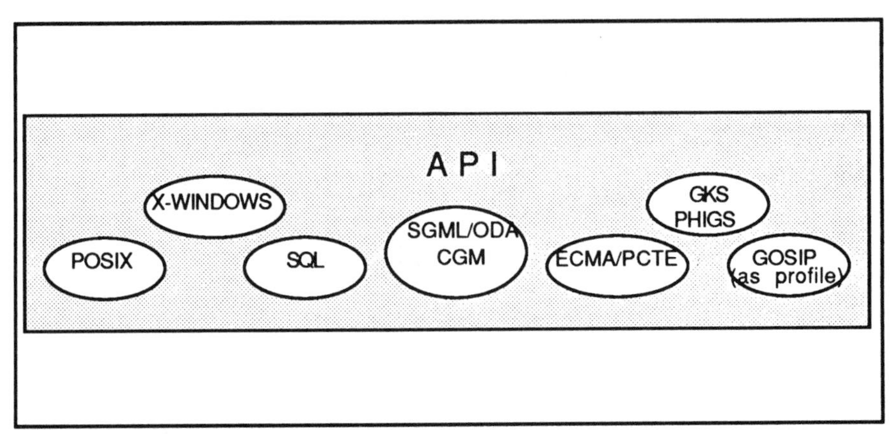

Figure 7. The Application Program Interface of the Open System Environment

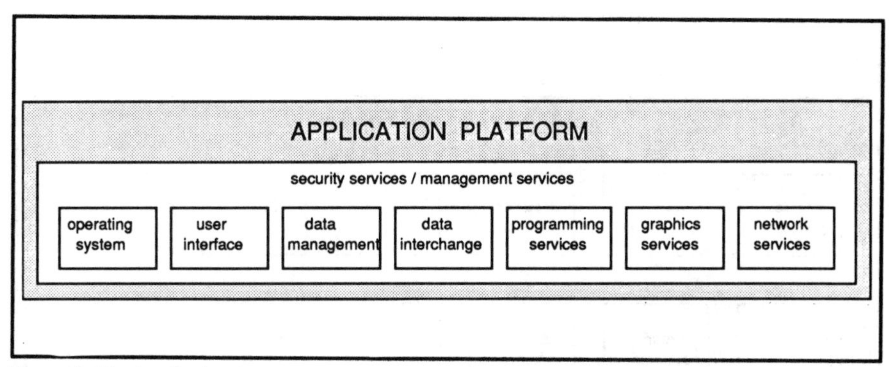

Figure 8. The Application Platform of the Open System Environment

Common Tool Environment) may be used. Graphics services provide the interfaces for programming two- and three-dimension graphics in a device-independent manner. The standards included in this service area are the Graphical Kernel System (GKS) and the Programmer's Hierarchical Interactive Graphics System (PHIGS). The network services include data communications, transparent file access, personal/microcomputer support, and distributed computing support. [15]

External Environment Interface

The External Environment Interface (EEI) links the application platform and the external environment between which information is exchanged. The particular services comprise the human/computer interface, the information interface, and the communications interface. [16] The EEI assures interoperability between devices and the hardware platform. Interoperability of application software operating on heterogeneous hardware/software platforms is necessary for performing some user functions and for data sharing. Specifically, the EEI supports information transfer between the application platform and the external environment. Data interchange services are provided by standard ports such as SCSI-II (Small Computer System Interface) and RS-232D. Data management will use Remote Database Access (RDA), which will most likely be done through network communications via distributed environments. The operating system will also communicate with external devices through network communications via distributed environments.

External Environment

The External Environment necessary to run the software is determined by the users' needs. Users determine whether CD-ROM, video disc, TV, etc. are to be part of a particular "system." Figure 9 shows the Open System Environment with sample devices in the External Environment layer. The human end-user would be an important external entity with which the application platform exchanges information.

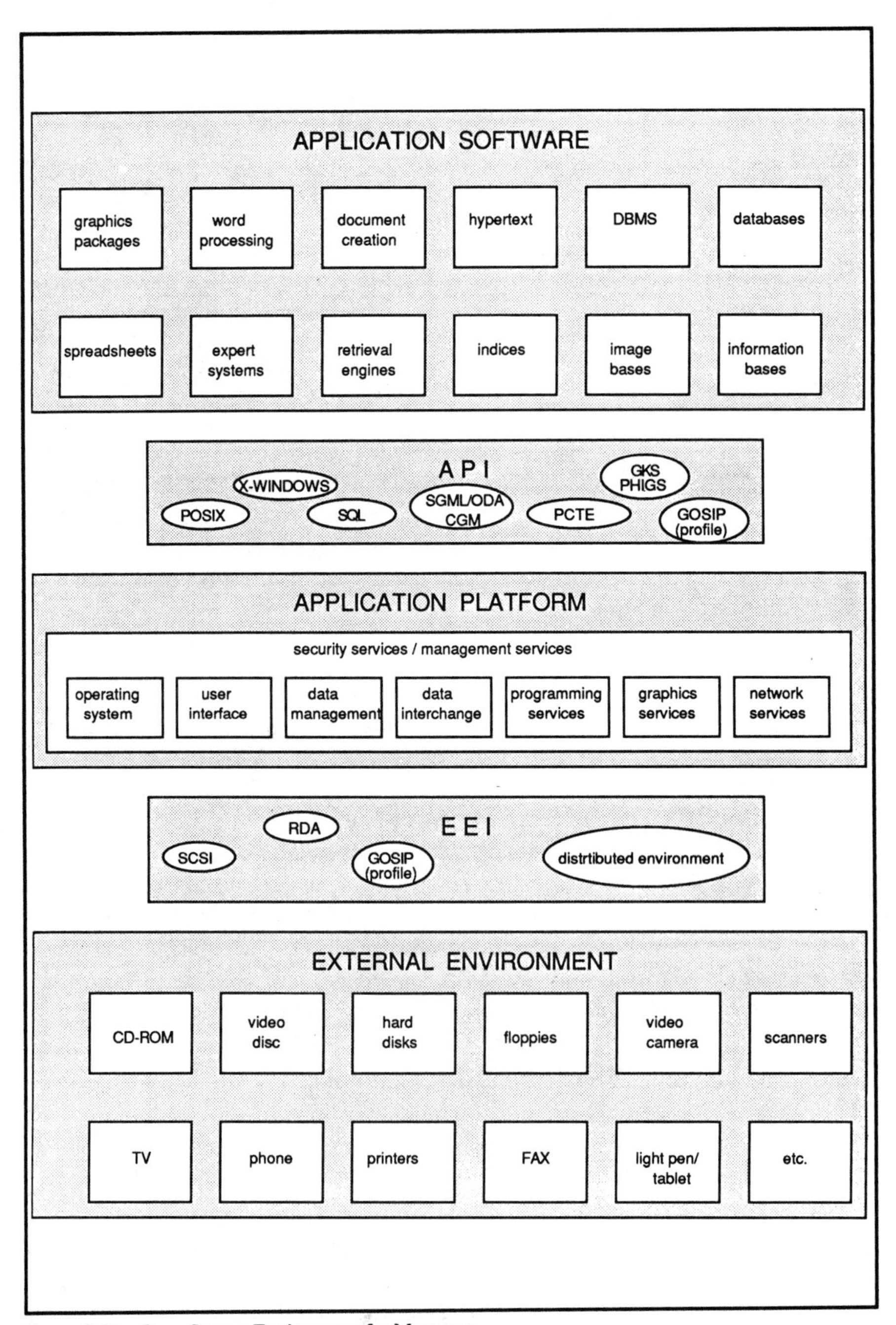

Figure 9. The Open System Environment for Museums

A MIGRATION STRATEGY FOR AN EXISTING SYSTEM

In 1989 a hypertext system, Catalogued Objects and Information for Numismatists (COIN), was presented. [17] The system is viable and if augmented could meet the needs of a researcher in a particular museum environment. The following discussion illustrates how that limited system could be placed in the Open System Environment.

Figure 10 shows the architecture of the COIN system. The interaction among software packages depends on the hypertext interface, which opens applications and keeps track of a limited amount of data from transactions. To the user this function is similar to the services that would be available with an OSE; however, the functionality of COIN is limited. Much more useful would be a system with structured data which could be used and reused for various purposes. The Standard Generalized Markup Language (SGML) would provide more efficient use and reuse of the text portion of this hypertext system.

The graphics in the COIN system are limited to scanned black and white photographs and line drawings. A better quality visual representation of the objects is necessary. These representations could be placed on video disc or CD-ROM. Video disc would al-

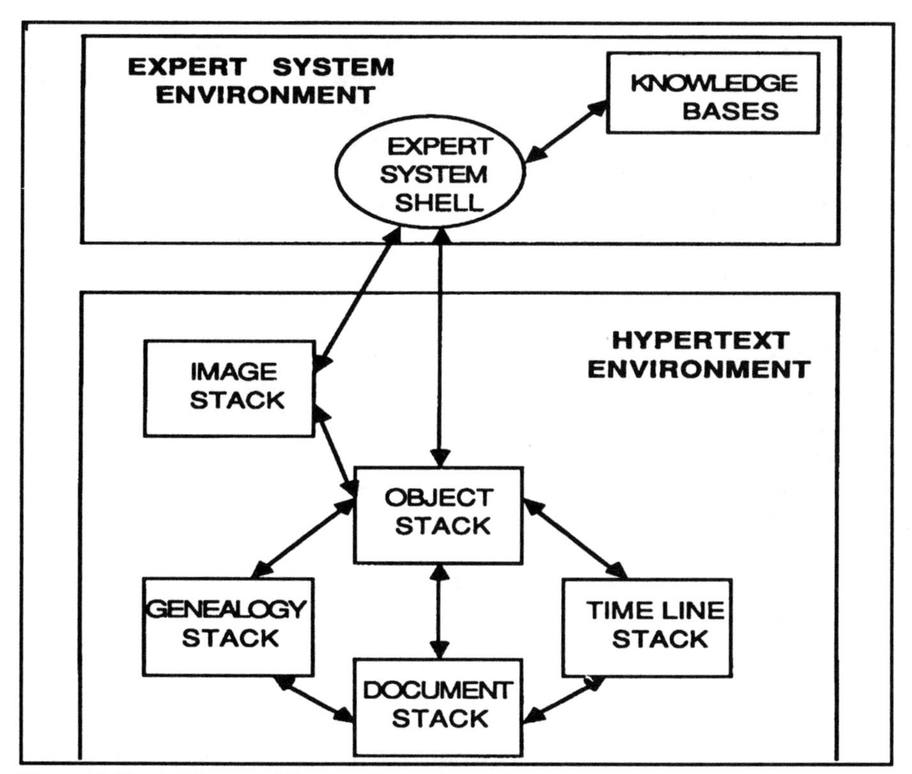

Figure 10. The Architecture of Hypertext System for Numismatists

low full-motion video sequences while CD-ROM offers a convenient and inexpensive alternative. Several groups are working on extensions to the existing CD-ROM standards [18] that will allow this storage medium to be an important component of the OSE. Algorithms for encoding images and video have been developed and are "near-standards." These include JPEG (Joint Photographic Experts Group) and MPEG (Moving Picture Experts Group). JPEG is a standard for compressing and decompressing digital, continuous-tone still-images. [19] MPEG is a standard for compression of video and the associated audio-on-digital storage media. This allows full-motion video to be a computer data type which can be integrated with text and graphics. [20] Other work includes the development of boards and chips that will allow video to be transmitted over digital channels and even software compression of video clips.

Work is also progressing in the area of hypertext. Hypertext/hypermedia extensions to ODA (ISO/IEC JTC1/SC18/WG3: Technical Requirements for ODA/Hypermedia, N1817) and SGML (ISO/IEC JTC1/SC18/WG8: HyTime and SMDL, ANSI X3V1.8m) are being furthered. In addition, MHEG (ISO/IEC JTC1/SC2/WG12: the Multimedia and Hypermedia information coding Experts Group) is working on object-oriented methods. [21] The need to harmonize these activities is of concern. A recent proposal towards that end was presented in March 1991. [22]

In order to move the COIN system to an OSE, several steps must be taken. The text must be taken out of proprietary files used by the hypertext and expert systems and be placed in generic SGML files. Likewise, the images must be placed in CGM or another standard format. The hypertext interface could then be used to read in these files to emulate the current system—an advantage in that the text and image files would have a life beyond the current software application. A more important advantage is that these files could be used in other applications. Still unclear is how to preserve the link structures among the multimedia components.

SUMMARY

Humanities scholars such as art historians and museum professionals need a variety of resources. Much of their work concerns the major tasks of classifying and interpreting objects. The researchers need to work with these objects, although several object surrogates may be found to facilitate their work. These surrogates may include textual descriptions, line drawings, photographs, and video sequences. A number of surrogates for each object is desirable. Once a preliminary classification is made, the object must be interpreted. Further comparing of objects might be undertaken and published materials consulted. A system for linking related materials of various data types (i.e., multimedia) is necessary.

NOTES

1. The mention of commercial products in this chapter intends only to describe the research environment and does not imply recommendation or endorsement by the National Institute of Standards and Technology.

2. Marie C. Malaro, *A Legal Primer on Managing Museum Collections* (Washington, D.C.: Smithsonian Institution Press, 1985), p. 3.

3. Ibid., 45.
4. Ibid., 43.

5. Richard Brilliant, "How an Art Historian Connects Art Objects and Information," *Library Trends*, 37/2, Fall 1988, 121-7.

6. Judi Moline, "Towards a Knowledge Representation Framework for the Arts and Humanities," Draft of PhD Dissertation for Doctor of Philosophy in Information Transfer in the Graduate School of Syracuse University, 1991.

7. Gary Fisher, "Application Portability Profile: The U.S. Government's Open System Environment Profile," NISTSP 500-187, National Institute of Standards and Technology, April 1991, 4.

8. IEEE, "Draft Guide to the POSIX Open Systems Environment," Unapproved Draft P1003.0 / D11, Technical Committee on Operating Systems and Application Environments of the IEEE Computer Society, March 1991, 20.

9. The Open System Environment Concept is being developed by the Systems and Software Technology Division of the Computer Systems Laboratory, NIST.

10. IEEE, 21.

11. Ibid., 24.

12. Fisher, 7.

13. Judi Moline, Allen L. Hankinson, and Lawrence A. Welsch, "Multimedia Courseware in an Open Systems Environment: A Federal Strategy," NISTIR 4484, National Institute of Standards and Technology, December 1990, 26.

14. IEEE, 22.

15. Fisher.

16. IEEE, 22.

17. Judi Moline, "Chapter 10: The User Interface: A Hypertext Model Linking Art Objects and Related Information. *Interfaces for Information Retrieval and Online Systems: The State of the Art.* Edited by Martin Dillon. (NY: Greenwood Press, 1991), pp.133-158, and Judi Moline, "Linking Information to Objects: A Hypertext Prototype for Numismatists," *Visual Resources*, (1991), 7:361-377.

18. Myron Rubinfeld and Lawrence A. Welsch, "A CD-ROM Architecture: An Open Systems Environment Perspective," NISTIR Draft, National Institute of Standards and Technology, April 1991.

19. Gregory K. Wallace, "The JPEG Still Picture Compression Standard," *Communications of the ACM*, 34(4):30-44, April 1991, 31.

20. Didier Le Gall, "MPEG: A Video Compression Standard for Multimedia Applications," *Communications of the ACM*, 34(4):46-58, April 1991, 47.

21. Edward A. Fox, "Guest Editor's Introduction: Standards and the Emergence of Digital Multimedia Systems," *Communications of the ACM*, 34(4):26-29, April 1991, 27.

22. Jon A. Stewart and Carol Young, "Proposed US Position on Standardizing Hypermedia Structure and Time-Synchronized Multimedia Content," Personal/DEC Contribution dated March 6 by the Digital Equipment Co. representatives to X3V1 TG3, TG5, 1991.

APPENDIX A: LIST OF ACRONYMS

The following acronyms used in this chapter are provided here for reference.

API—Application Program Interface
CASE—Computer-aided Software Engineering
CD-ROM—Compact Disc-Read-Only Memory
CGM—Computer Graphics Metafile
COIN—Catalogued Objects and Information for Numismatists
ECMA/PCTE—European Computer Manufacturers Association/Portable Common Tool Environment
EEI—External Environment Interface
GKS—Graphical Kernel System
GOSIP—Government Open Systems Interconnection Profile
ISO—International Standards Organization
JPEG—Joint Photographic Experts Group
MPEG—Moving Picture Experts Group
ODA—Office Document Architecture
OSE—Open System Environment
PHIGS—Programmer's Hierarchical Interactive Graphics System
POSIX—Portable Operating System Interface for Computer Environments
RDA—Remote Database Access
SCSI—Small Computer System Interface
SGML—Standard Generalized Markup Language
SQL—Structured Query Language

Judi Moline
Computer Scientist
National Institute of Standards and Technology
Technology Building, Room B266
Gaithersburg, Maryland 20899

CHAPTER

14

ARCHIVISTA: NEW TECHNOLOGY FOR AN OLD PROBLEM

Gerald Stone

INTRODUCTION [1]

Archives, like libraries and museums, are empowered to acquire, organize, preserve, and make available that which each specializes in collecting. The National Archives of Canada, formerly the Public Archives of Canada, is one of the country's oldest federal cultural agencies. Established in 1872, it has a legislated mandate to acquire, conserve, and facilitate access to public and private records of national significance and to be the permanent repository of federal government and ministerial records.

The Documentary Art and Photography Division of the National Archives has responsibility for developing and managing the Archive's graphic materials. These holdings number over 15 million items, and include about 13 million photographs; 250,000 works of documentary art, including paintings, drawings, watercolours, prints, posters, and medals; and nearly a million philatelic items, which were transferred from Canada Post, the national mail service.

These holdings are increasing exponentially, taxing the ability to control, conserve, and provide physical and intellectual access to them for staff and the general public alike. During its first century, the National Archives acquired slightly more than 2.5 million photographs and works of documentary art. [2] Last year it acquired one million such items! This month alone (April 1991) 1,170,000 photographs were acquired from the *Gazette*, a Montreal daily newspaper.

In 1986, the Canadian Museum of Caricature was established as a program of the National Archives of Canada under the management of the Documentary Art and Photography Division. One chief aim of the new museum was to increase public awareness of the existing body of original cartoon drawings, which had been collected and preserved by the National Archives since the early 1900s. A new gallery was opened in June 1989 in the Byward market area of Ottawa, close to the National Gallery. The gallery has provided a showcase for an ambitious program of acquisition, exhibition, and publication, and it received its 50,000th visitor about two years after its opening.

PLANNING ARCHIVISTA

Not by chance, a prototype of the ArchiVISTA system was installed in the gallery at its opening. In planning activities for the Canadian Museum of Caricature, we decided to strive to provide an online visual catalogue of the nearly 20,000 editorial cartoons and political caricatures that had been amassed. The development path—beginning with a detailed survey of the collection itself, a needs assessment and feasibility study, and a Request for Proposal, including detailed system specifications—is described in the Spring 1990 issue of *Library Trends.* [3] Accordingly, only a few points for planning an imaging system are discussed here.

First, the importance of knowing both the characteristics of the material for which an imaging system is designed and its intended purpose cannot be overemphasized. A survey can greatly aid in understanding the material for which the system will be used: the size range of documents; their physical condition, especially any structural or other weaknesses inherent in the material; their image characteristics, colour, and tonal range; and other details. Also important to know is who will be using the system, for what purpose, and where. These factors are crucial in developing or assessing a set of system specifications, helping to define acceptable limits for response time, resolving power, the type of scanning equipment to be used, and much more. The purpose of our system, we decided, is to facilitate access to our archival, graphics holdings—not to preserve but to give access to them. And, as discussed later, not just caricatures.

Also, after evaluating various technical means, it becomes necessary to decide and commit to a certain approach. Our choice was between analog media such as silver-based photography, microfilm, and videodisc on the one hand, and digital optical disc technology on the other. We opted for the latter because of its high resolution; digital error correction capabilities that minimize loss of image quality in copying and over an extended period of time; portability of data; integrated descriptive and image files; and possibilities for decentralized access.

SYSTEM OVERVIEW

ArchiVISTA is a complete imaging system built around the AT&T VISTA graphics processor board. It consists of two subsystems, both of which operate on a 80386-based, IBM AT-compatible microcomputer equipped with a 19-inch high resolution image monitor (1024 x 768) and 14-inch data monitor. The capture subsystem uses digital imaging techniques; and, although the retrieval subsystem primarily uses analog video techniques, the digital images are also available to it. Both permit the image to be printed or viewed, including panning across or zooming into a part of the image. The PC/DOS route was chosen, not because it is necessarily the best graphics computing environment, but because it enables the system to be more easily integrated with the National Archives' office support system.

The capture subsystem is primarily concerned with the capture of images by a digital camera system and storing them to optical disc. It also builds a capture database to manage how and where the images are stored. Digital WORM (Write Once-Read Many) 5.25-inch optical discs are used as the capture medium, although this may change as new formats or media develop or become standardized.

The retrieval subsystem is concerned with building a retrieval database by linking the stored images to descriptive data imported from the National Archives' bibliographic system, MINISIS. The images, residing on videodiscs, can then be searched or browsed using various retrieval screens. Public retrieval screens provide easy-to-understand access to the caricature database, offering browsing and searching capabilities as well as a tutorial. The browse feature allows the user to scroll through and select from a list of all the available subjects or artist names currently in the database. The public search facility is used to specify more selective search criteria than is possible with the browse feature, including up to five different subjects, artist's name, name and place of publication, and date range.

Staff retrieval screens provide more possible search criteria so that staff personnel have greater flexibility and searching capability. Boolean operators can be used between search fields to narrow or expand a search statement. A second screen can be called with more descriptive and administrative control data such as storage location and access restrictions. Another feature allows four pictures to be simultaneously viewed and compared. Also, in the staff mode, digital images can be called up from the optical disc drive, providing better quality images than videodisc for viewing or printing.

PILOT PROJECT

In our first pilot project, we scanned 20,000 original cartoon drawings on site. These ranged from smaller than 11 by 15 inches up to 34 by 44 inches. Seventy percent were line art and continuous tone drawings scanned in black and white at 1 K (1024 x 768), 8 bits per pixel. Twenty-five percent were drawings with dry transfer materials (e.g. Lettratone), which were scanned in black and white at 2 K (2048 x 1536), 8 bits per pixel. Five percent were color images, scanned in color at 1 K, 32 bits per pixel.

All the drawings were scanned border to border to preserve any inscriptions or annotations which the cartoonist may have made. A second, more detailed scan was made when an image had a very large border area, so that important details would not be lost. It was also important to impress upon our contracted camera operator our archival concerns. This began with ensuring that food and drink, cigarettes, even chewing gum, were strictly taboo anywhere near archival documents, original cartoons included. It also surprised our operator that we wanted him to capture as faithfully as possible the original document, even when he thought he could "improve" it by selectively filtering out stains or smudges.

Persistence and patience are vital to the success of any systems development project, but especially so when using highly sophisticated, but unproven, state-of-the-art technology. For example, the lights were too hot, too uneven, or, in the case of fluorescent tubes, flickered too much, causing alternating dark and light bands in scanned images. Problems in compressing and decompressing images were also encountered—the procedure took too long and caused objectionable interference patterns. Rather than sacrifice quality, even though it increased media costs, we decided to store all images digitally without using any compression algorithms.

Scanning of the 20,000 caricatures began in January 1989, four months after a contract was awarded to Fifth Dimension CAD/CAM Systems of Ottawa, and was completed by the fall. In all, 30 of the 5.25-inch, double-sided WORM optical discs were used to store the images. Although a prototype of the retrieval system was up and running at the Canadian Museum of Caricature's gallery since its opening, it was not until April 1991 that a complete, videodisc-based retrieval system was installed, giving access to the 20,000 scanned images.

ACCESS OR PRESERVATION?

As previously stated, our use of ArchiVISTA is not for preservation so much as for access. Preservation and access are two separate things, and the latter, giving public access to original, rare, or valuable material, hardly aids in their preservation. This is an age-old dilemma with which archivists, librarians, and museum curators have had to contend.

The purposes for which researchers access archival material also vary. Most of our users are interested only in the *content* of the original and are usually satisfied with a reproduction or copy. Only a few users really want to *see the original* archival document for its evidential value, as, for example, to examine in detail the paper or other support that an artist used.

The ArchiVISTA system, using optical disc technology, provides a promising means of greatly improving access to the informational content of visual archival holdings and of easily furnishing a copy, either printed or on screen, all without further recourse to the original once it has been scanned. The original, properly stored after scanning, is better preserved through subsequent reduced handling. This is an added benefit, a consequence of the ArchiVISTA system, but not its main purpose.

I would like to expand this idea. The National Archives of Canada has a Preservation Copying Division. Until recently, 80 percent or more of its Photography Services resources have gone into making 4- by 5-inch duplicate or copy negatives to service ad hoc public demand for copies of original photographs, drawings, paintings, and other archival holdings. This activity has detracted from its original purpose of copying those archival holdings most in need of being preserved, which includes an estimated 1 million nitrate and diacetate photographic negatives.

Conservators and curatorial staff at the National Archives agree that optical disc imaging technology cannot yet replace silver-gelatin negatives as a preservation master copy of original photographs. But we do believe that most of the 25,000 or more photographic copies of our graphics archival holdings, mostly photographs, that the public orders each year can be satisfied by printed output from an optical disc imaging system.

We are now modifying and testing ArchiVISTA's capability to scan, store, and output photographic negatives and transparencies in black-and-white and colour. If successful, this process will enable the National Archives to shift its preservation copying resources to its original purpose without diminishing its public service role.

To be successful, we must be able to compress, without fault, image files to at least one quarter of their size. We need also to critically evaluate our videodisc-based retrieval system, with which we are not entirely satisfied, and determine if we can adopt a completely digital approach, perhaps using CD-ROMs. In other words, we have to sustain that commitment to optical disc technology which we have made thus far and develop it further until we are satisfied that we are deriving its maximum benefit.

DESCRIPTIVE STANDARDS AND SUBJECT INDEXING

Traditional methods of providing intellectual access begin to break down when applied to voluminous, archival collections of graphic material. How do you begin to describe and index the more than one million photographs that we may acquire in *just one month*? It doesn't really matter how many cataloguers we have. The task is impossible *if* we approach it with the textual, library-oriented, item-level bias that we, as good librarians, have had inculcated in us.

A new approach is essential, one that not only recognizes the benefit of describing archives at various collective levels of description but that also takes into account, as at least one study shows, [4] that a brief descriptive record with a picture offers as effective a means of access as a detailed, but purely textual, descriptive record.

Here, too, lies another area where an electronic imaging system holds great promise. Emphasis on describing the content of an image shifts from man to machine; the latter is not only much more objective and thorough, but also cheaper. The cataloguer's task is quickly becoming less that of physically describing an item or a file and more that of providing subject and other access points which lead the user to a facsimile of the original image.

To illustrate with a speculative example that cuts across media boundaries, the National Archives is developing a geomatics system for acquiring geo-referenced data in electronic form. We could, for example, digitize the more than 30,000 copy negatives of still photographs of cities, towns, streets, and buildings already described and indexed by geographical subject headings. These subject headings, in turn, could be translated into geographical coordinates, providing a link to the geomatics system.

Think of the possibilities for the geographer or historian who wants to see our archival resources relating to a specific geographical area. A particular building might be examined in terms of its architectural plans, through aerial and other photographs and drawings, and at various points in time, from the sod-turning ceremony to its demolition—all at a single terminal. We could go further still, geo-referencing portrait files, the architect who designed the building, and the mayor of the city, to create rich, multilayered databases giving access to a wealth of information.

Subject indexing graphics materials is extremely labour-intensive and costly. Much research is currently being done on pattern recognition. It works something like this. Take a file of images—our caricature database, for example. Instruct the computer, via a set of programs, to analyze all records that share some common denominator (e.g., analyze all the caricatures indexed as Richard Nixon). Perhaps there are 200 such records. The computer would sort through and analyze each of these records, coming up with a kind of digital, iconographic fingerprint of Richard Nixon. Now, if there are any caricatures of Richard Nixon in the next batch of scanned images, the computer can automatically index them, based on its recognition of a known pattern.

Readers can surely envisage what this means for subject analysis as we know and practice it today. The challenge is to isolate and define visual patterns for the terms that we now use to index our holdings. Once done, what a radical difference it will make, multiplying access many times over that which we can today provide, and probably at a fraction of the cost.

A DIFFERENT POINT OF VIEW

We have thus far examined ArchiVISTA from an information manager's point of view. Let's now conclude with a sampling of comments from the general public, as written in the Canadian Museum of Caricature's guest book. I hope they convey something of the sense of pride and excitement that we, too, feel about this new-found technology and our use of it.

- Had a great time with ArchiVISTA!
- Fabulous - excellent - computer super
- Very nice computer system
- Especially liked the computer stuff
- Very impressive! Great software!
- Great start! Looking forward to seeing computer collection grow!

Compliments and praise may be well deserved, but complaints and criticism are also usually well founded. Just to assure you that the comments are not always flattering, we offer these from visitors (with our solutions in parentheses).

• Computer is incredibly *SLOW*! (The tutorial was painfully slow and has been speeded up.)

• The translation of the software is awful! (The user interfaces are in English and French. The French translation has since been corrected.)

• How do you work the computer? (The ArchiVISTA retrieval workstation in the museum gallery is intended to be totally self-serve. Even though an online tutorial is available, this comment suggests that written instructions in layman's terms should also be provided.)

As a federal public servant, accountable to Canadian taxpayers, I found the most gratifying comment the one from Dave M., of Hull, Quebec: "Taxpayers' dollars well spent!!!"

ACKNOWLEDGEMENTS

I wish to thank Leona Jacobs, Systems Librarian of the University of Lethbridge in Alberta, whose idea and encouragement led to this paper, and to Lilly Koltun, Director, Documentary Art and Photography Division, National Archives of Canada, for her careful reading of the text and enthusiastic support.

NOTES

1. This chapter represents the author's revised and enlarged version of his paper delivered at the Mid-Year Meeting of the American Society for Information Science, April 27, 1991, Santa Clara, California.

2. Public Archives of Canada, *Annual report, 1973/1974* (Ottawa: Information Canada, 1975), p. 80.

3. Gerald Stone and Philip Sylvain, "ArchiVISTA: A New Horizon in Providing Access to Visual Records of the National Archives of Canada," *Library Trends*, v. 38, no. 4 (Spring 1990), pp. 737-750.

4. M.E. Rorvig, "The Substitutibility of Images for Textual Descriptions of Archival Materials in an MS-DOS Environment," K. Lehman & H. Strohl-Goebel, eds., *The Application of Microcomputers in Information, Documentation and Libraries* (Amsterdam: North Holland Press, 1987), pp. 407-415.

Gerald Stone
Chief of Information Services
Documentary Art and Photography Division
National Archives of Canada
395 Wellington Street
Ottawa, Ontario
Canada K1A ON3

MEDICINE

CHAPTER
15

HYPERMEDIA IN MEDICAL EDUCATION: ACCENT ON THE LIBRARY'S ROLE

Naomi C. Broering

INTRODUCTION [1]

The unique capabilities of computers offer an opportunity for medical schools to cope with the information explosion and the amount of knowledge students are required to grasp. The growing number of medical discoveries, the complexities of the medical sciences, and the speed in which new knowledge is being created make computer workstations logical tools for future physicians. Forward thinking educators have turned to computers as a means of managing the growing mass of information.

At Georgetown University, the Macintosh computer has emerged as an important hypermedia tool in the medical education program, which is supported by the university's Medical Center Library. This chapter briefly traces the introduction of computers in the medical school curriculum and focuses on the library's role in two educational software development projects that illustrate visualization and the hypermedia approach to learning.

Medical students at Georgetown use personal computers in many courses. Applications include special exercises for basic science, preparation of papers in bioethics, clinical problem solving by searching the medical literature online, learning differential diagnosis with electronic diagnostic systems, and writing automated history and physical reports of patient encounters during clinical rotations at the University Hospital.

Using computers in medical education at Georgetown or at other medical schools, however, did not occur overnight. Their use represents part of a gradual transformation in instructional approaches that began in the early 1980s when computer advances made it possible to combine voice, images, and data at an affordable price. Since 1983, the year *Time* magazine announced the computer as the "Machine of the Year," computers have invaded medical education with a force more powerful than anything experienced in the past two decades. [2] Evidence of change has been occurring rapidly at local and national levels. We are witnessing a trend that profoundly affects our faculty, librarians, and students.

The immense impact of computers in medical education results from several environmental factors. Nationally, forceful recommendations calling for curriculum changes were made in recent years by four major health institutions: the American Association of Medical Colleges in the report on General Professional Education of Physicians (GPEP), [3] the National Board of Medical Examiners' announcement to implement computer-based testing in Part III of the national examinations [4], the Association of Academic Health Centers (AAHC) report on "Executive Management of Computer Resources in the Academic Health Center", [5] and the Robert Wood Johnson Foundation's grant program to transform medical education. [6]

Not until Harvard University's "New Pathway" curriculum has there been such a powerful institutional commitment to prepare medical students to use these new tools. [7] With growing frequency, special medical and basic sciences disciplines are revamping teaching styles to de-emphasize memorization and to use computers as memory extenders. The National Library of Medicine's (NLM) support for the Integrated Academic Information Management System (IAIMS) program certainly has served as a vital "change agent" at the participating institutions. IAIMS has accelerated the introduction of medical informatics at Georgetown and it has become increasingly apparent that other academic medical centers are planning a similar course of action.

COMPUTERS IN THE MEDICAL CURRICULUM

The IAIMS project has played a major role in the dynamic use of computers at the medical center. The library spearheads the IAIMS project with a vigorous program to encourage faculty to develop educational software, including providing some instructors with computers to experiment in new teaching methodologies. As a result several courses have been changed to include computer applications, and we now have a growing effort to integrate computers in existing courses.

The integration of medical informatics in the curriculum at Georgetown is informal. There is no identifiable track, nor specific computer courses. Nonetheless, computers have permeated the student's educational experience in a variety of settings (classroom, library, and clinical environments), because their use is considered essential in preparing modern physicians.

For nearly ten years Georgetown medical students have received opportunities in the library on basic computer use. They have gained extensive bibliographic searching experience through the Library Information System's (LIS) online catalog and the mini-MEDLINE SYSTEM since 1982. [8] They have used the library's collection of computer assisted instruction (CAI) programs for independent study and self assessment. The students are taught to use microcomputers in the library's Biomedical Information Resources Center (BIRC), which was expanded to include two computer classrooms and open workstations of nearly 80 computers (Macintosh, IBM, and AT&T).

COMPUTER APPLICATIONS IN BASIC SCIENCES INSTRUCTION

The basic sciences were the first to benefit from many of the CAI programs developed in the 1970's. Some excellent clinical programs, such as the MEDCAPS series and the Massachusetts General Hospital programs, expanded the use of CAI in the early 1980s. Programs began to surface in the mid 1980s that took advantage of hypermedia/hypertext capabilities, making the basic sciences field a natural leader for innovative approaches in medical education. Still, it took a special effort by the library to fund software development before our faculty became actively involved in creating software. The SuperPATH Project in pathology and the Electronic Textbook in Human Physiology described in this chapter are examples of these efforts.

SuperPATH

In 1987, Georgetown began an experimental project to introduce PathMAC, an information system developed at the Cornell University Medical College, into the medical school's second year pathology course. Several changes, including hardware and software modifications, were made to adapt the programs to Georgetown's needs. By 1989, the Georgetown version of a hypermedia/hypertext "electronic" program in pathology evolved as "SuperPATH."

SuperPATH is an ongoing joint project between the Medical Library and the Department of Pathology. It is conceived as a powerful adjunct to traditional classroom methods in helping second year medical students learn the increasing body of information about pathology and to develop skills needed for medical problem solving. Basically, SuperPATH combines the latest technologies of hypertext and imaging to enhance teaching and learning by integrating digitized images of pathology slides with lecture notes, glossaries, and literature.

Two sections of SuperPATH have been completed: Autoimmune Diseases and Neuropath. The latter completely replaces lectures formerly conducted in a didactic classroom environment. Now that the students study from the computer programs, faculty members are free to cover other materials in class or to allow students to use their time differently. Since SuperPATH began in 1989, the students have been attending the Clinicopathologic Conferences (CPCs) held in the hospital. This experience bridges the gap between information learned in pathology class and application of this knowledge at the clinical level. Prior to SuperPATH the relationship was less apparent; consequently, students concentrated on memorization to pass a course rather than understanding medical concepts that they would need to apply in practice.

The SuperPATH courseware employs Apple Macintosh computers and SuperCard. The Neuropath program format uses the latest version of SuperCard. Although the section on Autoimmune Disease still uses the Guide software for the hypertext portion, it is being converted to operate the same as Neuropath. The hypertext approach organizes information so that it is closer to the way people actually think and work rather than by

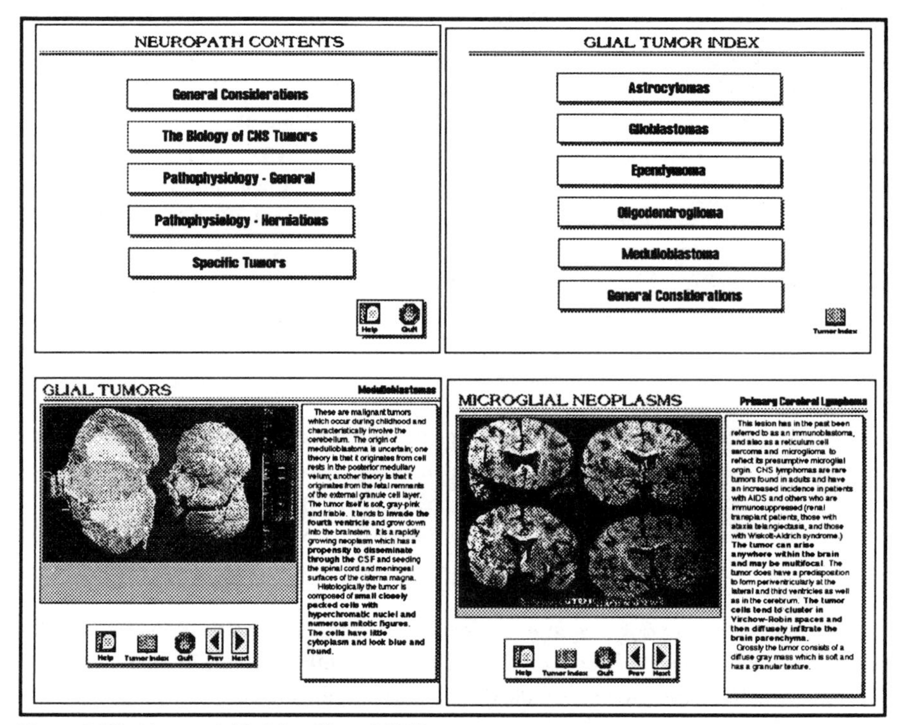

Figure 1. The Neuropath Module of SuperPATH

traditional linear methods. The routines that link digitized images to text have been revised so the program can function more easily at sites other than the library.

Pathology slides selected by faculty are scanned using a Barney scanner. Documents and digitized full color images of medical slides are captured and stored on a 600M-byte hard disk (WREN drive). They are accessible through a file server connected to the workstations via Ethernet used in the Library (see Figure 1).

SuperPATH currently uses three unique hypermedia capabilities of the Macintosh—incorporates color images, uses windows, and integrates text with graphics. The following figures illustrate how the system works and the powerful manner in which it supplements traditional learning in Pathology.

The SuperPATH system was first used during the 1990 Spring Semester with modules on autoimmune diseases and central nervous system tumors. By 1991, the system began to receive heavy use and the students have requested enhancements, including print capabilities. The BIRC needs more workstations to accommodate high peak times during examination periods. Future plans for SuperPATH include the creation of several CPCs, creation of a pathology "interesting case" database, and new modules on lymphomas, gene mapping, and infectious and special disease pathology.

The Electronic Textbook in Human Physiology

The "Electronic Textbook" is another cooperative computer project between the Library and a Medical School department. The Library obtained a grant from the U.S. Department of Education to develop with the Physiology Department a prototype Electronic Textbook in Human Physiology using a Hypermedia/Hypertext approach. The purpose was to enhance learning and visualization in human physiology by developing a prototype knowledge base of core instructional materials stored in digitized format.

The Electronic Textbook goes beyond SuperPATH because it uses sound and animation to simulate certain human physiologic functions. It combines into one source the major instructional materials needed by students, i.e., faculty lecture notes, text, illustrations, animation, glossaries, slides, and sound. The program is based on the principle that humans more readily comprehend certain physiological concepts by viewing them as dynamic images rather then the static pictures and words with which they are usually presented. Currently nearing completion is a self-instruction program in cardiac physiology.

The following has been achieved in the Electronic Textbook:

• Using Macintosh computer graphics capabilities, we have developed colored animations that can demonstrate heart functions

• Heart sounds and textual information have been integrated with the animations, allowing students to study the moving heart in detail and step through the animations focusing attention on necessary detail

• Voice comments by the faculty have been included to emphasize specific items of information that the students should learn

• The program includes textual materials from lectures and examples of 16-part multiple choice questions with immediate feedback to selected answers

• Sections on electrical and mechanical events of the cardiac cycle are already completed.

The Macintosh computer graphics allow demonstration of these concepts with colored animations, enhanced with sound and text. Students can study the moving heart in detail, and can step through the animations to focus attention on necessary detail. Currently, the program includes pre- and post-test questions that provide immediate feedback to selected answers. The Einthoven Triangle, a section on electrical and mechanical events of the cardiac cycle, is a difficult concept that is far easier to comprehend using visual animation techniques.

The system uses Macintosh IIcx or IIci computers with 5M bytes of RAM and 80M-byte drives. The software approach, called HyperBook, uses standard off-the-shelf software such as Studio 8, Macromind Director, and Microsoft Word. Course content and animations are developed by faculty, while screen designs are created by the Library's programmer. The Library has also entered lecture notes and a glossary/dictionary in a separate module, which is being linked to the active learning routines of the electronic textbook in Phase II.

The Physiology Department has conducted two unveilings of the program. It was introduced during a full-class lecture last year, which was conducted as a demonstration for students. The instructor engaged in a dialogue with students about the cardiac functions and then demonstrated the process to the class. The second session was conducted in April 1991 in place of a Physiology lab. The students, divided into five sections, were taught how to run the program and were assigned several exercises. This latter approach was extremely successful. It generated a lot of discussion and enthusiasm for a subject which was previously considered unexciting. Plans are to extend the labs next year.

The following illustrations depict some of the routines and visuals students encounter during the learning exercises. The pre- and post-test answers are scored so students can monitor their own progress (see Figure 2).

Self-instruction materials in endocrine and renal physiology are planned for the next phase. The faculty has already begun to design animation routines for these human functions (See Figure 3). While animations appear simple and entertaining, the preparation of useful animations are extremely time consuming. They require a screen-by-screen, step-by-step analysis of the process before it can be linked together. Faculty admit they have been forced to review the human processes repeatedly to assure accuracy. Generally, the easier the program appears to the student, the more difficult it has been to program and design.

An anonymous survey was conducted during the initial computer-based laboratory session on the Electronic Textbook. Student reactions were unanimously positive. A few comments include:

> *"I enjoyed learning from the Electronic Textbook;* . . .
>
> *" The ability to see an "action picture" of concepts helps to reinforce and apply knowledge;"* . . .
>
> *"The best part is to visualize the "big picture" and then go back and break it down into components."*. . .
>
> *"I like the fact I can go at my own pace. On the preliminary quiz I only got two correct answers. At the end of the program, I got eight correct answers. The pre- and post-quizzes were helpful."*. . .
>
> *"The sounds which accompanied the animations made it easier to understand what is actually going on inside the heart, and in what order."*

Imagine medical school students saying these things about a basic science class! It seems unbelievable, but we received complimentary remarks from nearly 200 medical students who attended a recent physiology class held in the library's computer classroom. Similar statements have been made informally about our courseware in pathology and a system under development in histology.

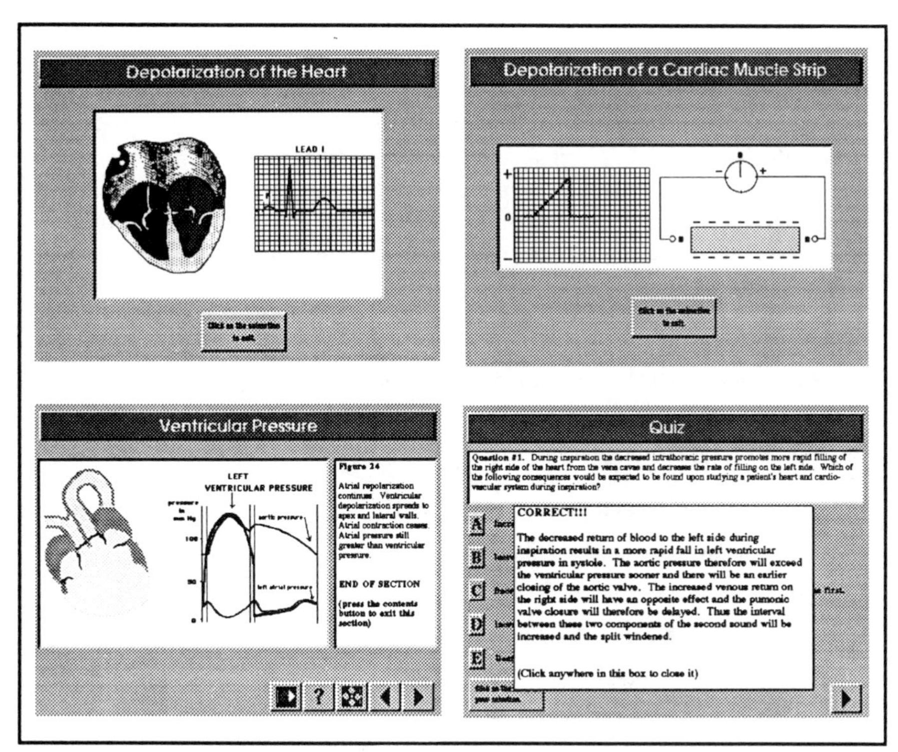

Figure 2. The Electronic Textbook in Human Physiology

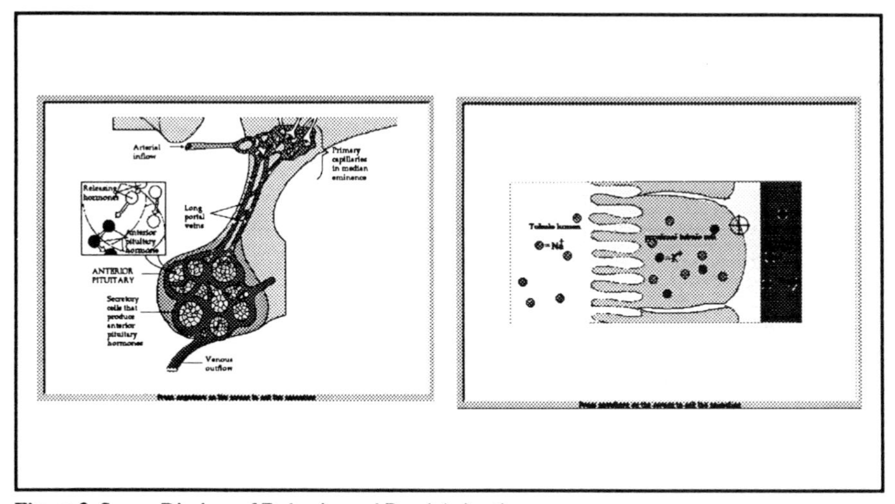

Figure 3. Screen Displays of Endocrine and Renal Animations

SUMMARY

Generally, I believe the multimedia approach to learning has been broadly accepted in medicine. The introduction of hypermedia techniques using Macintosh computers has further enhanced the effort to improve visualization in the learning process. The ability to store, manage, and retrieve large amounts of information rapidly, coupled with images and sound, has revolutionized the way we can teach and students can learn. These methodologies are especially applicable to medicine because it is a highly visual and information intensive field.

The time and investment required to develop comprehensive courseware in this tremendously complex discipline is beyond the capabilities of one institution. Our experience in developing software has made it obvious that we cannot possibly afford to create electronic textbooks for the entire medical school curriculum. Therefore, Georgetown and eleven other medical schools that are developing courseware using the Macintosh platform have formed the North East Medical School Consortium (NEMSC). The members share programs that they have individually developed. The members are:

- Cornell University Medical College
- Dartmouth Medical School
- Georgetown University Medical Center
- Harvard Medical School
- Johns Hopkins University School of Medicine
- Mount Sinai School of Medicine
- New York University Medical Center
- SUNY Health Science Center at Syracuse
- University of Pennsylvania Medical School
- University of Rochester Medical School
- Yale University School of Medicine

The NEMSC group recently developed a magneto optical disk of the software that the schools are willing to share. While this is an experiment in sharing diverse programs, we believe it will lead to development of standards and design tools for medical courseware.

Something we did not anticipate are the new opportunities for libraries in the consortium. Each of the images, animations, simulations, sounds, and textual materials in the courseware must be indexed properly for future retrieval. We are now exploring the best mechanisms for undertaking this activity. Plans are to have the medical librarians of each of the eleven schools participate in indexing their contributions to the consortium, and we are currently exploring the most suitable approach.

ACKNOWLEDGEMENTS

The author gratefully acknowledges the invaluable assistance of Lawrence Lilienfield, MD, PhD on the Electronic Textbook in Human Physiology; and Elliott Kagan, MD and Robert Wolov, MD on the SuperPATH project. Special thanks are also extended to Shoukoufeh Larijani for the illustrations, editing, and preparation of the manuscript.

NOTES

1. This chapter represents part of a longer manuscript on hypermedia accepted for publication in *Academic Medicine* in 1992.

2. N.C. Broering and P. Mistry, "IAIMS at Georgetown University: From Strategies to Action," proceedings of a symposium sponsored by the National Library of Medicine, U.S. Department of HHS, Bethesda, MD; March 12, 1986: 24-28.

3. AAMC. "Physicians for the Twenty-First Century: The GPEP Report," Washington, DC, 1984.

4. National Board of Medical Examiners. "CBX: Computer Based Examination," presented at the Symposium on Computer Applications in Medical Care, Washington, DC, October 31, 1982.

5. T.E. Piemme and M.J. Ball, "Executive Management of Computer Resources in the Academic Health Center: A Staff Report." Washington, Association of Academic Health Centers, January 1984, p.34.

6. "Preparing Physicians for the Future: A Program in Medical Education," The Robert Wood Johnson Foundation, News Announcement, August 23, 1991.

7. D.C. Bok, "Needed: A New Way to Train Doctors," *Harvard Magazine*, 1984 May-June.

8. N.C. Broering, "The miniMEDLINE SYSTEM: A Library Based End-User Search System," *Bulletin of the Medical Library Association*, 1985 April; 73(2):138-145.

Naomi C. Broering
Dahlgren Memorial Library
Georgetown University Medical Center
3900 Reservoir Road
Washington, DC 20007-2197

CHAPTER
16

Conversion of Artwork to Electronic Form: A Case Study of Costs and Aesthetic Factors

Valerie Florance and Rob Duckwall

INTRODUCTION

Numerous full-text electronic databases are now available for purchase or online access. [1] Many are reproductions of existing printed books developed through "conversion" of a printed product into machine-readable form. Conversion products developed from existing published materials are rarely exact, complete reproductions of the original. Most can be characterized as either *partial* or *engineered* conversion products.

Partial conversion retains most elements of the original, but fully or partially excludes others. Converted popular textbooks, dictionaries, and other reference works often exclude graphics, [2] a practice that has historically been justified in terms of technological barriers: the large size of graphics files, the difficulty of transmitting large graphics files to remote sites, the poor resolution of monitor screens, and so forth. [3] Typically, text in such files is presented on screen in unbroken, scrollable pages, with inserts to indicate missing figures or tables. [4]

Engineered conversion produces changes in the presentation format, the graphics elements, and the arrangement or content structure of the original document. [5] These products generally show page design features not present in the original, including graphical elements such as buttons or "hot links" that indicate inter- and intratext relationships.

Graphic images are an important part of medical knowledge, providing students and physicians with vital information such as the form, location, and characteristics of human anatomy, results of laboratory procedures, or actions of physiological processes. [6] Thus, a conversion product based upon a medical text must provide access to quality reproductions of images and text.

The most basic measures of successful conversion are accuracy (nothing is missing) and conceptual comparability (the intellectual content is preserved). In assessing the quality of graphics conversion, accuracy and information content are reflected in what may be termed aesthetic qualities of the original:

- fluid lines and crisp edges
- effective contours and shading
- readable text labels
- clear leader line terminal points.

For certain kinds of images (e.g., cross-sectional anatomical drawings), lines, contours, and shading are content-bearing components—they are part of the substance of the knowledge being transmitted. Thus, the conversion goal of aesthetic comparability demands both accuracy and stylistic fidelity to an original.

CONTEXT FOR THE STUDY

Since 1987, staff at the Welch Library's Laboratory for Applied Research in Academic Information has collaborated with faculty of the Johns Hopkins University School of Medicine (JHUSOM) to create knowledge bases which support their research and practice needs. [7] During the past two years, Laboratory staff members have worked with Drs. L. Randol Barker, John R. Burton, and Philip D. Zieve to create a full-text, machine-readable database based upon the *Principles of Ambulatory Medicine* (PAM), a popular medical text they edit whose third edition was published by Williams & Wilkins in late 1990.

Chapter text and tables of contents for the latest edition were generated from the SGML-encoded textual component of the PAM database. [8] The PAM database is intended to support a number of information products and services (e.g., online search and display, production of typography files, etc.). The rationale for adding a graphics component is simple and compelling: images are an integral part of the medical knowledge represented in the book. The work reported here results from preliminary analysis related to the development of a graphics component for the PAM database.

OBJECTIVES AND METHODS OF STUDY

The study objectives were to explore issues surrounding the conversion of existing artwork to electronic form, develop and test criteria for evaluating the aesthetic outcome of artwork conversion, identify and test artwork conversion methods, and document the conversion costs for creating PostScript files of PAM artwork. The choice of equipment, methods, and evaluation criteria was guided by the following requirements:

- faithful re-creation of the original, to the finest detail
- comparable quality to the original
- comparable quality of screen and print versions of converted artwork.

Preliminary evaluation of scanner-generated bit-map images from two chapters of the book's second edition indicated that their aesthetic quality was inadequate for on-screen viewing: text was often unreadable, detail and shading was lost, some lines were thick and clumsy-looking on standard computer monitors, etc. A conversion method was sought that could produce output of comparable on-screen and print quality, and machine-readable files that could support a range of output media. A plan was developed to identify and test conversion methods by producing editable, PostScript files for one chapter of PAM line art.

About 25% of the images in the *Principles of Ambulatory Medicine* are drawings, ranging from simple line art to finely-shaded, text-labelled renderings (the term artwork is used hereafter to describe these images.) A review of artwork in the book's third edition led to the selection of Chapter 63 for the test. Chapter 63 contains five figures as follows:

Figure 63.1: Coronal section of shoulder anatomy. A detailed drawing with cross-hatching, finely-lined shading, and numerous text labels. Leader lines connect text labels to specific points within the drawing.

Figure 63.2: Topographical localization of pain and tenderness. Figure contains 4 parts. Part A is an anterior anatomical view of the shoulder and Part B is a posterior anatomical view of the shoulder. Both are line drawings with variable line weights, cross-hatched shading, and fine dots for detail. Leader lines from number labels point to fairly clear areas within the drawing. Parts C and D, photographs, were not used in the study.

Figure 63.3: Range of motion exercises. A simple outline-type line drawing without shading or fine detail. Motion is indicated by small arrows. Line weight variation does occur.

Figure 63.4: Normal shoulder arthrogram. Excluded from the study because it is not a drawing.

Figure 63.5: Points of neurovascular compression. A diagrammatic drawing using screened shading to highlight and differentiate anatomical parts and labelled insets to magnify important details. Leaders to the insets terminate within the drawing.

The characteristics of the five drawings selected for the study are summarized in Table 1.

Conversion Procedures

Four conversion methods were selected for testing, each employing a slightly different mix of equipment, skills, and procedures (Table 2). All four methods employ the Adobe Illustrator program.

Mouse method: the artist uses the Apple Scanner to create a scanned image that serves as a tracing template within Adobe Illustrator. The template can be turned off

TABLE 1: CHARACTERISTICS OF DRAWINGS*

Characteristic	63.1	63.2A	63.2B	63.3	63.5
Contour Effects					
Crosshatch Shading	✓		✓		
Screened Shading	✓				✓
Finely-lined Shading	✓	✓	✓		
Differentiated Screen Shading					✓
Line Weight Variation		✓	✓		
Minute Details	✓	✓	✓	✓	
Labelling					
Text Labels	✓				✓
Single Character Labels		✓	✓	✓	
Leaders into Drawing	✓	✓	✓		✓

**Principles of Ambulatory Medicine, 3rd Ed. Chapter 63*

and on, allowing the artist to review the progress of the sketch. Setting the scanner at 150 dpi produced the best template image for this method.

Tablet method: employs the Wycom Stylus Tablet by which the artist uses a stylus to trace an enlarged photocopy of the original drawing. The stylus, shaped like a pencil, is a more familiar drawing tool for most artists than the mouse. Calibration of the stylus affects the speed and ease of the work. This approach requires use of a large-screen monitor for editing work, and produces large-scale output which must be rescaled for viewing on standard monitors.

Auto method: the completed drawing is produced in a single step by a computer-based drawing program, Adobe Streamline, which creates a tracing from an Apple Scanner scanned image. The Streamline program treats text as an object, outlining the letters as if they were details of a drawing. Since no editing is done to the electronic image, the work can be done by a technician rather than a trained artist. A 300-dpi scan is used as the template for Auto method drawings.

Mixed method: the artist begins with an auto-drawn sketch created by Adobe Streamline and edits the electronic image with drawing tools within Adobe Illustrator. Thus, the procedures for Auto method are used, followed by final processes of the Mouse method.

All artwork conversion for the project was done by a trained artist. Aesthetic criteria were based upon evaluation of the original drawings and bit-map images of them. The final products of each conversion method were evaluated independently and jointly by the artist and an observer. The artist's journal and observer's log provided documentation of costs, aesthetic factors, and other issues that arose during the study.

TABLE 2: ARTWORK CONVERSION METHODS STUDIED

Characteristic	Mouse	Tablet	Auto	Mixed
Process				
Scanned original	✓		✓	✓
Traced sketch	✓	✓		
Hand finishing	✓	✓		✓
Skills				
Special equipment set-up	✓	✓	✓	✓
Art training	✓	✓		✓
Computer-based drawing	✓	✓		✓
Equipment				
Macintosh II*	✓	✓	✓	✓
Laserwriter II	✓	✓	✓	✓
Applescanner	✓		✓	✓
Adobe Illustrator	✓	✓		✓
Adobe Streamline			✓	✓
Supermac large-screen monitor		✓		
Wycom Stylus Tablet		✓		

**High-resolution RGB Monitor, 5 MB RAM, 40 MB Hard disk*

Aesthetic criteria

Four aesthetic criteria were developed for evaluating the conversion output, based upon characteristics of the drawings themselves. The criteria address both the "textual" correctness (accuracy, legibility) and the stylistic comparability (crispness, fluidity) of the conversion products as compared to the original.

Crispness refers to the clarity of the rendering in terms of sharpness and discrimination among fine details. A crisp drawing has clear separation between lines in cross-hatching and fine-lined shading. Leader line terminal points are distinguishable from surrounding imagery. Edges and curves are sharp.

Accuracy reflects the capability of the method (not the artist) to produce and/or preserve all details or elements of the original. An accurate drawing has all shading, differentiation, and line weight variations of the original, and no contour features have been introduced by the conversion method itself.

Fluidity refers to the shape and flow of lines in the drawing. Fluid lines show curves and straight lengths identical to the original, without jaggedness or line breaks introduced by the conversion method.

Legibility describes the quality of text included within the drawing (as opposed to text captions). Legible text is neither distorted nor unreadable; letter shapes and spacing are identical to the original.

Visual inspection of the scanned bit-map images from the book's second edition revealed five types of problems introduced during the conversion process. Each affects one or more of the contour or text features of a drawing:

- *Blocking*—merging into a single line or clump. Blocking occurs mainly in crosshatching and fine-lined shading
- *Drop-out*—the disappearance of details present in the original
- *Blurring*—leader line terminal points indistinguishable from the surrounding material
- *Deformation*—text is cropped, crowded, or otherwise unreadable
- *Distortion*—shape and weight of lines differ from the original.

Table 3 links these problems to the aesthetic criteria used for judging printed and on-screen output. For example, blocking is a *Crispness* problem, while distortion is a *Fluidity* problem.

Each conversion method was judged by visual identification of problems in its on-screen and printed output by comparison to the originals. For each aesthetic criterion listed above, the problems were used (when applicable) as measures for judging quality. [9] Numeric values were assigned and overall aesthetic scores computed for each conversion method. The skill of the original artist and the appropriateness of a particular drawing technique for on-screen display were not factors in the evaluation process.

TABLE 3: AESTHETIC PROBLEMS CAUSED BY CONVERSION

Criterion	Characteristic	Problem
Crispness	Crosshatch shading	Blocking
	Finely-lined shading	Blocking
	Leaders into drawing	Blurred ends
	Minute details	Blocking
Accuracy	Minute details	Drop-out
	Screen Shading	Drop-out No differentiation
	Line Weight Variation	Levelling False Variation
Fluidity	Line flow	Distortion
Legibility	Text Labels	Unreadable Deformed

TABLE 4: TIME REQUIRED TO COMPLETE DRAWINGS

	(Hours)				(Minutes)			
	Mouse		Tablet		Auto		Mixed	
Figure	**Sketch***	**Total**	**Sketch**	**Total****	**Sketch**	**Total**	**Sketch**	**Total**
63.1 Shoulder anatomy	2.50	**9.50**	0.25	**7.25**	5	**5**	5	**35**
63.2A Anterior shoulder	1.25	**4.00**	0.20	**2.95**	5	**5**	5	**20**
63.2B Posterior shoulder	1.13	**3.75**	0.20	**2.83**	5	**5**	5	**20**
63.3 Range of motion	1.25	**3.50**	0.17	**2.42**	5	**5**	5	**5**
63.5 Compress points	1.75	**3.88**	0.25	**2.38**	5	**5**	5	**n/a**

** Adjusted to account for learning curve*
*** Based on mouse-method finishing*

RESULTS AND DISCUSSION

The Mouse and Tablet methods require complete re-creation by hand of the original drawing. Both require the artist to trace a template to create the initial sketch, which can be edited using tools provided by the drawing program. Although finishing takes the same amount of time for these methods, completion of the initial sketch is about 5 times faster in the Tablet method. Since the output of these two methods is virtually identical, examples and comparative data are presented only for the mouse method.

Table 4 compares Mouse and Tablet time requirements to those of the Auto and Mixed methods. If the auto-drawn sketch requires a significant amount of editing, the total time for Mixed method may approach that of the Mouse method. The sizes of output files are displayed in Table 5. Bit-map scan sizes are provided for each figure, as a point of comparison to the final PostScript output. The difference between the Auto and Mixed method file sizes for Fig. 63.1 reflects the replacement of the "outlined" text objects created by the Adobe Streamline program with standard 12-point text. The large size of the Mouse method files (Figure 1) shows the effect of the eyelashing technique used to create line weight variation in Figs. 63.1, 63.2A and 63.2B. (Please see this chapter's Figures 1 through 8 beginning on page 184.)

The four methods varied significantly in the aesthetic quality of the output. Minor crispness, fluidity and legibility problems are present in all on-screen output for all methods, due to the 72-dpi resolution of computer monitors used in the study. In

TABLE 5: FILE SIZE OF COMPLETED DRAWINGS (KILOBYTES)

Figure		Scan	Mouse*	Auto	Mixed
63.1 Shoulder Anatomy		23	160	98	61
63.2A Anterior shoulder		19	57	27	24
63.2B Posterior shoulder		20	57	27	24
63.3 Range of motion		20	43	28	29
63.5 Compression Points		21	21	27	27**
	Total	**103**	**338**	**204**	**162**

** Tablet drawing sizes are equivalent*
*** Estimated*

Table 6, conversion problems identified with output of each method are indicated. The Mouse method produced screen and print output with the fewest conversion problems (Figures 2, 3). Print output from the Mouse method was completely comparable to the original. [10] Auto method produced the poorest results (Figures 4, 5). Although print output from an Auto method drawing showed fewer problems than screen output, neither was comparable to the originals, and screen output of Auto method was judged unacceptable for Figures 63.1 and 63.5. The Mixed method provided accept-

TABLE 6: EVALUATION OF OUTPUT FROM CONVERSION METHODS*

Criterion	Characteristic	Mouse method		Auto method		Mixed Method	
		Screen	Print	Screen	Print	Screen	Print
Crispness	Crosshatch shading			x	x	x	x
	Fine-line blocking			x	x	x	x
	Blurred leader ends			x			
	Minute detail blocking	x		x	x	x	x
Accuracy	Screened shading drop-out			x	x		
	Undifferentiated screens			x	x		
	Fine-line drop-out			x			
	Minute detail drop-out			x			
	Line Variation levelling			x	x		
	False line variation			x			
Fluidity	Line distortion	x		x		x	
Legibility	Unreadable text			x			
	Deformed Text	x		x	x		

**Figures 63.1, 2B and 5 for mouse and auto; Figures 63.1 and 2B for mixed*
x= problem present

TABLE 7: SCORES FOR AESTHETIC QUALITY OF PRINT & SCREEN OUTPUT

	Print			Screen		
Criterion	**Mouse**	**Auto**	**Mixed***	**Mouse**	**Auto**	**Mixed***
Crispness	4	-2	-2	4	-3	-1
Accuracy	6	0	6	6	-5	6
Fluidity	1	1	1	0	0	0
Legibility	2	0	2	2	-2	2
Composite Output Score	**13**	**-1**	**7**	**12**	**-10**	**7**

1=Problems not present; - 1= Problems present; 0=Equipment-based problems
**Fig. 63.5 not available for Mixed method*

able results, reducing Auto method crispness problems, and eliminating accuracy and legibility problems introduced by the Auto method (Figures 6, 7). Mixed method could eliminate all Auto method problems, of course, but the time required for such finishing could approach that of the Mouse or Tablet method.

A weighted score was developed for each artwork conversion method, based upon the presence or absence of aesthetic problems in each output medium (Table 7). The scores for Mouse and Mixed methods are consistent across screen and print output, while Auto method scores show more variation. Where low resolution of the viewing screen was the primary factor contributing to an aesthetic problem, such as line distortion in Figure 63.5, all methods were given a zero score for the problem factor.

Factor rankings for each method appear in Table 8. The Mouse method ranks highest on aesthetic factors, but its salary costs are the highest of the three methods, and the output files are the largest. Auto method has the lowest cost, but the aesthetic quality of output is the poorest of the three methods. Equipment costs, project time, and salaries were identified for each method and a 200-image estimate computed (Table 9). [11]

TABLE 8: RANKINGS FOR CONVERSION METHODS

Factor	Mouse	Auto	Mixed
Aesthetic Factors	1	3	2
Salary Costs	3	1	2
Equipment Costs	2	1	3
Project Cost	3	3	2
File Size	3	2	1

Aesthetic Factors: Best = 1; Cost Factors: Lowest = 1

TABLE 9: COST ESTIMATES FOR A 200-IMAGE PROJECT

Item	Mouse	Tablet	Auto	Mixed
Equipment Cost	$9,850	$10,070	$9,800	$10,070
Salary Cost*	$24,640	$17,840	$200	$1,680
Total	**$34,490**	**$27,910**	**$10,000**	**$11,750**
Storage (MB)	13.5	n/a	8.2	6.5
Staffing	Artist	Artist	Tech	Artist

** $25/hour for artist; $12/hour for technician*

Several other issues affect the conversion process through their impact on an artist's working environment. Although these factors were not incorporated in the weighted scores presented in Tables 7 and 8, they could negatively affect the overall efficiency of the hand-crafting methods.

Visual Quality of Working Copy: Figure 8 provides an example of the working drawing an artist sees [12] while editing a file in Adobe Illustrator. Although the template and editing blocks can be hidden in order to view the finished product, the artist must draw within this cluttered visual environment.

Size of Working Copy: The Tablet method requires a large-screen monitor if the drawing is to be viewed in its entirety. The resulting output does not display adequately on a standard monitor. Conversely, if the artist does not use the large-screen monitor, the sketch is too small for proper editing of details.

Learning Curve for Tools: An advanced course in the use of Adobe Illustrator reduced completion time for hand-crafted drawings by about 75%. If the project artist is not familiar with the drawing program or other equipment used in the conversion work (e.g., the scanner), time must be allowed for trial-and-error. The existence of technical support staff to assist the artist is virtually mandatory.

Time to Completion: In the Mouse and Tablet methods, line weight variation was created by breaking a line into numerous segments whose thickness could be assigned individually. Although successful in duplicating the fluidity of original lines, this process increased the editing time by an order of magnitude.

Table 10 summarizes aesthetic and environmental factors for each artwork conversion method tested.

SUMMARY AND CONCLUSION

Our comparison of four artwork conversion methods indicates that at least three conversion approaches exist for creating PostScript files whose print and screen output are aesthetically comparable to a printed original. There is an inverse relationship

TABLE 10: PROBLEMS OF ARTWORK CONVERSION METHODS STUDIED

Problem	Mouse	Tablet	Auto	Mixed
Task Execution				
Visual quality of working copy	✓		n/a	✓
Size of working copy		✓	n/a	
Learning curve for tools	✓	✓		✓
Screen-print output difference			✓	✓
Lengthy time for completion	✓	✓		
Aesthetic Problems				
Blocking of fine detail			✓	
Features missing			✓	✓
Line distortion*			✓	✓
Text distortion*			✓	

** distortion beyond that attributable to screen resolution*

between cost and aesthetic factors, such that the most inexpensive method produces output with the poorest aesthetic scores. Existing artwork can be reproduced exactly, in every stylistic feature and detail, but the time required for exact reproduction increases project costs by about 200%. The goal of exact re-creation requires artistic expertise to assure quality of the final products. Differences exist in the quality of screen and print output within each method, particularly for the Auto method. Stylistic features of a particular drawing may exaggerate these differences; for example, the differences between print and on-screen output for Auto method drawings of Fig. 63.2A are minor, while differences for Fig. 63.1 are significant.

The study suggests a number of planning considerations that one must address before beginning a graphics conversion project.

1. The primary medium of output (e.g., print or on-screen viewing) must be selected. Automated drawings produce adequate print output, but the on-screen representation is unacceptable; thus, Auto method would not be appropriate for an information product whose primary dissemination is via online access. Further, the output medium must be communicated to the artist who does the drawing. If the artist judges the developing or completed drawing only by print output, serious problems in the on-screen version may be ignored. Conversely, drawing techniques that enhance the on-screen presentation may reduce the attractiveness of the print product.

2. The extent of conversion must be carefully considered. Is all artwork in the original to be converted, or will some images be deleted from the online version? In the latter case, text "engineering" may be required to delete explicit and implicit references to graphics that have been eliminated. If all images are to be converted, a decision is required about their exact representation. If exact re-creation of the original

is planned, a hand-crafted method employing an artist should probably be chosen.

3. Graphics "engineering" may be required to take advantage of the new delivery medium. [13] For example, Figure 63.3, Range of Motion Exercises, attempts to show two exercises for improving shoulder mobility. This image might more effectively provide the user with the same information if it was converted to an animated sequence. Additionally, certain types of shading and detail might be more attractively represented by a different technique. For example, the crosshatch shading in Figure 63.1 might be replaced by a shading approach more suitable to medium- and low-resolution screens.

In terms of cost efficiency, conversion seems an attractive option for producing machine-readable information resources. By repackaging existing information products whose market is already established, conversion can reduce or eliminate the creation time, production, and dissemination costs that accompany the publication of new hardcopy texts. Philosophically, conversion depends upon the assumption that no important relationships exist among form, function and content (e.g.., that a change in form will not subvert the informational value of the message). Although the validity of the cost-savings hypothesis is easily tested, the latter assumption remains unproven. [14] Assuming that graphics conversion projects aim to provide information seekers with access to machine-readable images whose quality and usefulness are comparable to a printed original, then the informational roles of graphics in a text, and of elements within an graphic image, must be considered. [15]

Although the screen resolution of standard monitors is adequate for delivery of readable, attractive text, it may not be adequate for displaying certain kinds of artwork, where fine features, contours, sharp-edges or shading are necessary to convey all, or part of, the information. In such a situation, the conversion procedure may result in an ineffective or even inaccurate machine-readable image. By testing and evaluating the aesthetic outcomes of a method before conversion begins, database developers can assure that their efforts to include graphics will enhance, rather than degrade, the quality of the final product.

NOTES

1. K.Y. Marcaccio, Ed, *Computer-Readable Databases. A Directory and Data Sourcebook*, 7th Edition (Detroit: Gale Research, Inc.,1991), xiii.

2. See, for example the electronic edition of D.J. Weatherall, J.G.G. Ledingham, and D.A. Warrell, Eds., *Oxford Textbook of Medicine*, 2nd edition (Oxford: Oxford University Press, 1990).

3. L.F. Lunin, "Electronic Image Formation," *Annual Review of Information Science and Technology*, 22 (1987) 79-224; S. Bulick, "Future Prospects for Network-Based Multimedia Information Retrieval," *Electronic Library* 8 (No. 2, 1990) 88-99.

4. The *Principles and Practice of Infectious Disease* (PPID file) of BRS Colleague's Comprehensive Core Medical Library (CCML) is an example of this approach.

5. See, for example, R.J. Glushko, "Transforming Text into Hypertext for a Compact Disc Encyclopedia," *CHI '89 Proceedings* (New York: Association for Computing Machinery, 1989), 293-298; R. Furu-

ta, C. Plaisant, and B. Shneiderman, "A Spectrum of Automatic Hypertext Constructions," *Hypermedia* 1 (No. 2, 1989) 179-195.

6. Lunin, "Electronic Image Formation," 200.

7. For a discussion of the knowledge management model, see R.E. Lucier, "Knowledge Management: Refining Roles in Scientific Communication," *EDUCOM Review* 25 (No. 3, 1990) 21-7.

8. Further development of the PAM database requires the conversion of graphic and tabular materials from the printed 3rd edition into machine-readable form; the work reported here addresses the graphics portion of that effort. The book contains about 500 tables and 200 graphic images, including charts, photographs, drawings, and graphs.

9. For example, cross-hatched shading is an evaluation criterion for Crispness. If cross-hatched shading was blocked, then the conversion method received a "present" score for blocking. If blocking did not occur, an "absent" score was assigned.

10. In Fig. 63.5, mouse method produced better-quality print copy than the original, which had been reproduced in the textbook from a negative of the original artwork. By recreating the drawing, the artist was able to reintroduce differentiation between vessels which was not clear on the printed page.

11. Equipment costs are based on original prices paid, some of which reflect educational discounts. Current costs may differ, since all of the hardware was purchased before the beginning of the study.

12. A screen-dump utility was used to simulate what the artist sees on the screen. The gray fill for the subdeltoid bursa (see, for example, Figure 3, Mouse method print output) does not appear in screen-dumped images but *does* appear on the screen.

13. J. Martin, *Hyperdocuments and How to Create Them* (Englewood Cliffs, NJ: Prentice-Hall, 1990).

14. See, for example, P.C. Duchastel, "Research on Illustrations in Text: Issues and Perspectives," *Educational and Communication Technology Journal* 28 (No. 4, 1980) 283-287.

15. E.R. Tufte, *Envisioning Information* (Cheshire, CT: Graphics Press, 1990).

ACKNOWLEDGEMENTS

Partial support for PAM artwork conversion project was provided to the Laboratory for Applied Research in Academic Information by the National Library of Medicine (contract N01-LM-8-3531), and by Apple Computer, Inc. Rob Duckwall received a William T. Didusch scholarship from the Art as Applied to Medicine Department during his work on this project. Thanks to Chung Sook Kim for suggesting several improvements to the text, and to Paul Calhoun for technical assistance.

Valerie Florance,
Senior Research Assistant,
Laboratory for Applied Research in Academic Information,
William H. Welch Medical Library,
The Johns Hopkins University

Rob Duckwall,
Medical Illustrator,
Art as Applied to Medicine Department,
The Johns Hopkins University School of Medicine

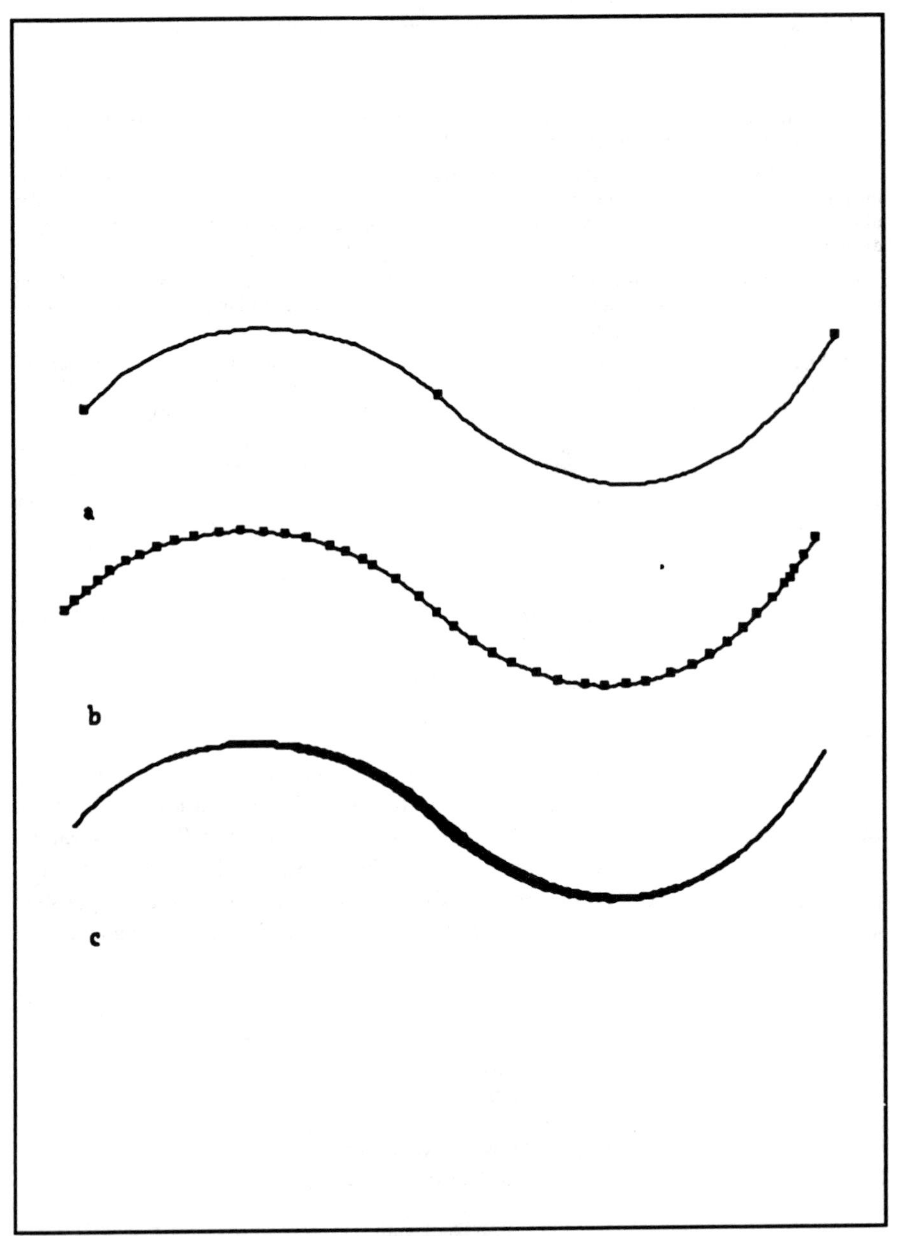

Figure 1. Eyelashing Technique. The drawing program produces lines of a single weight. This technique produces a line whose weight varies, as one might find in a pen-and-ink drawing. A line is broken into editable segments, as in (b). Each segment is assigned a weight, resulting in (c). The more segments, the smoother the weight gradation.

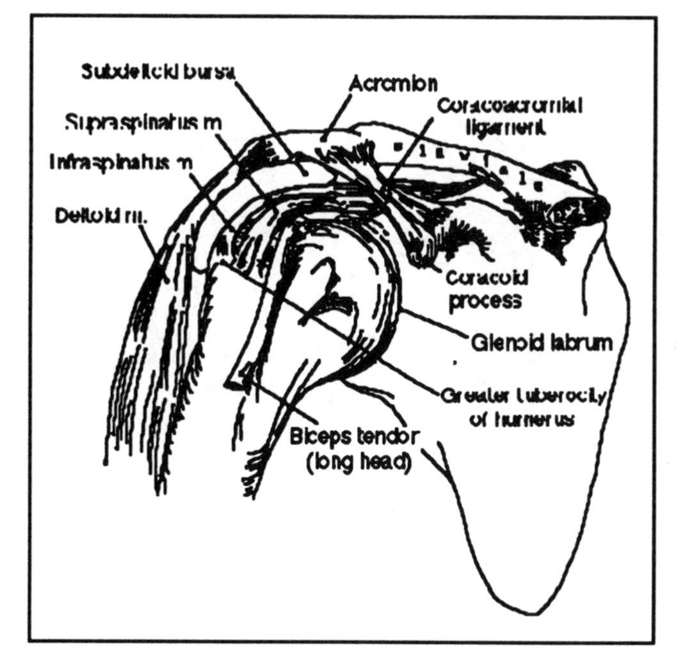

Figure 2. Mouse method screen output for PAM figure 63.1. Distortion of lettering is obvious on the upper text labels, plus some blocking in the cross-hatched areas. Actual screen image has gray-tone shading in the subdeltoid bursa.

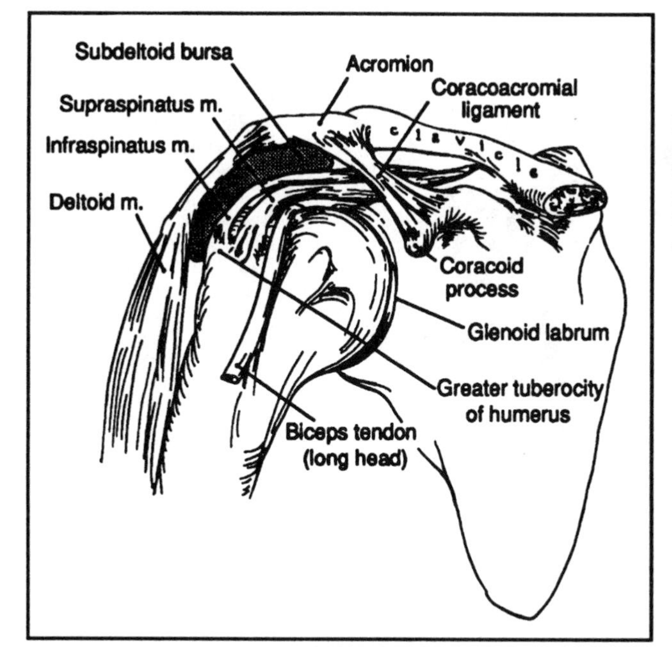

Figure 3. Mouse method print output for PAM figure 63.1. All features of the original are present; lines, text, and shading are crisp and fluid.

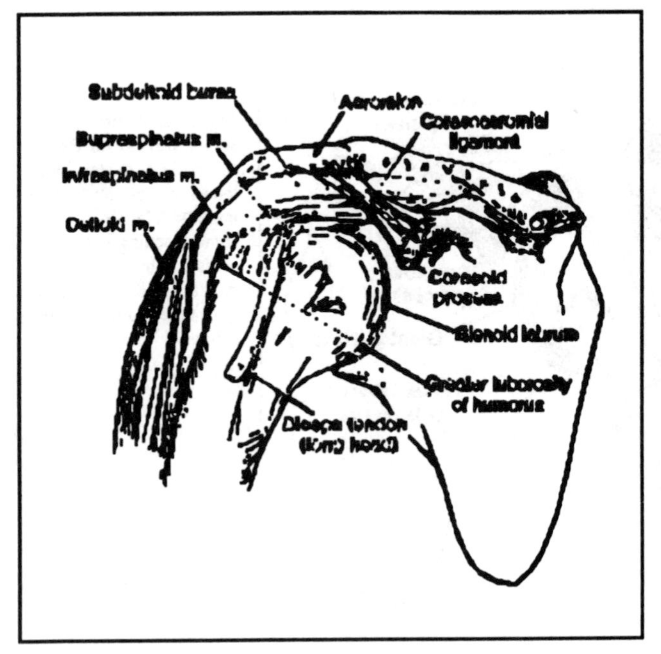

Figure 4. Auto method screen output for PAM figure 63.1. Text is illegible, features are missing, and substantial blocking of cross-hatching is visible. The poorest quality output of all methods. Actual screen image has gray-tone shading in the subdeltoid bursa.

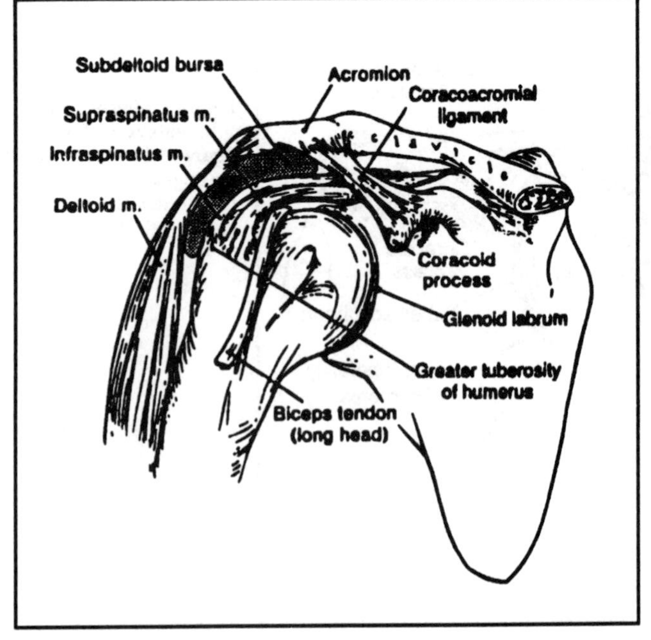

Figure 5. Auto method print output for PAM figure 63.1. Significantly higher quality output, from the same electronic image as the screen dump in Figure 4. Some fine details are missing, and minor distortion of letters is visible, e.g., the letter `t'.

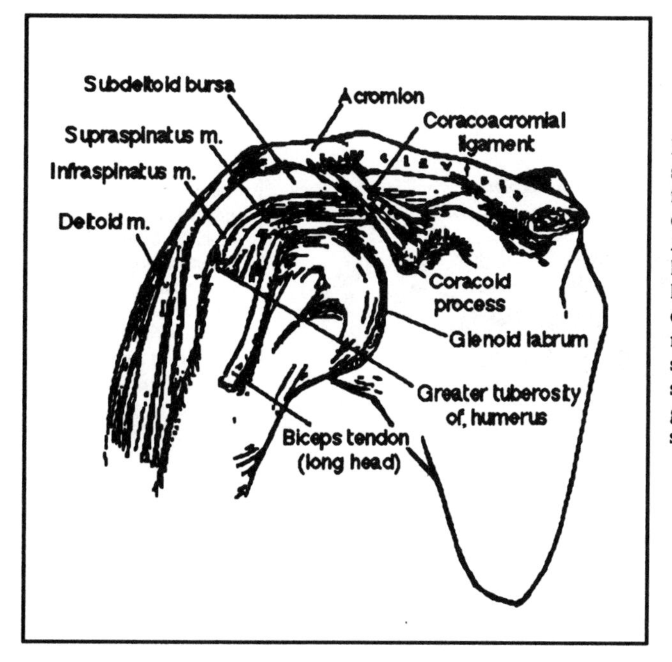

Figure 6. Mixed method screen output for PAM figure 63.1. Using the electronic image from Auto method, the artist has replaced text, clarified leader lines and their end-points, and reintroduced some shading details. Actual screen image has gray-tone shading in the subdeltoid bursa.

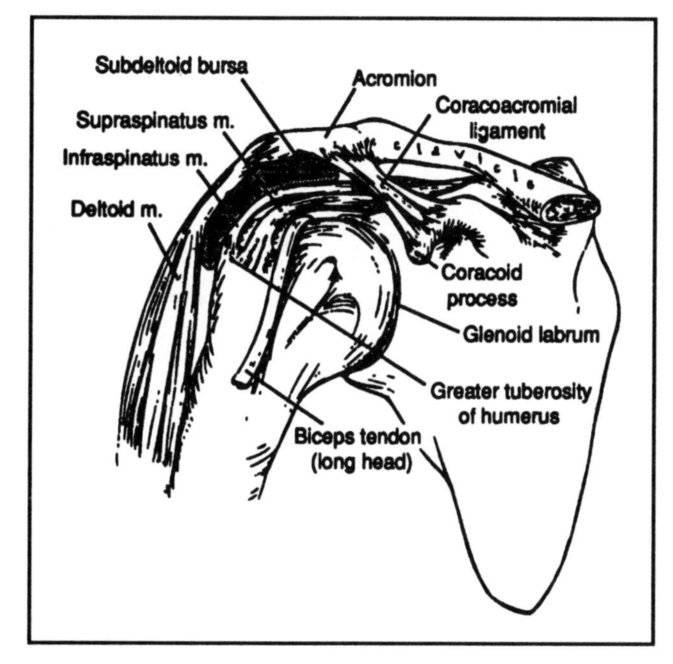

Figure 7. Mixed method print output for PAM figure 63.1. The text distortion is gone, labels were replaced. Except for the thickening of lines and minor blocking, the image is roughly comparable to the Mouse method print output and to the original.

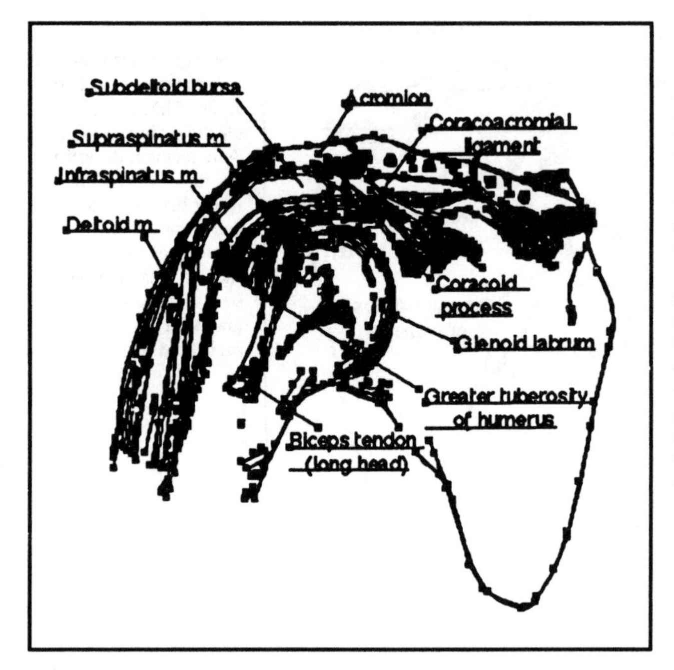

Figure 8. Editing View of PAM figure 63.1. When editing an electronic image, the segments are visible. For drawings with many eyelashed lines, the details of the image are difficult to distinguish. This image also has the template, or tracing copy, visible, so the artist can compare the electronic version to the original. The template causes the "double vision" effect.

CHAPTER
17

NAVY MEDICAL PRACTICE SUPPORT SYSTEM: PROVIDING MULTIMEDIA INFORMATION TO THE MEDICAL PRACTITIONER

Douglas M. Stetson

INTRODUCTION

Many Navy medical practitioners provide health care in quite isolated settings. These individuals lack access to the information sources and collegial support that characterizes most medical practice. A group of government and private sector facilities has developed a prototype Medical Practice Support System (MEPSS) to provide isolated practitioners with rapid access to medical information which might otherwise be unavailable. The system features a computer stored patient record, an electronic medical library, interactive video instruction, and medical diagnostic assistance. It uses commercially available hardware and specially developed software to integrate all functions into a unified user interface. This chapter discusses the system development plan, the importance of the user input, and testing plans.

BACKGROUND

When physicians are puzzled about the condition of one of their patients, they can find help easily. Hospitals and medical school libraries provide some of the information a physician might need, but formal and informal consultation with other medical practitioners are also important information sources. Even the most rural physicians have networks of consultants they contact regularly.

The situation in ships at sea is different, in that a physician is often the only medical officer on a particular ship. Perhaps newly graduated from medical school and having recently completed their internships in major hospitals, these physicians are well qualified, but they have never practiced alone. When in port, they can reach any consultant they require, albeit with some difficulty. At sea, their only means of communication is the radio telephone or written radio messages. These communications are never entirely private and may be altogether unavailable because of military requirements.

On submarines, the isolation is more pronounced. Submarines seek to remain undetected and radio communication risks revealing their locations. For this reason, communication from submarines at sea is severely limited. The practitioner aboard a submarine must be convinced, and convince the captain as well, that a patient's condition warrants breaking radio silence to obtain a consultation or to arrange an evacuation.

Medical evacuations at sea are complicated operations that are not undertaken lightly. They involve disruptive diversion of ships, aircraft, and personnel. A patient or a member of the evacuation party may be washed overboard. Occasionally lives are lost.

Specially trained, independent duty hospital corpsmen provide all health care to submarine crew members underway. Although they are not physicians, they have considerable medical experience and intensive training for their assignments. They have little experience, however, with severely ill patients. Like other medical practitioners, they prefer to transfer patients to more sophisticated facilities early in the course of an illness when they feel serious complications might arise. Elective transfers are sometimes arranged primarily because the practitioner and the commanding officer are concerned that the patient might suddenly become worse and require an emergency evacuation later.

The Naval Submarine Medical Research Laboratory (NSMRL) has developed several expert medical diagnosis systems to provide submarine corpsmen with the benefits of a telephone consultation with a physician without breaking radio silence. The computer programs guide users through patient evaluations and offer diagnostic opinions. Several studies have shown that the value of the programs lies more with their ability to guide the users through a careful patient evaluation than in the diagnoses they generate. [1, 2, 3]

Cooperating with other government and civilian agencies, the NSMRL Medical Informatics Group has built upon the standalone diagnostic programs to create a multimedia medical information system for isolated medical practitioners. We call it the Medical Practice Support System (MEPSS) to emphasize that the system is dedicated to the practice of medicine, not its administration.

APPROACH

After first determining system requirements, our research group assembled a prototype based on off-the-shelf hardware and commercial software development tools. We will take the prototype to several user locations to learn what changes should be made before we build the next prototype.

System Definition

1. A meeting of potential users, researchers, and sponsors worked out the requirements for the information system. Our goal was to provide information from a variety

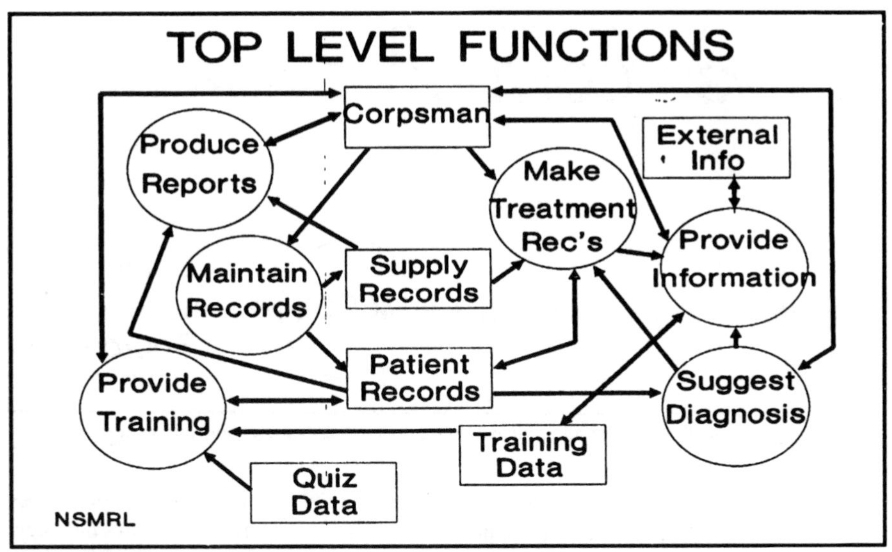

Figure 1. Corpsman/user as a component of an information system

of sources under a single user interface. We wanted to be able to use different types of expert systems in a single system in order to take advantage of existing diagnostic software and new products which might be produced. We wanted to assist the practitioner with routine chores, help with diagnostic dilemmas, and provide professional training. We felt that the system must be both easy to use and maintain, and must avoid reliance on any particular vendor. Finally, we determined to make the system compatible with SAMS, [4] an existing, computer-based shipboard medical administration system.

Each of the meeting participants was an important contributor. The users described what they lacked in their present situation and focused on features they felt would be most valuable. The researchers drew on their knowledge of what was available. The sponsors added the essential elements of enthusiasm, approval, and financial support.

2. A user representative, a systems analyst, a software engineer, and a medical informatics investigator developed the formal system specification. [5] This document proved important in coordinating the work of the several participating sites. The formality of creating a written system specification also helped clarify our thinking about the proposed system. For example, we had all presumed that the patient would not be included in the information system, but some of us had presumed that the user should be seen as part of the system itself, sharing information with other system elements as shown in Figure 1. The diagraming process made this assumption explicit. When we saw that this concept implied that the patient would be cared for by a computer information system (instead of a practitioner), we adopted the view in Figure 2, emphasizing that the system serves the practitioner, and the practitioner, alone, cares for the patient.

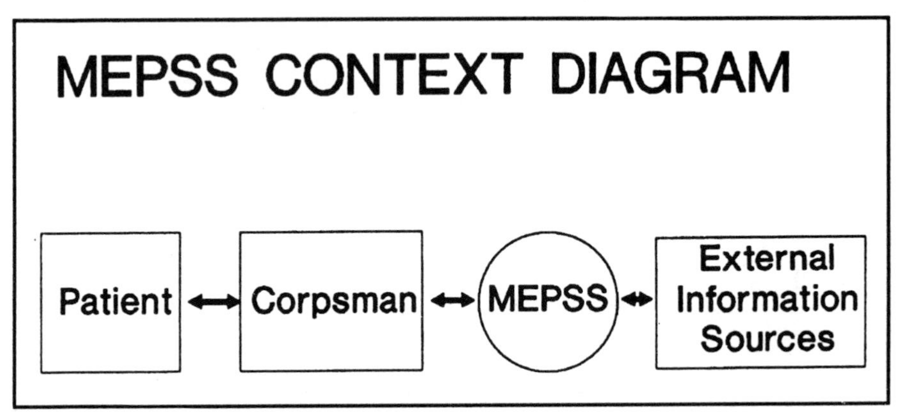

Figure 2. Illustration of intended relationship between patient, corpsman/user, and information system

Figure 3 illustrates the functions, data stores, and data flows of the proposed system. The diagram includes the corpsman to illustrate the direction of data flows between the corpsman and system elements. This diagram, and others with more detail, focused and coordinated the efforts of our decentralized development staff.

The formal system definition specifically mandated an open system architecture. It did not specify hardware, a programming language, or an expert system type. In building the prototype we have tried "C", MUMPS, Clipper, [6] and ENABLE [7] as integrating vehicles. We have also included rule-, probability-, and neural network-based expert systems.

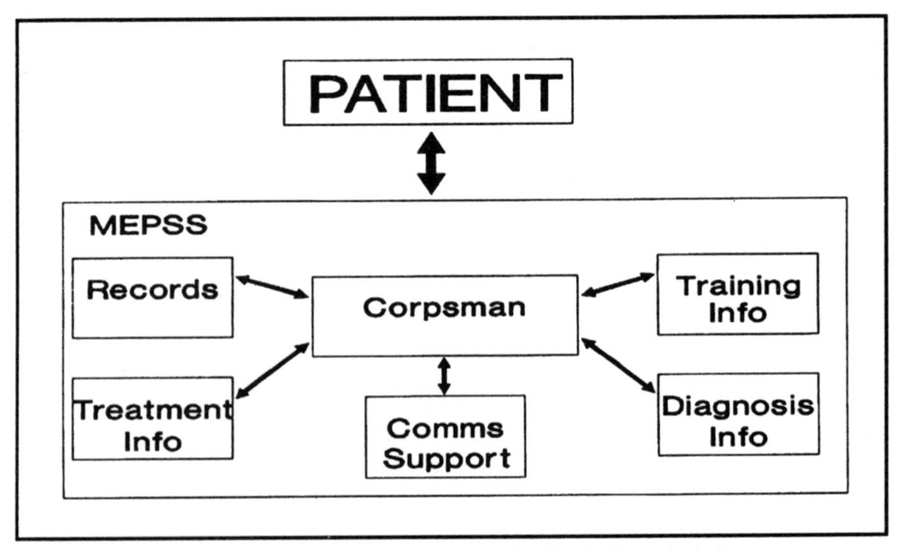

Figure 3. Graphic system specification of MEPSS. Further detail underlies each circle

System Description

MEPSS includes five modules: a computer-stored medical record, a computer-generated diagnosis and treatment advice, a computerized medical library, an interactive video instruction system, and a communications facility.

Medical record. A computer stored patient record is the kernel of the system. It stores information collected by the diagnostic modules. The information is compatible with the patient record maintained by SAMS (SNAPS Automated Medical System). SAMS, an extensive administrative facility in use aboard Navy ships, handles report generation, tickler files, and other administrative requirements. The SAMS input screens and patient record serve as the primary user interface. All MEPSS functions either depend on or emulate SAMS to communicate with the user. By using the existing system, MEPSS avoids duplication of functions and development efforts.

Diagnostic systems. These modules consult the patient record for information they need to reach a diagnostic opinion. The demonstration prototype includes two independent diagnostic systems. Others will be added as they are verified.

Library. The electronic medical library module will help shipboard practitioners get reference material more easily. All Navy ships must carry specific medical publications including copyrighted text books and references, Navy specific publications (e.g., environmental health and sanitation regulations applicable to ships), and military administrative material (e.g., how to arrange evacuation of a patient). On smaller ships, the libraries are too large to fit in the storage space where the corpsmen work. As a result the practitioners frequently store some of their books far from their usual work area and may not be fully familiar with their contents.

The MEPSS library contains the entire text of references it comprises. The entire text of the library is indexed. A user can search for information with Boolean statements. Searches may be limited to a particular reference, a selection of references, or they may cover the entire library.

By making full text searching rapid and easy, the library makes information from seldom used manuals realistically available to the practitioner. For example, if a crew member in the Persian Gulf were suddenly ill, a simple search strategy such as "FEVER (and) DIARRHEA (and) TROPICS" would recover most of the related information available without the user even knowing which references aboard the ship were the most appropriate or what material they contained.

Practitioners sometimes rely on their memories rather than consulting a reference when they feel that the search will take too long or be unproductive. By making useful information easily available, MEPSS may help busy practitioners provide more appropriate care.

Interactive training. The training modules use video disk-based interactive instruction programs. Medical personnel practicing alone at sea have no opportunity for structured continuing medical education. Computerized interactive video programs offer medical practitioners stimulating, auditable instruction which can be used to meet licensing and other administrative requirements. More important, the training is interesting enough to be used spontaneously and it presents a professional challenge for corpsmen. MEPSS includes the Navy Computer Assisted Medical Interactive Video Instruction System (CAMIS). [8] CAMIS offers over 30 productions ranging from introductory material for junior hospital corpsmen to sophisticated programs teaching Advanced Trauma Life Support for physicians. Some productions are suitable for patient education. All productions incorporate sound, video images, and computer-generated graphics.

Communications. The communications support module makes data from off-site sources available to the user when communication lines are available. The features include formatted packaging of medical information for compact transmission to supervising medical personnel, interpreters for access to on-line databases, and provision for communications through bulletin boards.

PROGRESS

Our group has assembled a prototype multimedia information system focused on the needs of clinical practitioners. We have combined patient record keeping with several expert systems, graphics, interactive video, and an electronic medical library.

Hardware Selection

To avoid creating a unique system that would require reliance on products from specific vendors, we have used off-the-shelf hardware that adheres to generally accepted standards. Specifically, we selected IBM 386 AT-compatible computers, which are widely used in the Department of Defense, VGA monitors (640 x 480 pixels x 256 color resolution), and commercial laser disk players.

Video graphics incompatibilities caused the greatest hardware difficulties. We intended to display images from three sources: our electronic medical library, CAMIS, and commercially available CD-ROM based medical libraries. Because of space limitations on ships, we also restricted ourselves to a single, compact, video display.

Developers and manufacturers do not agree on an appropriate resolution for displaying medical images. Some use 640 x 480 x 16 colors. Others insist on 1024 x 760 x 256 colors. Special tasks require still finer resolution. Monitors with this very high resolution are becoming more common but remain relatively expensive. Many thousands of standard VGA monitors capable of 640 x 480 x 256 color resolution are already in use.

Providing full motion video and computer-based graphics on a single monitor was also a development difficulty. Until recently, various vendors used incompatible techniques for providing television images on a computer screen. Users had to select a particular display platform, and then were able to use only video productions compatible with that platform. A recently distributed Interactive Video Instruction Association proposed standard [9] may bring some relief to this area. The standard (also known as Military Standard 1379D of 5 Dec. 1990) provides that any IVIA-compliant interactive video production can be displayed on any hardware platform which also meets the IVIA standard.

We have elected to try the 640 x 480 x 256 color resolution in our prototype. CD-ROM based libraries we have used provide images at this resolution. It is also the maximum resolution available from the video overlay board we are using.

The MEPSS prototype comprises a Dolch PAC 386-20 microcomputer with a Sony VGA SMI-3081 video/graphics overlay system, a Sony LDP 1410 laser disk player, and an IBM 8513-compatible VGA monitor.

Software Development

MEPSS was written in Clipper to provide information exchange between MEPSS modules and the SAMS (Version 7.0) patient record. Written in FoxPro, [10] the SAMS record shares the dBase [11] compatible files used by Clipper. Exchanging data between MEPSS and SAMS eliminates duplicate data entry requirements.

Diagnostic assistance software included in the first prototype addresses two clinical domains: abdominal pain and ocular disorders.

The abdominal pain component was based on a freestanding program developed and written in QuickBASIC [12] at NSMRL. [13] It was rewritten in Clipper to take advantage of the SAMS file format. A probabilistic system employing Bayes' rule, it evaluates information provided by the user to determine the relative likelihood of several causes of abdominal complaints. In the prototype it is supplemented by a dedicated neural network that distinguishes appendicitis from other disorders. [14]

The ocular disorders component of the diagnostic module is an example of a rule-based expert system. NSMRL developed the rules for the eye component using EXSYS Professional, [15] an artificial intelligence shell program. We selected EXSYS because it offered both backward and forward chaining capabilities and provided several different ways to control execution of the rules.

The Applied Physics Laboratory at The Johns Hopkins University created a custom designed inference engine in "C" and Clipper that performed all input and output functions for the diagnostic module and performed all inference functions. It executed the rules for the ocular disorders component and also performed the calculations for the neural network and the probabilistic algorithms that support the abdominal pain component. Using this custom inference engine facilitated smooth integration of the ocular module into MEPSS and avoided the need to use proprietary code in the final system.

A single supervisory shell, written in Clipper, integrates the three expert systems (probability-, neural network-, and rule-based). This single user interface makes the facilities of very differently operating diagnostic systems available to the user transparently. This approach will allow us to incorporate other diagnostic systems developed with different tools and using different technical approaches without requiring the user to become familiar with different interfaces.

We used the X Windows [16] operating system to incorporate a subset of an electronic medical library developed at the University of Florida. [17] The library features full text indexing, a Boolean search engine with dictionary and wild card selection facilities, and the facility to limit a search to any selected volume in the library.

MEPSS functional description includes a maintenance facility. This utility will ensure that changes in the knowledge bases can be made without assistance of professional programmers. Subject matter experts, familiar with inference techniques used in the system, will be able to add, delete, and modify the parameters used to describe the clinical conditions in the program.

Although MEPSS will first be used by hospital corpsmen, we used the same clinical terminology as physicians use when describing the clinical conditions. To ensure all users are comfortable with this vocabulary, we included an extensive hypertext help facility, which provides instant explanations of key terms. The explanations, themselves, include other key words which can be further explored to ensure that the users are confident that they understand the program.

In addition to supporting communication with SAMS, MEPSS diagnostic modules provide two written reports. The first is a standard clinical note suitable for incorporation into the patient medical record. The second is a specially formatted radio message suitable for transmission to a supervisory medical authority.

Use of Graphics

Our experience with the standalone abdominal pain diagnostic program showed that diagrams and charts helped assure error-free data entry and clarified output interpretation. We extended our use of graphics by including drawings and diagrams that illustrate clinical findings. This enabled us to convey complex and unfamiliar ideas in single screens. We used hypertext techniques to provide the amplifying graphic information without cluttering the question screen or impeding experienced users.

We also use the graphic information in the CAMIS video disk library. Users can call up photographs, full motion demonstrations of examination techniques, or animations depicting therapeutic maneuvers. The computerized library contains the scanned images of all graphics included in the library publications. Users locate images by searching their captions or by finding them in association with related text topics.

User Input to Development

Direct user participation at all stages of development is critical to producing a computer-based system that users will actually use. MEPSS has been able to take advantage of user input in several ways.

The SAMS development team employs a standing SAMS User's Group which regularly meets to discuss possible enhancements and to comment on its user interface. Version 7.0 of SAMS serves as a basis for the MEPSS user interface and embodies several years of expressed user preferences.

In making the standalone diagnostic programs available to the naval fleet, the developers at NSMRL have conducted numerous training sessions with experienced practitioners. Information from questionnaires and other comments from these sessions influenced selection of features we incorporated in the system.

Our most valuable user input was the objective and subjective data collected during formal system usability testing described in the next section.

Testing

A medical information system offering diagnostic assistance requires testing of both its usability as a computer system and its clinical accuracy.

We conducted formal usability testing on one of the diagnostic modules to determine whether users would express overt preferences for a particular interface. [18] The study involved three presentations of the same diagnostic program. Each version asked the same questions and provided the same responses, but each was packaged in a different user interface. We collected user responses with video cameras, questionnaires, and structured interviews. The study revealed that users expressed a clear preference for one interface over another. More important, however, despite the different versions of the systems requiring and providing identical information, users rated as most trustworthy the version they found most friendly.

Clinical testing of the diagnostic assistance modules is reported elsewhere. [19, 20] Complete clinical testing for the diagnostic modules will consist of three elements: subject matter expert evaluation judging the scope and appropriateness of the program as well as their view of the validity of its responses; testing of modules against clinical case descriptions from medical literature; and testing against clinical material collected from patient contacts. Additional testing will evaluate a module's accuracy when parts of the input data are missing or inaccurate.

PLANS

Near term plans include expansion of the demonstration electronic medical library; inclusion of additional diagnostic modules addressing gynecologic disorders, dental pain, chest pain, psychiatric disorders and trauma; and providing direct access to text, graphics, sound, and video segments from the video disk sources. These video disk sources can supplement system input and output functions. For example, when the system asks the user for details of a skin rash, it could display photographs of typical rashes and ask if one is similar to the one the user is seeing. Similarly, the system could provide the user with the typical lung sounds of a patient with pneumonia, or it could demonstrate how to examine a patient's abdomen. When offering treatment advice, the system can display video clips of unfamiliar procedures.

In addition, we intend to use industry standard methods for integrating medical measuring devices with MEPSS. For example, if an intelligent electrocardiogram machine is attached to the system, the machine-generated interpretation can be entered directly into the medical record without the user performing any transcription. The chest pain diagnostic module will then be able to use information the machine provides in reaching a diagnostic recommendation. Since electrocardiographic information is valuable in evaluating chest pain, this enhancement would be particularly useful for any user inexperienced in electrocardiogram interpretation.

Later, we expect to take advantage of emerging capabilities in plain language processing and speech recognition. We intend to make all MEPSS functions available to the user transparently in the context of the patient being examined and with consideration of the behavior patterns of the practitioner. The system will accept spoken patient record notes, provide background review of the proposed diagnosis and treatment plan, and pre-select appropriate text, image, and audio material for display.

SIGNIFICANCE

This system is centered on medical practitioners and their expressed requirements. It is not a medical administrative program providing clinically useful information as a by-product of some primary administrative function. It differs from other systems designed to improve information access in providing expert diagnostic advice. Its primary purpose is to improve clinical decision making by providing intelligent access to large amounts of information. The information resources in the system can be readily adapted to provide information and advice which is specifically tailored to the training and skills of the user, and to the medical care support capabilities of the clinical location. Instant access to appropriate information, particularly in isolated settings, will significantly help practitioners provide the best health care.

CONCLUSION

A prototype medical information system is available that can bring a wide range of medical information to medical practitioners promptly and with little effort. By assisting practitioners in rapidly obtaining precisely the information needed in a particular situation, the system can help improve the quality of decisions, reduce time lost to unnecessary referrals, and improve practice quality for the user by reducing administrative burdens. Development of such systems requires close cooperation with potential users at all stages and detailed testing before release.

ACKNOWLEDGMENTS

James S. Newacheck, LCDR, MSC, USN, and Boris Shajenko, Naval Submarine Medical Research Laboratory, Groton, CT 06349-5900.

Russell Eberhart and Roy Dobbins, The Johns Hopkins University, Applied Physics Laboratory, Laurel, MD.

William Pugh and Antonio Gino, Naval Health Research Center, San Diego, CA.

William Peratino, Naval Health Sciences Education and Training Command, Bethesda, MD.

William Underhill, Luneria Corporation, Alexandria, VA

Ralph Grams, Ph.D., University of Florida, Gainesville, FL.

Roger Kirouac, LT, MSC, USN, Naval Management Systems Support Office, Norfolk, VA.

DISCLAIMER

This work was supported by Naval Medical Research and Development Command Work Unit No. 63706N M0095.005-5010. The opinions and assertions contained herein are private ones of the authors and are not to be construed as official or reflecting the views of the Navy Department or the naval service at large.

NOTES

1. I.D. Adams, M. Chan, et al, "Computer-aided diagnosis of acute abdominal pain, a multicentre study." *British Medical Journal*, 293, (1986) pp. 800-804.

2. F.T. de Dombal, "Computer-aided diagnosis of acute abdominal pain. The British experience." *Revue d'Epidemiologie et de Sante´ Publique.*, 32, (1984) pp. 5056.

3. F.T. de Dombal, "Computer-aided decision support in clinical medicine." *International Journal of Biomedical Computing*, 24, (1984), pp. 9-16.

4. The SNAPS Automated Medical System (SAMS) is distributed and maintained by the Navy Management Systems Support Office, Norfolk, VA.

5. D.M. Stetson, R.C. Eberhart, et al, "Structured specification of a computer assisted medical diagnostic system." Proceedings of the Third Annual IEEE Symposium of Computer-Based Medical Systems, Chapel Hill, NC, (June 5-6, 1990), pp. 374-80.

6. Trademark of Nantucket Corp.

7. Trademark of Enable Software, Ballston Lake, NY.

8. CAMIS is distributed and maintained by the Naval Health Sciences Education and Training Command, Bethesda, MD.

9. Phillip Dodds, Scott Lewis, et al, "Recommended practices for interactive video portability (working document)." Published by the Compatibility Committee of the Interactive Video Industry Association, Washington, DC, April 1990.

10. Trademark of Fox Software.

11. Trademark of Ashton-Tate.

12. Trademark of Microsoft Corporation.

13. D. Southerland, K. Fisherkeller, et al, "ABDX: a decision support system for the management of acute abdominal pain. Version 3.0. Programmer's manual." Naval Submarine Medical Research Laboratory Report 1148, (31 October 1989).

14. R.C. Eberhart, R.W. Dobbins. "Neural network versus bayesian diagnosis of appendicitis." Proceedings of IEEE Annual Conference, Philadelphia, PA, (Nov. 1-4, 1990).

15. Trademark of EXSYS, Inc., Albuquerque, NM.

16. Trademark of Microsoft Corporation.

17. The Clinical Practice Library of Medicine was developed by Ralph Grams, University of Florida Medical School, Gainesville, FL.

18. E.F. Chouinard, B.L. Ryack, et al, "A comparison of the usability of three versions of a computerized medical diagnostic assistance program for abdominal pain." Poster session presented at the Human Factors Society Annual Convention, (October 1990), Orlando, FL. Naval Submarine Medical Research Laboratory Report 1172 (1991).

19. F.T. de Dombal, "Final report on modification of the de Dombal computer-based systems for diagnosis of abdominal pain to optimize its accuracy when applied to the United States Navy submarine force population." (Sept. 1980) (private communication).

20. J.C. Horrocks, A.P. McCann, et al, *British Medical Journal* Vol. 2, (1974), pp. 5.

Douglas M. Stetson
Captain, Medical Corps
United States Navy
Naval Submarine Medical Research Laboratory
Groton, Connecticut 06349-5900

Libraries

CHAPTER

18

THE *RIGHTPAGES*: AN IMAGE BASED ELECTRONIC LIBRARY ALERTING AND DISTRIBUTION SERVICE

Guy A. Story
Lawrence O'Gorman
David Fox
Louise Levy Schaper
H.V. Jagadish

INTRODUCTION

In 1990, AT&T Bell Laboratories began an electronic alerting and library testbed project called the *RightPages.* [1] A partnership between Research and the AT&T Information Services Network, the *RightPages* is an image-based system with the objective of bringing an electronic analog of the library to a user's desktop computer. This facility includes both delivery of document material as well as a personal—albeit electronic—research librarian to alert the user to new library material matching the user's interest profile.

One of the characteristic features of the *RightPages* is that it offers a "look and feel" similar to that of traditional libraries, but augmented with some of the features that computer imaging, networking, and databases enable. For instance, users may choose to rely on the automatic alerting capability to direct their reading; or may "browse the stacks," perusing images of journal covers and tables of contents, and choosing articles in this way. When a user makes a selection, the article appears exactly as in the original—it is simply a scanned image of the original. Spatially associated with the scanned image are results of optical character recognition (OCR) and page layout analysis. These enable contextual access and searching of the article contents.

Relevant to this project is the goal of testing publishers' readiness to license their publications for image-based systems. AT&T has traditionally respected copyright compliance in paper copying, [2] and will continue to do so for electronic copying. AT&T's history of compliance has served to put some publishers at ease. It should be

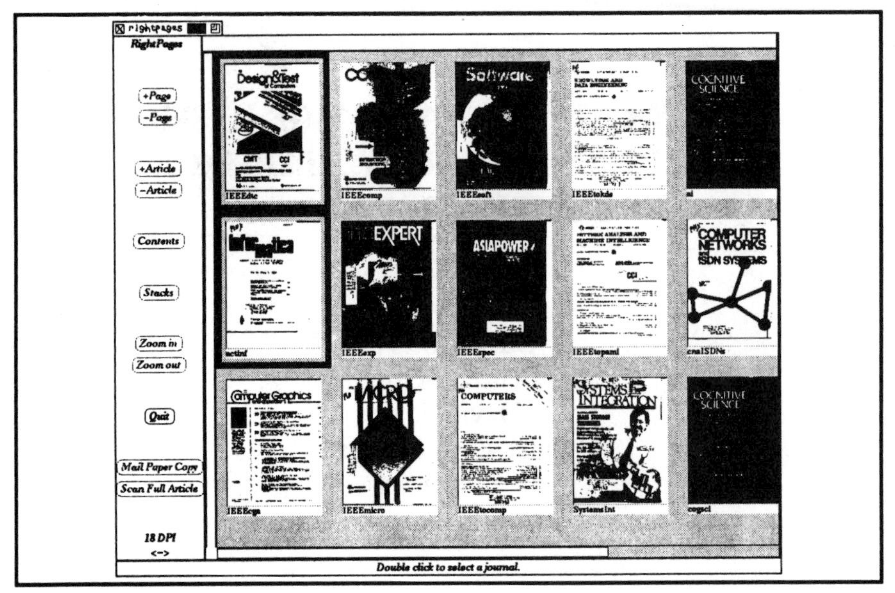

Figure 1. Display of front covers

understood that any organization embarking on an electronic digitization project containing published content in any media must obtain permission from the copyright owners. Much has been learned that is useful to others engaged, or about to be engaged, in similar projects. Since the *RightPages* is still in its beginnings, these findings are preliminary.

About 60 researchers participating in this test have reading access on their personal workstations. As members of this community develop familiarity with the system, we will observe their use, modify the system accordingly, and continue to improve the underlying processing for better effectiveness and speed of delivery.

THE USER INTERFACE

When new articles match a user's personal profile of keywords and phrases, that user is alerted via electronic mail and prompted to run the *RightPages* user interface. This interface presents the user with the "stacks," an array of small images of periodical front covers, corresponding to the issues present in the database (Figure 1).

The interface highlights the covers of issues in which matches were found, called "alerts." Clicking the mouse on a cover brings up an image of the table of contents page, and the system highlights the regions on the page corresponding to the articles matching the user's profile (Figure 2). Clicking on any of those regions brings up the first page of the article (Figure 3).

One feature of this interface is that the table of contents images "know" the re-

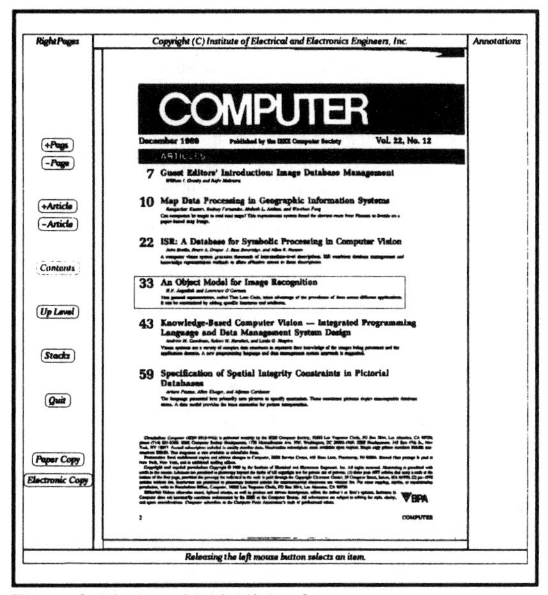

COMPUTER

December 1989 | Published by the IEEE Computer Society | Vol. 22, No. 12

ARTICLES

7 Guest Editors' Introduction: Image Database Management

10 Map Data Processing in Geographic Information Systems

22 ISR: A Database for Symbolic Processing in Computer Vision

33 An Object Model for Image Recognition

43 Knowledge-Based Computer Vision — Integrated Programming Language and Data Management System Design

59 Specification of Spatial Integrity Constraints in Pictorial Databases

Figure 2. Display with highlight of contents

gions on the page image that correspond to the articles. Each of these regions acts as a hypertext-like link to the appropriate article page, allowing the user to go directly to the desired page image without having to move sequentially through the intervening pages.

An initial design decision was made to scan only the first page of each article when a periodical is first entered into the system. Although in part a labor-saving decision for this testbed, the rationalization, as yet unproven, is that the first page will provide enough material both for the alerting function and for users to decide whether they wish to see the entire article. We will re-evaluate this decision based on system use and user feedback.

In the initial release, the user may order a complete copy of the article in either paper or electronic form. If the user orders an electronic copy, the system issues a request for the entire article to be scanned. Then the system alerts the user that the entire article is now available in the *RightPages* database, and that by bringing up the *RightPages* interface in the same way as before, the entire article can be viewed. This article is then available for other users as well; in effect the database is gradually populated with full articles that are in demand.

Besides following the alerting pointers, the *RightPages* user may browse any other articles in the same issue,

RightPages | Code. TLC exhibits several advantages in | Annotations

An Object Model for Image Recognition

H.V. Jagadish and Lawrence O'Gorman

AT&T Bell Laboratories

Attempt to go to a null node.

Figure 3. Display of first page

or may browse journals and articles throughout the stacks. We hope that, just as in traditional libraries, our interface design encourages exploration and serendipitous discovery of other articles of interest.

The *RightPages* interface appears to the user as presenting bit-map copies of articles, but actually has "smart" images whose text contents are available for online text searching. This is done by spatially associating the results of OCR with the visible bit-map image (see Figure 3). Furthermore, we have designed text search techniques that are tolerant of OCR errors. Since the system always presents the original typeset page image and not an attempted recreation of it after OCR and other recognition analyses, the *RightPages* interface is "fail-soft."

DOCUMENT PROCESSING DETAILS

The *RightPages* is implemented in the C++ programming language using the InterViews [3] graphical interface toolkit. It runs on top of the X Window system [4] on workstations and terminals that support X.

Periodicals first enter the *RightPages* system when an operator scans them using a graphical scanning interface. Pages are scanned at 300 dpi, currently at one bit per pixel. Grayscale processing is necessary to extract text and figures for some images, therefore grayscale scanning and processing will be provided in the near future.

For each periodical the operator indicates the title, volume, issue, and date. Research is underway to automate the recognition of the link regions corresponding to the article entry on the table of contents pages, but in the system's initial release the operator must sweep out these regions with the mouse and indicate the links to each of the article pages.

Once captured, a page image undergoes a number of processing steps before its text content is ready for the database. First, the image is cleaned using a filter for removing "salt-and-pepper" noise. [5] Next the image undergoes optical character recognition. Last, the system attempts to improve the results of OCR by using contextual information and word combination probabilities. [6] The ASCII text for article pages is dispatched to the process that matches against user profiles.

The original 300 dpi image resolution is, of course, too high for typical bit-mapped displays, and so the image is subsampled to resolutions matching the small number of monitor types currently supported. This subsampling process attempts to filter the image and remove pixels while maintaining, at least in a browsing scenario, the text's readability. [7] User feedback will be helpful in evaluating the effectiveness of these methods.

The subsampled images, OCR results, and results of the (currently manual) page layout analysis are coordinated in the interface so that while the user is presented with the image, machine-supported enhancements are present at all times. Providing new enhancements is a goal of ongoing research in the coordination of multiple document representations.

As described below, one of the licensing provisions calls for the system to provide usage statistics. This data is of paramount interest to the publishers participating in the project, but it also interests us, since certain assumptions about user habits and behavior have affected the system design. All user activity is logged, and periodic usage reports are generated from the log.

COMPONENTS OF THE LICENSING AGREEMENTS

The attempt by AT&T Bell Laboratories to obtain license agreements to scan, store, and transmit images of technical journal articles for the *RightPages* project has been time consuming and only moderately successful. Site licenses for sixty technical journals and conference proceedings have been obtained thus far.

AT&T entered into an agreement with the Copyright Clearance Center (CCC) to participate in its experimental program in which the CCC obtains licenses and authorizations from publishers for the electronic transmission of their materials. Most authorizations were obtained under this agreement, although a few bilateral agreements exist with publishers. The former approach was preferred as it offered a standardized contract, agreement process, and payment method. Our agreement with the CCC for paper photocopying has provided a viable model for electronic copying.

The agreements used are significantly more restrictive than those recently made by AT&T and vendors of ASCII full-text databases. With the *RightPages*, as in any image-based retrieval system, publishers are licensing not just text, but the whole "look and feel" of the journal—text, graphics, print, and layout. Perhaps that is why publishers may be more wary of making agreements involving electronic copying of images, or it may be simply that most publishers of highly technical journals have not routinely made their content—ASCII or image—available in a private networked environment.

Our general experience was that publishers were unprepared to respond readily to our requests. Some were unsure about the CCC's future role in electronic delivery and preferred bilateral agreements. Others lacked an understanding of the stakes involved and were unable to respond to our request. Most feared undervaluing their content; the wide variations in royalty pricing indicated differing strategies. All lacked a process for handling such a request—not knowing what to do with it led to months where the request was passed from desk to desk or simply died.

Overall, however, publishers indicated an interest to be involved in projects, such as *RightPages*. They recognize they stand to learn much from these fledgling electronic libraries. Building partnerships with publishers and encouraging their active participation in *RightPages* has been fruitful for both parties.

The AT&T licensing agreement with the CCC for *RightPages* has the following components:

- CCC will obtain licenses and authorizations from publishers.
- AT&T-BL has the right to convert material to electronic form by scanning, to store materials electronically, and to transmit materials to two sites.
- AT&T-BL has the right to print one copy on paper or transfer material to another electronic medium and to use materials for private files not to be resold.
- The agreement term is two years.
- AT&T-BL must use best efforts to verify the accuracy of materials.
- AT&T-BL must place a copyright notice at the start of each material.
- AT&T-BL must prepare and issue periodic reports.
- AT&T-BL will pay the CCC royalties and CCC, in turn, pays rights owners.
- AT&T-BL must notify the CCC of any infringement or unauthorized use.
- AT&T-BL will maintain all subscriptions during term of agreement.

At the time of this writing, 11 out of 34 publishers responded to the authorization request. Agreements have been made with 10 of those; others were declined because of high royalty fees.

PLANS FOR THE FUTURE

RightPages is a testbed project, and the system currently does not offer services and features that approximate the variety and breadth of those found in commercial systems. We modestly hope that *RightPages* proves usable in the simple scenarios for which it was designed and that it provide a testbed for experiments in document analysis, modeling, and management. Following are a few near-term goals:

- A set of typical navigation bells and whistles to help users cope with a growing database
- Page layout analysis to automate the table of contents linking
- Inexact online text search, based on the OCR post-processing techniques
- Novel article classification and user profiling schemes
- Inclusion of the internal documents database
- Further hypertext-like enhancements to conventional documents
- Expansion to other media, applying similar data modeling approaches.

NOTES

1. L. O'Gorman, G.A. Story, and D. Fox, "An Electronic Library Alerting and Distribution Service," *Proceedings of Workshop on Syntactic and Structural Pattern Recognition* , Murray Hill, NJ, 1990, p. 493.

2. Louise Levy Schaper, "Copyright Compliance in the Electronic Age: Practical Uses", *Proceedings of*

the Twelfth National Online Meeting, New York, NY, May 1991.

3. Mark A. Linton, Paul R. Calder, and John M. Vlissides. "InterViews: A C++ Graphical Interface Toolkit," *Technical Report CSL-TR-88-358*, Stanford University, July 1988.

4. Robert W. Scheifler and Jim Gettys, "The X Window System," *ACM Transactions on Graphics*, 5(2), April 1986, pp. 79-109.

5. Guy A. Story, Lawrence O'Gorman, David Fox, Louise Levy Schaper, and H.V. Jagadish, "The RightPages: An Image-Based Electronic Library for Alerting and Browsing," *Computer*, IEEE, 1992 (in press).

6. Mark A. Jones, Guy A. Story, and Bruce Ballard, "Integrating Multiple Knowledge Sources in a Bayesian OCR Post-Processor," First International Conference on Document Analysis and Recognition, Saint Malo, France, September 1991.

7. Lawrence O'Gorman and Guy A. Story, "Subsampling Text Images," First International Conference on Document Analysis and Recognition, Saint Malo, France, September 1991.

Guy A. Story
Lawrence O'Gorman
David Fox
Louise Levy Schaper
H. V. Jagadish

AT&T Bell Laboratories
Murray Hill, New Jersey
(908) 582-5571

CHAPTER

19

Multimedia for Training Library Staff

Peter Stubley, Michael Leslie
and Darren Umney

INTRODUCTION

Multimedia is poised to make a significant impact in learning methods in higher education over the next few years, which in itself will have a bearing on library provision. Nonetheless, there has been little investigation of the specific library uses of multimedia.

Beginning in October 1990, Sheffield University Library has worked on a project to investigate the application of multimedia to libraries. The project is funded from a two-year research contract worth £53,000 ($94,000) from the British Library Research and Development Department. The Multimedia in Libraries Project has as its primary aim the production and evaluation of a multimedia demonstrator for librarians and information workers. In particular, the demonstrator is intended to examine a range of issues in library staff training. Given that the use of multimedia by librarians has so far been limited, a second aim of the research is to incorporate within the demonstrator a "reference" subset to enable others to see how, in broad detail, a multimedia presentation can be constructed so that they will be encouraged to use the techniques.

The prototype demonstrator is nearing completion, all the work having been carried out on an Apple Macintosh IIci with 8 megabytes of RAM and an 80-megabyte hard disk, printing to a Personal LaserWriter NT. In its final version, this basic configuration will likely be supported by ancillary hardware such as a 24-bit colour board, motion video board, colour scanner, CD-ROM player, and video camera. Two software packages have been used: MacroMind Director and Aldus SuperCard.

TERMINOLOGY

In the opening paper of the Online Conference 1990, John C. Gale of Information Workstation Group, quoting Dave Miller, another industry watcher, described multimedia as "a slippery term", [1] which certainly allows marketing people the latitude to express precisely what they are selling without fear of contradiction. Some say that only animation (without audio) is needed to justify the term; others that it combines graphics and audio, with moving images being optional. Most agree that some form of interactivity is essential. Worlock [2] also tackles slipperiness (or "sloppy thinking" as he calls it), but from a more belligerent standpoint, stating categorically that "to qualify as multimedia, a product must use multiple media; and it must be interactive." This approach conveniently eliminates desktop video and presentation graphics—neither of which are interactive. As far as *our* use of the term is concerned multimedia is *not* (or not necessarily):

- hypermedia
- presentation graphics
- desktop video

but it *is* the integration of:

- moving images
- graphics
- colour
- sound
- text

LIBRARY STAFF TRAINING AND MULTIMEDIA

The area of librarianship chosen for investigation is the "reference interview," the term librarians use to describe the interaction between library staff and enquirers at the reference desk. This is the most important link in the information chain because only by a full understanding between the two parties can the precise information needs of enquirers be satisfied.

The reference interview offers many opportunities for misunderstanding between a librarian and an enquirer, and the prototype—as well as the final—demonstrator shows how different interactions can lead to different results. The prototype concentrates on four aspects of the reference interview which, as explained later, comprise the four modules of the training package:

- nonverbal communication
- query negotiation
- bibliographic search strategies
- feedback

In defining these aspects, it should be clear that our target audience of trainees are professional librarians, particularly those involved in Reader Services activities, irrespective of experience, but especially recently qualified professionals together with library school students.

STRATEGIC NODES

To ensure that an integrated and professional training package is produced, important decisions have to be made throughout the whole design process. We have referred to these major decision points as "strategic nodes," not because they act as branching points within a system, but because they are crucial to its overall structure and design. The *Oxford English Dictionary* defines a node as "a central point in any complex or system," which seems to fit our usage in spite of conflicting with the more standardised use of the term as a branching point in hypermedia systems. We have identified four strategic nodes as:

- navigation
- representation
- interactivity
- modularity

Navigation

Much research has been carried out on the navigational problems of hypermedia systems, [3] the real possibilities of being "lost in hyperspace" having become one of the prime concerns for those working in the area. The problems primarily relate to the nonserial possibilities of exploration of hypertext documents; solutions can encompass the incorporation of a stable base point, facilities for backtracking, and the

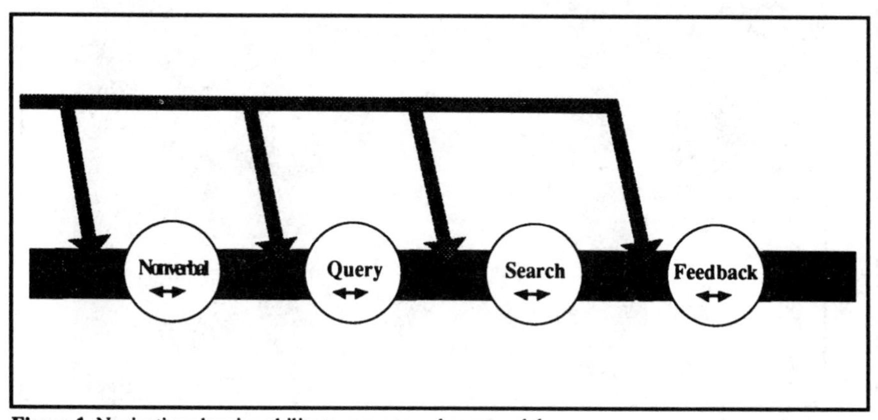

Figure 1. Navigation showing ability to move to a chosen module

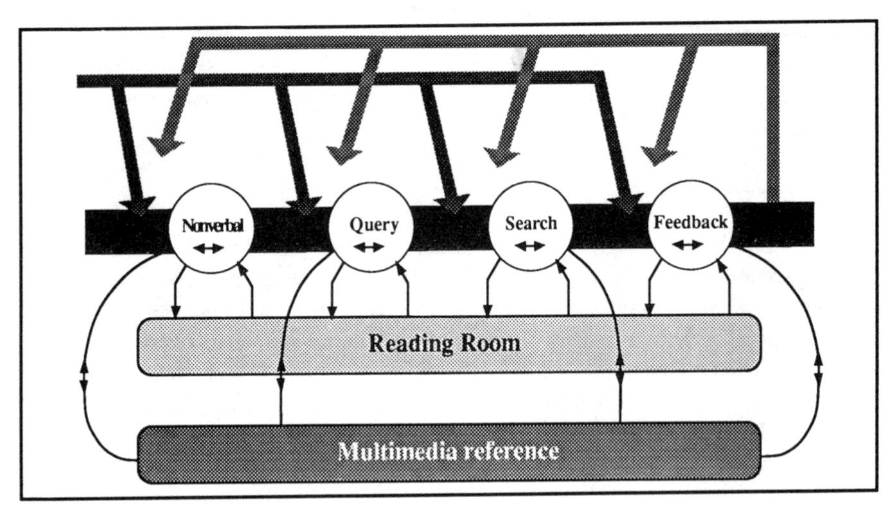

Figure 2. Navigation showing possible paths through the demonstrator

use of graphical and typographical cues.

By contrast, the researchers envision that this multimedia demonstrator will be essentially linear in use, though trainees will have the option of moving directly to the

Figure 3. Screen dump showing navigation compass

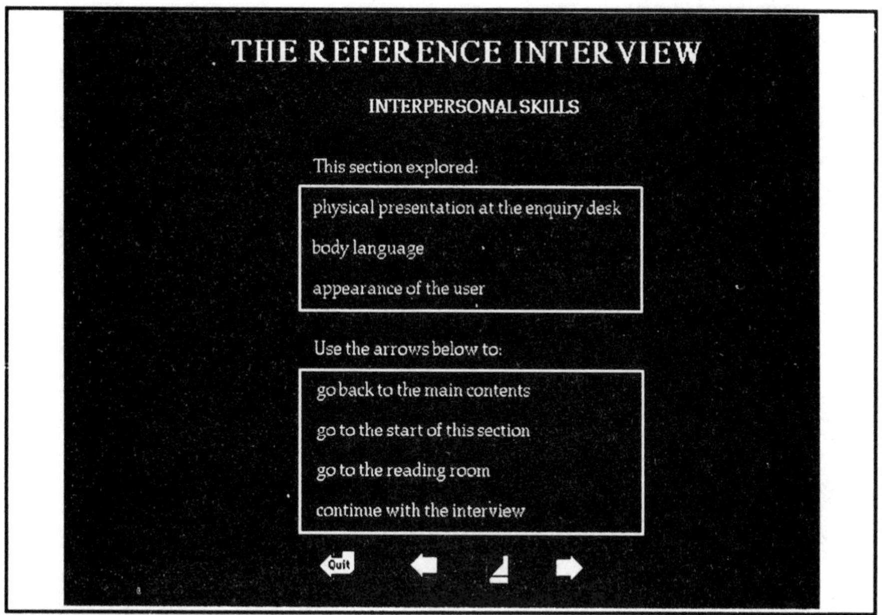

Figure 4. Screen dump showing reinforcement screen

module that concerns them most (Figure 1). At the same time, through the intention of building into the demonstrator a reference capability for both multimedia systems and the reference interview, hypermedia elements and the strategies for dealing with them will form a vital part of the whole. Finally, it is possible for trainees to return to the start of a module and repeat the exercises if necessary (Figure 2). Our discussions have likened the reference interview to a major road running the length of the demonstrator with minor roads providing a fuller view of the surrounding countryside. In some instances, possibly, offering alternative routes to the final destination.

Movement through the demonstrator is achieved by means of the navigation compass in the bottom left corner of the screen (Figure 3) coupled with reinforcement screens at the end of each module (e.g., Figure 4).

Representation

To be an effective training aid, the demonstrator must hold interest and present interactions that closely represent real-life situations. This is easier said than done where the main issues are interpersonal skills. Rushby [4] points out that "computer-based learning has traditionally concentrated on applications in mathematics, the hard sciences, aspects of business studies, and similar, fairly clear-cut topics with a high numerical content." In spite of this, "some components of the overall training could be delivered through technology if it were possible to humanise the interaction

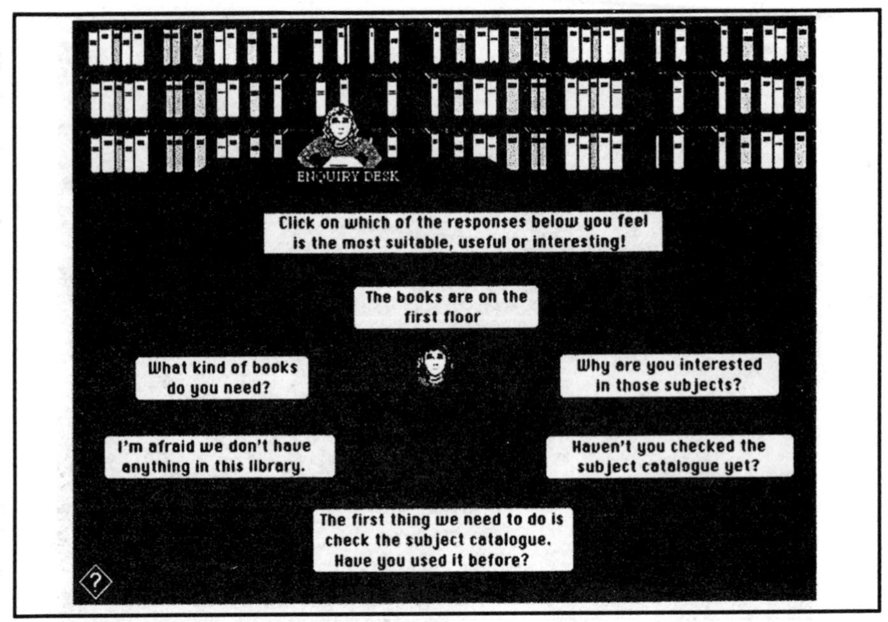

Figure 5. Screen dump showing possible responses to query

and enrich it with the nonverbal cues that are a crucial part of interpersonal communications."

At first glance, this humanising of the interaction would appear difficult, if not impossible, through animation, which has been considered one of the prime components of a multimedia presentation. Animation, when applied through the popular format of the cartoon, may be considered primarily to exaggerate reactions to situations; though no doubt exceptions exist, the format is not generally used as a vehicle for conveying subtleties of communication skills.

Nonetheless, it is not unknown for professional training films and videos to incorporate elements of exaggeration and simplification to transmit their messages more effectively. In the prototype demonstrator, animation is used to portray the librarian working at a reference point and being approached by the researcher, and this initial contact, together with the first responses of the librarian, are presented with humour that has so far been well received by demonstrator users. It is difficult for us to see how subsequent scenes could be handled adequately through animation and we intend to incorporate video into the demonstrator's final version. This work will start when we have completed our evaluation of the full-motion video boards now entering the market, so that the integrated training programme can be used from a single monitor.

While video may be considered a more suitable medium for presenting interpersonal skills, it brings its own problems. Not least of these is cost. No commercially available videotapes covering all aspects of the reference interview have been found but, in any case, integrating a tape made for a different purpose into a *multimedia* presentation would prove difficult if not impossible. Consequently, the video sequences must be created from scratch, using professional (or semi-professional) scriptwriters, actors, and camera operators to produce a professional product. None of this comes cheap, although we are hoping to use the services of University of Sheffield's Audio Visual and Television Centre.

For most enquiries the reference desk is only the starting point. Whether the enquirer is led to his answer immediately, or the librarian carries out the search at a later time, there is a need to move away from the desk into the stock. We are considering attempting to achieve this effect by using a "walkthrough" package, although it has two drawbacks. First, these are standalone applications that are difficult to integrate into a presentation created through another program such as Director. Second, the workload imposed on the computers make these appear more like "crawlthroughs" taken by a drunken hedgehog.

Two methods are used for representing text. Where a quotation directly relates to a graphic, a text box is superimposed on the graphic within Director. When the trainee wishes to consult relevant papers in detail, he or she moves to the "reading room," created in SuperCard because of Director's text-handling limitations. The trainee can consult papers within the reading room from abstract to full text displayed one page at a time. Notes can also be taken and transferred to disk for subsequent consultation.

Interactivity

Like many complex enquiries received at the reference desk, the one being posed within the demonstrator does not necessarily have a single correct bibliographical answer. Similarly, while there may be a single preferred response at the interpersonal level, a range of alternatives may be equally successful in eliciting details from the enquirer and providing a satisfactory conclusion to the reference interview. Responses depend on individual situations and just as *representing* real-life situations is not an easy task, similar difficulties exist in rationalising the virtually infinite number of ways in which librarians receive queries. In reducing these to a number manageable by a particular hardware/software configuration, the multimedia designer risks losing essential subtleties that may reduce the effectiveness of the training experience. This type of training aims at developing coping mechanisms that will enable trainees to respond to situations outside the limited number presented in the program. Having said that, it is essential that training covers the main types of response and that trainees are led to understand the broad categories of these and their effect.

In the prototype the primary focus of interactivity resides in the query negotiation module. After the researcher approaches the desk and asks a question, the trainee is invited to make a free-text response. This is followed by a screen containing predetermined answers tailored to cover systematically responses of the following types (Figure 5):

- why?
- open question
- closed question
- jargon
- directional
- inclusion
- listening

Once the trainee makes a choice, the system indicates the category of response coupled with an explanation/definition, together with the possibility of moving directly to associated reading in the reading room. The effect of the response is then continued to its logical conclusion. In addition to the existing response categories, we are investigating the possibilities for incorporating transactional analysis into the demonstrator although it likely will not appear in the prototype.

Modularity

Modularity has been imposed both by the current limitations of our software/hardware configuration and by its having been designed into the system to enable trainees to choose their own starting point or select those areas of special relevance. In a system with 8 megabytes of RAM, a 6-megabyte limit applies to the continuous segments that can be constructed within Director—what the application refers to as "movies." The result is that each training module, with its high colour graphics and animation content, consists of several movies called up sequentially from the hard disk—with, in most cases, significant time delays. We do not yet know if this limit will disappear with increases in RAM size.

Designed modularity is important for three reasons. First, it enables the prototype to be designed and constructed in manageable chunks that can subsequently be strung together. This design has the advantage that both debugging and changes can be achieved more easily. Second, if the trainee has too little time to work through the complete programme or has difficulty with a particular technique, he or she can approach the training one module at a time; i.e., the process encourages self-paced learning. Finally, a modular system more readily permits the bolting-on of additional modules at a later date.

CAUSE FOR CONCERN

At the time of preparing this chapter, the Project Team was in process of evaluating full-motion video boards for the Macintosh; or, rather, attempting an evaluation.

Reports and reviews, together with sightings at computer shows, began in late 1990 in the U.K., but by April 1991 it had still proved impossible to organise a comprehensive, comparative demonstration.

Several dealers expressed interest in demonstrating full-motion video, usually indicating a preference for one board or another, but they then disappointed, either by being unable to arrange the demonstration in the final event or by proving incapable of answering questions essential to our potential use (e.g., "Can specified sections of videotape be accessed from a VCR from within Director?"). One dealer organised a session with a distributor of a particular board who still could neither answer our questions nor provide practical proof that we could achieve our ends using his product. What he did show us was an array of effects that was truly staggering but of little practical use, such as the ability to graft two moving heads onto the same body. In our experience few library users with this apparent disability come in and ask questions at the reference desk.

We suspect that the problem is not just the dealers, although they are not blameless and are implicated sometimes by their own inaction. From a researcher's point of view the real problem lies with the computer industry, which has been pushing multimedia for more than a year without having in place a solid hardware and software foundation. It is as if, as alchemists, they possess the hermetic mysteries which they must not reveal to lesser mortals. Alternatively, with regard to multimedia, computer dealers are like the Rosicrucians described by Eco [5] who, to protect themselves, deny their faith when interrogated. Thus, computer dealers that claim to understand multimedia almost certainly do not, but, at the same time, it is impossible to uncover the true holders of the multimedia mysteries because they are afraid, or unable, to reveal themselves.

IN CONCLUSION

Staying with Eco, [6] in one small passage, he includes a dialogue about the Creation (modified as presented below) between two principal characters:

"Creation is a process of divine inhalation and exhalation. God takes a deep breath, holds it, and emits a long luminous hiss."

"A hiss of light?"

"God hissed and there was light."

"Multimedia."

In other words, it has taken since the Creation to bring us to a point where we are beginning to appreciate the problems associated with applying multimedia to personal computers. Let us hope that we do not have to wait as long before we have truly useful training products.

NOTES

1. J.C. Gale, "Multimedia: How We Get from Here to There." Presented at *Online Information 90: 14th International Online Information Meeting, London, 11 December 1990.* Organised by Learned Information.

2. P. Worlock, "Time for the M-word," *Macworld* (UK edition), March 1990, p. 104.

3. A. Simpson, "Lost in Hyperspace: How Can Designers Help?", *Intelligent Tutoring Media*, vol. 1, no. 1, 1990, pp. 31-40.

4. Nick Rushby, "From Trigger Video to Videodisc: A Case Study in Interpersonal Skills." In D. Laurillard, *Interactive Media: Working Methods and Practical Applications.* Ellis Horwood (1987), pp. 116-131.

5. Umberto Eco, *Foucault's Pendulum.* London: Pan (1990), p. 199.

6. ibid, p. 219.

Peter Stubley
Sub-Librarian
St. George's Library
University of Sheffield
Sheffield, England

Dr. Michael Leslie
Lecturer
Department of English Literature
University of Sheffield
Sheffield, England

Darren Umney
Research Associate
St. George's Library
University of Sheffield
Sheffield, England

CHAPTER
20

MANAGING HYPERTEXT-BASED INTERACTIVE VIDEO INSTRUCTION SYSTEMS

Bor-sheng Tsai
Christine M. Chamness
May Ying Chau

INTRODUCTION

The combined use of hypertext and interactive video to assist teachers as well as bibliographic instructors is gaining momentum. New models or systems have been continuously in development. As these systems gain greater prominence, it is urgent that their costs, effectiveness, technical problems, and related aspects be thoroughly explored. This chapter presents the experiences and observations of the authors cumulated from their teaching, research, technical operations, and public services. Examined are current commercial products, situations in library adoption, technical considerations, compatibility and interface problems, advantages, and related issues.

The authors' research centers on the application and promotion of computer literacy in regard to use of an interactive video system in academic environments. Part of this study (a summary of literature and on-site visits) also serves as a preliminary research for the set-up of interactive video equipment in the Purdy Library's Media Center at the Wayne State University.

OVERVIEW OF THE TECHNOLOGY

Interactive video learning systems integrate computer technology to enhance educational programs. Text, images, and sound are presented at the same time. Sound is changed from analog signals (a continuous range of amplitudes or frequencies) to digitized formats (discrete electrical pulses using a two-state or binary system). [1] These signals then became acceptable to the computer and are reconverted to analog form so that they are audible. Images are digitized and are presented on the screen with high quality. [2] Interactive video systems may also interface with computer programs so that they can communicate with each other. Networking with remote terminals is also possible.

Although the computer is the heart of the system because it can command other components to perform designated functions, it must be guided by a software program. For example, any user who wants to view a particular sequence of frames stored in the video disc can enter a request. The software then instructs the computer to command the video disc player to present the audio visual information in the specific sequence stored in the disc. The videodisc player will allocate the particular sequence of frames as instructed and display them on a screen. Seeing the presentation, the user responds and may make selections via the graphic guides. The software then instructs the computer to branch to an appropriate point in the instructional program after analyzing the user's response. [3] Consequently, the user is led to participate further in the learning program via a sequence of interactivity.

There are three levels of interactivity in interactive video systems. **Level I** enables the access of individual frames and makes possible the creation of a "slide show". [4] The only equipment needed is a basic video player. **Level II** enhances Level I by incorporating a computer element into the videodisc player. Simple branching in the program is possible. **Level III** provides the greatest interactivity. A separate microcomputer is connected to control the video player. [5] This level allows the interspersing of computer text and graphics with videodisc images as well as sophisticated branching and answering processing (e.g. the VERALEX IVD Programs at the Law Library, Wayne State University).

Interactive video instruction is advantageous because it requires the learner's frequent response, thus demanding a student's attention. This system allows individuals to learn at their own pace in an environment in which the user can choose among, or respond to, exercise questions and receive system feedback. Research shows that students may not learn more from the interactive video system but they can learn faster and retain the information longer. [6]

Instructors can also benefit because the computer records each student's responses and progress. These records can assist teachers in determining where the learners should next be directed.

A major concern in setting up an interactive video system is the cost. Equipment and devices are expensive to acquire and to maintain. In addition, an interactive videodisc system is designed for individualized user-machine interactive learning. Such an approach contradicts traditional classroom methodology of teacher-student interaction. Conflicts and resentment may become hindering factors. Therefore, a constant communication and promotion of the system may be required to promote acceptance. [7]

ACCEPTANCE FOR THE NEW TECHNOLOGY

The hardware for the interactive video system consists of a TV monitor; a personal computer with monitor, keyboard, and hard disk drive; and a videodisc player. As a special (such as law or medical) academic library that is part of the university library system, the funding was acquired through this special library's own proposal for new technology. The IVD learning system we have introduced and now in use is gaining university-wide publicity. The special software for the interactive video system used in the Law Library was originally distributed by VERALEX, Inc., a subsidiary of Lawyers Cooperative Publishing Company. These videos are mainly produced at the Harvard Law School. The one-year leasing rate to use the videos, currently 17 volumes in all, is $3900.

Lawyers are strongly print-oriented. They are moving into the electronic age with LEXIS/NEXIS and WESTLAW, legal databases, computers, fax machines, and CD-ROM products. Video presentations of courtroom action are training new lawyers in courtroom tactics by simulating real situations where split second timing is necessary and critical. These videos are now being used to train law school students, new associates in law firms, and attorneys in government practice. Continuing education for attorneys is mandatory and the interactive video is just one form of that education.

Most librarians, on the other hand, are eager to promote new technology either in the academic setting or in private law firms. Librarians, however, need instruction to aid not only the students or new associates in use of the system, but also to promote the system to the law school faculty, other interested academic disciplines, and law firm partners for continuing education purposes. Wherever librarians understand and appreciate the value of this new format for educational purposes, they are more apt to promote its use and to finance new or improved products.

SOME SOLUTIONS

Vendors, Products and Costs

Most of the vendors we have contacted are willing to provide current information in general and special technical information as well. For the convenience of this study, a list of courseware and vendor names are compiled from the *IBM Multimedia Courseware Catalog*. This catalog indicates that the IBM-compatible courseware market is divided into five major areas: Education, Health/Medical, Management/Professional, Data Processing, and Industrial Technology. Apple-compatible vendors that we have contacted have produced courseware mainly related to education.

The videodisc itself plays an important role in the interactive video system. Each videodisc contains 54,000 tracks on one side and are numbered. Individual frames or tracks can be accessed randomly or in sequence. There are two formats for putting information on the disc. The CLV (Constant Linear Velocity) format changes the speed of the disc during recording and playback. The purpose is to pack as much information as possible onto each track. It results in a linear playback time of one hour per side (such as movie presentation). This format limits the interactivity and options for fast random access or pausing at an individual frame. The CAV (Constant Angular Velocity) format, on the other hand, stores only one frame per track. It not only reduces the playback time (to about 30 minutes) but also allows the user to interact with the system through random access to any of the 54,000 frames on each side of the disc. The CAV disc contains still images such as slides or printed materials, but motion segments and live action in color or black and white are also available.

The cost for equipment set-up varies. Normally, an interactive video learning system can be assembled from older model computers. Based on IBM's *Multimedia Configuration Handout Version 27* (July 6, 1990), an IBM 8530-001 PS/2 Model 30 (640K bytes) microcomputer can be adapted to an IBM InfoWindow system configuration. Hardware required for adaptation are a 1503 GPIB Adaptor Card, a 5240 InfoWindow EGA Jumper Card, and a 5040 GPIB cable. The price for these devices is $1248. The Macintosh SE computer requires no additions except compatible cables for connecting the videodisc player and television set. Either computer (IBM or Apple), however, must have enough hard disk space for proper system operation. In some cases, expansion of hard disk space may be necessary.

Both Pioneer and Sony produce laserdisc players, and these products are compatible with both IBM and Apple computers. The price range of the laserdisc player varies from $900 to $4300. Any television set can be incorporated into the system as long as it can be connected to a videodisc player. The prices of courseware vary widely. License fees for the courseware is also a consideration. Buyers should work out a reasonable deal with the sales representatives and pay attention to discount packages.

Site Visits

During the following on-site visits, we reviewed several products:

Law School Library, Wayne State University. VERALEX Interactive Video Disc (presented by Veracorp, a Harvard Law School Interactive Video Project) is employed to provide a simulated courtroom situation. The entire system is controlled by the VERALEX Interactive Video Software Version 3.0 (contained on a floppy disk). This program guides the operation and enables the learner to interact during the presentation via a hypertext system. It also allows users to access various hidden texts to get additional information whenever needed. The key words in the text can be highlighted. A term chosen can be related to another term. For example, the learner can highlight a specific *Federal Rules of Evidence* on the screen. Hidden texts related to the key word (in this case, the text of the rule) appear and disappear simply by the user moving the cursor right and left. Pressing the enter key causes the program to resume its normal sequence.

During the presentation of the court drama, the system presents facts, documents (doctor's recommendation), and photographs to the learner. The prosecutor proceeds to question the witness. Whenever the student disagrees with the counselor's line of questionning, he or she can touch any key to stop the action. The judge on the screen will respond "overruled" or "sustained" to the user's objection. If overruled, the student can choose to see the hidden text and find out the reason. The software provides track control so that the learner can randomly access any segment of the presentation without going through all the sequential frames.

VERALEX provides a Level III interactivity between a user and the program. It is excellent courseware, needing only perhaps a more complete debriefing system at the program's end to measure the student's understanding of the whole case. Such a metric may be helpful for teachers to construct their instructional materials.

Medical Library, Wayne State University. The hardware system includes a Zenith computer, a video screen monitor, a Pioneer laserdisc player model LD V-6000, and connecting cables. The interactive video courseware used is the "Basic Medical Pathology Series," a product of National Library of Medicine Computer Assisted Curriculum Delivery System. It offers seven different topics and provides lecture-like presentations on each topic for a duration of about 30 minutes. Major concepts are explained and special terms are defined.

The topic we examined in this study is the "Cellular Alternation/Adaptation." The slides, which show alternation and adaptation of cellular morphological structures, are included as an essential part of the lecture. Function keys allow users to pause and to forward and reverse the frame sequence at any time during the presentation. Pretest questions are available in a multiple-choice format. Questions include definitions, concept verification, and cellular structures identification. The users can pass on any question they do not want to answer. True or false questions are also available. The grading system penalizes guesses. No points are awarded after the third attempt to answer. The user can end the program at any point. This program is useful for students who want to study at their own pace. Any unclear concepts can be repeated and slides can be viewed as often as needed. The interactivity of this program, however, is low—during the presentation, users cannot interact with the program through any form of input.

College of Education, Wayne State University. The hardware components used for the IVD program adopted by the College of Education include a Macintosh SE Computer, a Denon DRD-253 CD-ROM drive, an Edudisc Audio mixer, a Pioneer LD-V4200 laserdisc player, and a Panasonic TV monitor. Software includes Apple's HyperCard program disk and program courseware. The program product is Optical Data Corporation's "ABC News Interactive." Graphic navigators are used in the HyperCard system.

Icons are categorized into topics, tools, and navigation. Icons for topics give users a choice for different ABC News reports, such as Dr. Martin Luther King Jr.'s speeches. Icons for tools allow users to branch to control panels where "cut and paste," language selection, and frame sequencing are made possible. For example, users can look up the brochure and choose a particular event, or they can access the control panels. The user can simply type in the frame sequence number, and video information on the particular frame appears on the TV monitor. Navigation icons simply let users move in different directions (forward or backward) through the presentation.

This program has high interactive potential because frame segments can be selected and saved. Students can create video term papers from courseware by means of the options (e.g., frame selection) the program provides. Such projects were discussed in the

T.H.E. Journal [8, 9]. Another interesting feature is the program's bilingual translation capability. For example, a user can choose either English or Spanish as the language for the narration. This program is useful not only for explaining historical events but it may assist in learning foreign languages as well.

Detroit Public Library. The Detroit Public Library has set up an interactive video program—*Passport to Your Future*—for career guidance. Students can explore 425 occupations and access information on 3100 colleges and universities. This program is produced by the Library of Michigan.

The system operation method is mainly by touch screen. Users can interact with the system by touching the options provided on a menu screen. When one choice is "touched," a submenu may appear. Interactivity is in a linear format. A "slide show" with narrations is provided but users cannot disrupt the presentation at will. They must follow through the entire section—the program's major disadvantage.

This program provides low-level interactivity. It is user friendly for someone who is not highly computer literate. At least this program will not intimidate the general public.

Local Computer Stores. Several local computer representatives and vendors we visited were willing to make available their multimedia laboratories and computer clubs to aid the users or potential customers. Classes may be held there to expand the users' knowledge regarding computer literacy or multimedia aspects. These clubs help members keep up with the trends of image processing and to learn about new courseware products. Vendors such as Radio Shack, Apple, and IBM are very likely to house some laboratories for the users' convenience.

SELLING A NEW TECHNOLOGY

Experiences in using the IVD instruction system at the Law Library are presented as follows.

Budgeting

Acquiring a specialized subject interactive video system, such as VERALEX, was a collective development decision. The Law Library, for example, had been using the CALI (Computer-Assisted Legal Instruction) disks with an IBM-compatible computer for outside classroom instruction in "Evidence" class (although the CALI disks address other subjects as well as evidence). Interactive Video was judged to be a superior product for the instruction; therefore we have discontinued the purchase of the CALI disks. The Interactive Video system is superior in teaching legal concepts because of the electronic hypertext available with the *Federal Rules of Evidence* and full explanations of the correct answers. CALI requires students to have available a paper copy of the *Federal Rules of Evidence* while answering questions. Also, the scoring system on the Interactive Video system can pinpoint a student's weakness in understanding hearsay, opinion, or evidence by identifying which questions were answered incorrectly.

We believe that the Interactive Video system has surpassed the CALI system because students have advanced beyond the technology of CALI. The time to build the connection between the two (old CALI and new VERALEX Interactive Video) instruction systems is now. Our duty as an information professional is to escort the students quickly through this technical transition period.

Promoting

How can faculty, students, and practicing attorneys be convinced to use the system when the "printed word" has been the major force in their professional lives? They must comprehend the value of the system as a learning resource/tool that is worth the time spent. To promote that understanding, we have implemented a four-step approach.

First, we prepared the "Research Guide for the Interactive Video System" and placed it at the Reference Desk. This guide outlines the system's value, the hardware used, and the titles and subject matter of each video currently available.

Next, we sent a copy of the Research Guide to all Law School faculty members with a letter that recommends this system as an additional tool for their students to use. We also plan to contact faculty members in other departments on campus that would benefit from the system as well, e.g., Criminal Justice, Social Work, and Business Administration.

To make the system highly visible to students and faculty, we first placed it near the Reference Desk, but later moved it to the new Law Library Computer Laboratory. It is now in that Laboratory on a rolling table that can be wheeled into a group discussion room for students' use. A security cabinet has been equipped to house the hardware, which makes it easier to move the system to other rooms or buildings on campus. The reason for moving the system is that it distracts other students in the Laboratory. Consequently, a cabinet and headphones were purchased.

The fourth step—personal contact with faculty members and students—proved the most effective. This semester the system is being used by first year law students in the "Evidence" class and is recommended for the "Student Trial Advocacy Program." Demonstrations are being organized for other librarians on campus and for the faculty of the School of Liberal Arts as well.

A survey was prepared to gather an immediate response to the system by asking target questions. The survey is geared to find out three things: 1) the difficulty or ease in operating the system, 2) the difficulty or ease in following the logic of the legal scenario, and, 3) the value in reinforcing the legal concepts of evidence, hearsay, and opinion. The comments from the students have been quite positive and encouraging.

Managing

The maintenance of the interactive video system has evolved over time.The Library has replaced the floppy disk drive with a hard disk drive, purchased a set of headphones and a security cabinet, and paid the $3900 annual cost for the video disks and software disks to run the programs. Maintaining and updating the system as well as increasing its visibility to provide full availability for users need constant justification. Continuing promotion together with the survey of users and user statistics are vital in justifying system costs.

Cost Effectiveness

The cost effectiveness of IVD as a complementary instructing and learning tool is now under study. A full report based on statistical analysis of the data collected from the survey is pending. Thus far, the users' responses have been positive and encouraging. The system has performed well and the hardware interface has been effective.

BEHAVIORAL ANALYSIS OF TECHNICAL LIAISON

We have studied the three levels of the interactive video instruction systems, namely, the slide show level, branching level, and text-graphics interspersing and question-answering level. For coordinating the level of multicoaching systems (which may cover programs, programming languages, software packages, and audio-visual-textual objects), a clearer definition is desirable. The following model was designed to meet that goal. Starting from linear sequencing through dynamic interacting, to "using the computer's storage capabilities, it is possible to create permanent audio/visual-based curricula yourself," [10] particularly when a window system is not compatible with the need to play programs developed by several different sources. [11]

Model of Instruction Bonding

To improve interactivities among audio-visual-textual effects and software programs, a model of bonding is developed. [12]

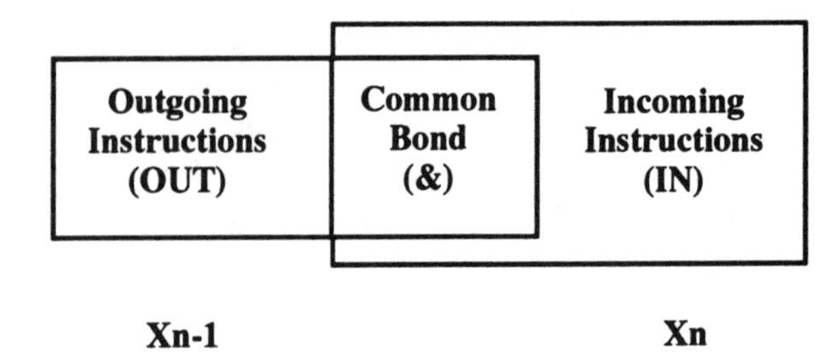

A set of mathematical formulas are represented as follows:

U = OUT + & + IN = Xn-1 + Xn - &
dX = IN - OUT = Xn - Xn-1
OUT = (U-&-dX)/2
IN = (U-&+dX)/2
& = U+dX-2*IN = U-dX-2*OUT

Where, U denotes the number of the union of two encountered party instructions;
Xn-1 and Xn denote the two consecutive sets of instructions within a special subject field;
OUT denotes the number of the old (forgotten/outdated) instructions;
IN denotes the number of the new (fresh/updated) instructions;
& denotes the number of the intersection or the conservation (retaining) of instructions;
and dX denotes the number of change of instructions.

"&" is the key "bonding" factor we want to emphasize. It provides the glue that can bond multimedia together. It is "fuzzy" because it constantly shifts and changes. During an instructional system's internal processing, "&" is concerned about the communication language(s) that this system applies in order to interconnect with other programs available within the same system. For example, the "bonding" commands used in popular Basic language may include LOAD, RUN, SAVE, MERGE, CHAIN, CHAIN-MERGE, SHELL, GOSUB, IF-THEN-ELSE, LOCATE, DRAW, MOVE, LINE, RESTORE, etc.

The significance of this bonding model is that it allows us to:

- Figure out the total population of the systems and software packages and languages we are currently and continuously dealing with (U = OUT + & + IN = Xn-1 + Xn - &)
- Locate the common interests in the instruction processes (& = U+dX-2*IN = U-dX-2*OUT)
- Calculate the differences that exist in the interactivities (dX = IN - OUT = Xn - Xn-1)
- Control the discrepancies resulting from the interconnection and interaction among multimedia (U-&-dX or U-&+dX)
- Be alert to the half-life of the strengths and weaknesses of the programs and instructions [OUT = (U-&-dX)/2, and IN = (U-&+dX)/2]

- Observe the periodical changes and, consequently, forecast new direction of the technologies (dX/dt).

Interactive SHELLing

A system managerial menu is traditionally used to assist internal interactivities. As an external structure of an interactive program is defined as a structure that is seen by the user "in the form of a network of pages," an internal structure is defined as a structure that is seen by the programmer "in the form of a frame program consisting of nested procedures." [13]

The user or the intermediator's understanding of DOS could substantially enhance this managerial assistance. Using the SHELLing capacity dwelling in many software programs could reduce the traffic jams among multiprograms' interconnectivities and interactivities. If the mainstream operating program consistently uses the same computer programming language, e.g., Basic, for internal program-program connections, the interfacing commands such as CHAIN, MERGE, and CHAIN-MERGE could be utilized. If the mainstream operating program needs to connect with sidekick software packages written in different programming languages during the entire instruction process, a hint screen in Basic to assist users in "SHELL-out" and "EXIT-in" is definitely useful. It allows Basic language programs to interface with diversified external media resources while the users are totally navigated by an instructional mainstream.

Hyper-Object Programming and Processing

A hyper-object oriented program can be developed using programming languages, authoring languages, or authoring systems. Basic, Pilot, and HyperTie are good examples. As Mr. Craig N. Locatis of National Library of Medicine points out:

> Although authoring languages are easier to use, they still require coding as well as knowledge of commands, syntax, and programming conventions. Authoring systems, on the other hand, are essentially "programmerless." They guide users and generate underlying programming code. [14]

Whenever an "object" approach is desirable, one may need to recognize that music or sound effects, graphics or visual effects, and characters or texts can actually be represented from the same set of programming source codes:

> Each frame on a videodisc has a unique address (number) and can be individually displayed as a still frame. This is true even of still frame make-up of a dynamic sequence. Each frame can contain text, photographic, audio, or digital information (i.e. programs)... However, the design of a videodisc program is more complex than ordinary instructional software because of the many options possible (e.g. multiple audio channels, motion or still frames, slow/fast motion, graphic overlays, etc.). [15]

Using Basic as an example, audio, video, and text elements, although different in output formats, could be coded, preformed and stored in three parallel special object libraries with unique memory addresses for later recalls. Subroutine programming and conditional branching may result in the preparation of a set of IF-THEN rules that allow users to access the branch instruction displaying systems more easily.

In using HyperTie software, the authology is similarly demonstrated in two modules: EDIT and BROWSE. EDIT "is used to create, edit, or test applications or application segment," and BROWSE is "a run-only package, which can present applications, but it cannot edit them." [16]

Instruction NarrowCasting

A special subject-oriented library will always attract local researchers to use its instruction system. The overall satisfaction of users relies on the *locality* of the "NarrowCasting of Subject Information." The focal points must then be on users' special needs. The analyses of their need would consider the forming of the subject schema as well as the quantity of needs and frequency of usage. "Instruction NarrowCasting" programs are developed by adopting the ready programmed formats and structures of the *Automatic Instruction Model* designed by Bor-sheng Tsai. This model and related works are soon to be fully reported.

Effective Technical Coordination

An effective technical coordination is useful in determining all possible reference angles that might be needed in supporting measurement and judgement. To satisfy this need, the subject information field must be explored, charted, and defined. The reference angles are then possibly determined (See Appendix A: Strategic Mapping):

> With new means of linking and mapping knowledge we can give our learners a sextant and the charts and notices to mariners.... It's now possible to provide the knowledge to sailors with better navigation aids. . . . by providing shell programs with built-in knowledge maps as frames of reference. [17]

To coordinate the communication traffic of multimedia, the first task is to control the direction of the *instruction photon movement.* To understand this concept and technique, one must conduct an orientation for analyzing multimedia. Recognizing the master control software program in the parallel system software is the first priority task. This master control software could be linked to the mainstreamed automatic instruction programs prepared or written by the instructional coordinators. The "Information Coordination System 4891A/C" was designed by Bor-sheng Tsai for this purpose. The videodisc, in this case, is "being treated as if it were an additional disk drive." [18] (See Appendix B: Information Coordination System)

The importance of "information coordination" was echoed by Austin Speed:

> . . . Frame Grabber is capable of storing a selected frame of video in its own memory configuration and converting it to an IFF (Interchange File Format) file to be used as a digitized image. This enhances the possibilities of combining live video images and computer generated elements as their interaction can be more closely coordinated. Frame grabbing also paves the way for image enhancement by using the computer's paint or color change feature to alter the image. [19]

Artificial Image Space Exploration

In a recent study, eight components are found indispensable in the recognition and orientation of a *Subject Knowledge Field*: scale, locus, bondage, direction, frequency, relative distance, boundary, and threshold. [20] These eight components are used not only for the exploration of a subject knowledge field but also for the construction of the MARM (Machine Readable Mapping) format, which can be used in defining artificial images.

Scale—a quantity control unit that defines the sizes of the images to be represented. The benefits from the scaling, in terms of changing the sizes of characters and pixels, are enormous.

Locus—the location of a focal point. For example, custom designed picture elements (pixels) representing alphabets can be coded in IBM Basica Logo. These alphabets are then stored in the assigned lower hierarchy of number lines for later routine recalling and for regrouping with other alphabets to form a word string. This word string is again stored in a higher hierarchy of number lines for other later routine recalls. These routine recalls include cumulative reusing and reclustering with other parallel strings. This type of snowball accumulation of instructional experiences from assigned number lines enables the microinstruction (and later microknowledge) field to expand progressively. A strategic map may be developed and regularly modified.

Bondage—the bonding of a word or word string. Any "authoring activity" that includes the processing of texts, images, sound effects, etc., is treated as an object and stored at the assigned accession line number, where a series of GOSUB subroutines recall the wanted pixels or objects to form the word or the subject wanted in a desired scale. A two dimensional statement, "LINE(X1,Y1)-(X2,Y2)," is used to bond the two named strings as *coordinated poles* and represent them on the monitor screen or on the voice synthesizer. The coordinates of Xs and Ys, or the locations of rows and columns can be determined by referring to the window framed scale for locations and coordinates.

Direction—the arrow pointer that indicates the "SENDER/RECEIVER" status. A DRAW statement with a formula, e.g., DRAW "M(X-3),(Y+3)", can be adjusted flexibly to show the arrow direction.

Frequency—the number of times an object (word or word string, sound, picture, or formula, etc.) occurs during the period of observation or composition.

Relative Distance—the measure of the numbers of links (arrows or middle agents) needed to complete a recalling or communication process. Since a coordinated pole ties together two named strings with a linear bond, it is considered one unit in the distance measure.

Boundary—the limit for subject knowledge resources, focused populations, sizes of communication symbols such as ALPHANUMERICS, and monitor screen windows in framed scale for row-column locations and X-Y coordinates.

Threshold—the gatekeeper for safeguarding desirable relations that usually are based on frequency of occurrence during intellectual contacts.

Based on the manipulation of these components, a strategic mapping format is developed for organizing instructional collaborations within a special subject instruction communications network. These instructional collaborations can serve as the skeleton (or generator pool) for the interconnectivity control inside this network. The *coordination* is always the main concern in human-machine cooperation. The locality, described in a previous section (see: Instruction NarrowCasting), depends heavily upon the above eight components.

In terms of technical development and control, these eight components are the logical variables to be reviewed constantly. After all, the interconnectivity preludes the interactivity. The coordination program serves as an *intelligent circuitry* to transfer and orient subject rules to users. It is not difficult to develop intelligent circuitry using the same programming language or within the same software package. Nonetheless, it is difficult to coordinate different software written by different programming languages that dwell in different kinds of disks at different locations. The instruction manager of multimedia systems who knows coding, DOS operation, and the characteristics of the involved instructional devices will be able to write or organize an intelligent CAI program for coordinating multimedia-related instruction representation processes.

RECOMMENDATIONS

The manager of the hypertext-based IVD instruction system may need to look at the following areas.

Software and Hardware Selection—No doubt, we must carefully choose software. Hardware devices such as hard disk, VGA monitor, scanner, hand-held camcorder with cassette storage, CD-ROM, video recorder and player, and laser printer, must be carefully investigated and compared before selections are made.

Interdisciplinarity—Interdisciplinary coordination is necessary in developing quality interactive videodisc courseware. Five professionals are involved: subject matter expert, instructional designer, video producer, software designer, and system engineer. Thus, the development of this type of information management system is costly and time-consuming. [21]

Epistemological Mastery—The students engaged in inquiry-oriented learning activities must:

> . . . learn to pursue knowledge embedded in the instructional system by developing a personal path of inquiry, . . . in which the student takes responsibility for learning how to learn. . . . We must determine if this method of instruction can promote automaticity, the building of associations, the generation of meaning, and the transfer of skills from one environment to another. [22]

User-Oriented Programming—Algorithms and programs must be "directed primarily at people and only secondarily at computers. ... When you finally do go on the machine, code in the highest programming language available to you." [23]

CONCLUDING REMARKS

Any intelligent interface must have three critical features. First, it knows the user's goal and can help the user to achieve it. Second, it can forecast the behavior and preferences of the user. And, third, it can access other components of the computer system when needed. [24] And an intelligent tutoring system should be able to provide a genetic graph. The extended genetic graph should be able to group "related knowledge into islands," to represent "the justifications of rules" and "planning knowledge," and it should be "a network of islands." [25]

The major drawback in managing an interactive video instruction system is the cost. Computers, videodisc players, monitors, input devices, and interface facilities are expensive, as are the production of the programs and system upgrades and maintenance. The system is designed for individualized user-machine interactive learning, which might contradict the traditional classroom approach of teacher-student interaction. Resentment and resistance are always factors.

Nevertheless, a faculty or instruction programmer may be attracted by the interactive video system simply because a custom designed instruction program is "integrated with the teacher's normal teaching techniques." The new instruction program "has complemented and improved traditional methodologies without threatening extant pedagogy." Therefore, "the integrity of their course material is preserved." [26] How to make this powerful tool more feasible for both instruction programmers and users is a continuous challenge.

NOTES

1. Richard W. Boss, *The Library Manager's Guide to Automation*. 3rd edition. (Boston, MA: G. K. Hall & Co., 1990), 54.

2. *Multimedia: Imagine the Possibility—Light, Camera, and Action*. Information package developed by IBM, 1990.

3. Robert Heinich, *Instructional Media and the New Technologies of Instruction*. 2nd edition. (NY: John Wiley & Sons, 1985), 182-187.

4. John Phillipo, "An Educators' Guide to Interactive Videodisc Programs," *Electronic Learning* (September, 1988), 70-75.

5. Robert Price, "Producing Interactive Videodisc Programs on a Shoestring Budget," *Ohio Spectrum*, 41 (Spring 1989), 17-20.

6. Zan Tamar Bailey, "CAI and Interactive Video Enhance Students' Scores on the College Level Academic Skills Test," *T.H.E. Journal*, (September 1990), 82-85.

7. S. Reisman, "Interactive Videodisc at California State University, Fullerton," *ERIC* ED 310 756.

8. CEL Educational Resources, "Optical Disc Technology: Video Term Papers Take the Place of Traditional Written Reports," *T.H.E. Journal*, (April 1988), 68-69.

9. Thomas Wilson, "The Video Term Paper," *Horizons* (March/April 1989), 93-94.

10. "Creating Your Own Courseware," *Interactive LaserDisc* (Spring 1990, Supplement to T.H.E. Journal), 13.

11. Scott A. Stewart, editor, *Interactive Video Primer: Medical Education* (VA: Stewart Publishing, Inc., 1990), 1-9.

12. Bor-sheng Tsai, *The Behavioral and Structural Analysis of a Special Subject Literature*. Ph.D. Dissertation (Cleveland, OH: Case Western Reserve University, 1987), Stage II: Spin/Bond.

13. J. Nievergelt, *Interactive Computer Programs for Education: Philosophy, Techniques, and Examples* (CA: Addison-Wesley Publishing Company, 1986), 71.

14. Craig Locatis, *Videodisc Repurposing* (Bethesda, MD: U.S Dept. of Health and Human Services, 1989), 17.

15. Greg Kearsley, *Authoring: A Guide to the Design of Instructional Software* (CA: Addison-Wesley Publishing Company, Inc., 1986), 37-38.

16. Arch C. Luther, *Digital Video in the PC Environment*. Second edition. (NY: McGraw-Hill Book Company, 1991), 281.

17. Richard N. Tucker, "Navigation: The Art of Knowing (Where You Were)," *The Interactive Learning Revolution: Multimedia in Education and Training* (NY: Nichols Publishing, 1990), 136.

18. Charles R. Miller, *Essential Guide to Interactive Videodisc Hardware and Applications* (CT: Meckler Publishing Corp., 1987), 22.

19. Austin H. Speed, *Desktop Video: A Guide to Personal and Small Business Video Production* (NY: Harcourt Brace Jovanovich, Inc., 1988), 238.

20. Bor-sheng Tsai, "Mapping Metrics for Subject-Object Coordinated Field Recognition and Representation," Paper presented to The Third International Conference on Informetrics, Bangalore, India, August 9-12, 1991.

21. Edward C. Beardslee, *Interactive Videodisc and the Teaching-Learning Process* (Bloomington, IN: The Phi Delta Kappa Educational Foundation, 1989), 18.

22. Carla Seal-Wanner, "Interactive Video Systems: Their Promise and Educational Potential," *Computing and Education: The Second Frontier*, edited by Robert O. McClintock (NY: Teachers College, Columbia University, 1988), 29-30.

23. J. Nievergelt, *Interactive Computer Programs for Education: Philosophy, Techniques, and Examples* (CA: Addison-Wesley Publishing Company, 1986), 142.

24. Eleanor L. Criswell, *The Design of Computer-Based Instruction*. (NY: Macmillan Publishing Company, 1989), 108.

25. Ira P. Goldstein, "The Genetic Graph: A Representation for the Evolution of Procedural Knowledge," *Intelligent Tutoring System*, edited by D. Sleeman and J. S. Brown (NY: Academic Press, 1982), 59.

26. Mark C. Fissel, "The Video Information System: Is It the 'Best Educational Tool Around?'" *T.H.E. Journal*, 18:5 (December, 1990) 59-61.

Appendix A: Strategic Mapping

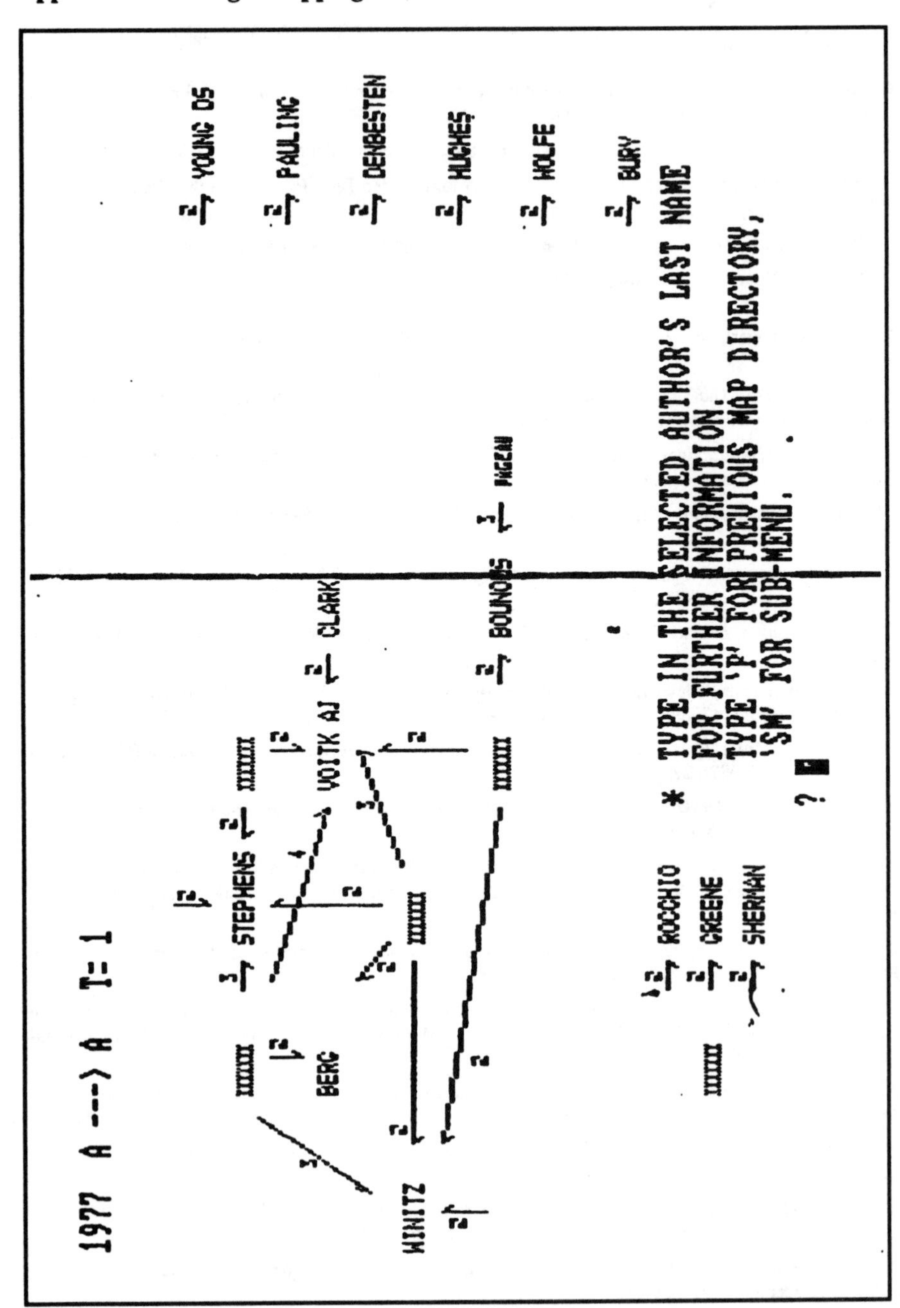

Appendix B: Information Coordination System

INFORMATION COORDINATION SYSTEM 4891A/B

Designed by Bor-sheng Tsai
Library Science Program
Wayne State University
315 Kresge, Detroit, MI 48202
(313) 577-6202

SHELL-OUT? (Type the NUMBER of your choice and ENTER)

0. DOS (Path-Finder$)
1. WSU-NET
2. LOTUS 1-2-3$
3. dBASE$
4. DisplayWrite$
5. WordPerfect
6. PrintMaster$
7. HyperTie$
8. Strategic Mapping
9. Inf-B/N/F-Casting
10. Anti-Virus
11. Multi-Lingu/Cultur
12. IVD-Gilbert File$
13. IVD-Seizure Case$
14. IVG-Prince Game$
15. VoiceMaster$
20. WINDOWS

NOTE: * To 'Exit-In,' you just type EXIT or the proper PASSWORDS at the C>.
** If you don't need to 'Shell-Out,' then press ENTER or F5.

Bor-Sheng Tsai
Assistant Professor, Library Science Program
Christine M. Chamness
May Ying Chau

Wayne State University
315 Kresge Library
Detroit, MI 48202

End Piece

CHAPTER

21

"BEING THERE," OR MODELS FOR VIRTUAL REALITY

Michael B. Spring

INTRODUCTION

The final chapter, which addresses models for virtual reality, originates in three areas of study—standards, interfaces, and modeling.

Standards

Several organizations are attempting to develop a reference model human/computer interaction that will assist in the development of standards. Spring, Jamison, Fithen, and Thomas [1] working with the Strategic Planning Committee of ANSI X3 have proposed the broad outlines of such a model. The effort, though still in its formative stages, is being shared with various constituents for comments. Virtual reality represents one radical direction for research on human computer interaction and, as such, it provides a test of the comprehensiveness of a reference model.

Interfaces

One focus of the interface projects at the University of Pittsburgh is the provision of a holistic experience for users. The goal is to make the interface and interaction as natural as possible: to create a virtual copy of the process or entity being modeled. In addition, the effort attempts to provide a level of intelligence behind the interface to assist users. This is not a new concept—others talk about the development of agents to operate on behalf of users. The agents of interest at Pitt are ones that collect data about how an interface is used and dynamically tailor the interface to better meet the needs of users.

Modeling

The third reason for interest in virtual realities is that no strong models yet exist. The need for models and the difficulty of model development is particularly fascinating for this chapter's author. Thus, we focus this final chapter mainly upon the development of models in the creation of virtual realities.

We address the problem of model development in five stages. First, historical references to virtual reality and examples from literature and cinema are reviewed to provide a conceptual background, or gestalt, for thinking about models. Second, the various terms used and some appropriate definitions are outlined. Third, a preliminary model is proposed in the form of the dimension of virtual reality systems providing a methodology for classifying the various projects discussed in the literature. Fourth, the candidates for base models for virtual reality are set out. Finally, the implications of two models are discussed—virtual reality as interface or interaction and virtual reality as space or environment.

SOME ANTECEDENTS OF VIRTUAL REALITIES

The creation of virtual realities is one more step in a tradition long engaged in by computer and information scientists—creating formal models of a process or entity to allow them to be translated into a form that can be programmed to operate on a computer. The goal is to formalize the laws by which a given reality operates—its ontology, as well as the laws by which people know about them—the epistemology. Anyone working in this new area would do well to keep in mind something Marvin Minsky said about AI:

> *Anything that you hear about computers and AI should be ignored, because we are in the Dark Ages. We're in the thousand years between no technology and all technology. You can read what your contemporaries think, but you should remember they are all ignorant savages.* [2]

A statement equally applicable to those who undertake the task of understanding and designing reality!

Just as we may view an encyclopedia as a nonelectronic predecessor to hypertext, so we may look to literary and noncomputer technological antecedents of virtual reality. This section begins with the oft cited direct references and then looks to conceptual antecedents in various media.

Historical References

Some observers suggest that virtual reality is first depicted in Vernor Vinges's *True Names and Other Dangers* in 1987. Others point to William Gibson's 1984 *Neuromancer* where the term "cyberspace" first appears. It is interesting to reflect on the word play in Gibson's choice of title—Neuromancer versus Necromancer—a one letter change. Recollect that a necromancer is one who conjures up the spirits of the dead for the purposes of magically revealing the future or influencing the course of events.

In these references to the science fiction literature, the user is connected to some alternate reality via some kind of brain wave sensors and stimulators. We have accepted the fact that at least for the foreseeable future the virtual reality interface will occur through the existing sensory channels.

Literary Antecedents

If we focus less on the technology and more on the process of being transported to some alternate reality, there are numerous literary examples of virtual reality. Frank Baum's *Wizard of Oz*, and Lewis Carroll's *Alice in Wonderland* surely depict worlds in which ontology and epistemology as we know them have been modified. The process of transferring between realities was depicted most dramatically in Stephen Donaldson's trilogy *The Chronicles of Thomas Covenant, the Unbeliever*. It would not be surprising if 1000 years hence historians trace a direct link between the interest of our generation in fantasy literature such as Tolkien's *The Lord of the Rings* and the subsequent efforts to create "virtual realities" in a computer mediated form.

In cinematic terms, *Being There* may be one of our first social commentaries on this new form of interaction. Peter Sellers provided a most entertaining performance as a person caught up simultaneously in two different realities—one consisting of his proximal, physical world and the other being his experience in the world as viewed by television.

The movie *TRON* provides an example of virtual realities in it's pure form as imagined by the early science fiction writers. *TRON* provides an alternative mechanism for engagement—incorporation versus sensors and stimulators—but is otherwise very pure if somewhat allegorical. There are several other movies in which experiences are created and stored on some electronic medium and replayed for the participant—*Brainstorm*, *Futureworld*, and *Total Recall* provide but three examples.

Technological Antecedents

Two technologies—television and computers—provide early examples of user-perceived virtual realities. Both have been providing a kind of transfer to another world for almost as long as they have existed.

The Computer Generically As A Virtual Reality. In some ways, computers have always engendered virtual realities for their users. It has been the norm, rather than the exception for years. Consider Soshanna Zuboff's [3] studies of automation. Her accounts of users suggest that even primitive applications of computer technology have the effect of creating alternate, if not virtual, realities for users.

> *In learning to work with this new equipment, it takes a while to believe that when you push a button, something is actually taking place somewhere else. You don't get the feeling that things are connected. How can pushing a button in here make something happen somewhere else.*

What strikes me the most strange, hardest to get used to, is the idea of touching a button and making a motor run. It's the remoteness. I can start it from up here, and that is hard to conceive. I can be up in the control room and touch the keyboard, and something very far away in the process will be affected. It takes a while to gain the confidence that it will be OK, that what you do through the terminal will actually have the right effects. (p. 82.)

TV as a Virtual Reality. We have all had the experience at one time or another of watching something on TV and getting the feeling of actually being there. I know that when my 4-year-old son disconnects from this world and connects to Bugs Bunny's world, the only way I can break the connection at times is to turn off the TV. It is interesting to watch the disorientation and reorientation cycle he goes through.

I know I had the feeling of participating in another plane during the Tiennamen Square demonstrations. I noted with interest as I prepared this piece that many colleagues who had watched the Tiennamen Square incident with great interest did not know how to spell the Tiennamen–a situation not dissimilar from what occurs in our neighborhoods: we may know a neighbor's name or a street name, but not how to spell it.

More recently, many of us led two lives during the Gulf crisis. There was a clear distinction between faculty with cable and faculty without. Those with were bleary eyed, those without were somewhat less affected, but no less desirous of an information fix. I would further suggest, based on anecdotal evidence, that this was a very difficult term for faculty and students—primarily because many of us were living in two realities.

Video Games as Virtual Reality. Video games represent a marriage of computers and graphics display screens that endeavor to provide a TV-like image. They also allow us to become an active force in a narrowly constrained alternative reality on a screen. In this case, we have not only incoming stimulation but the ability to influence the video environment via some kind of control. There is much to learn from the research here—and those engaged would do well to look to the pioneering work done by Sherry Turkle at MIT. Suffice it to say that what we call video games are a crude form of virtual reality. How they will affect our children is an important question, but one for another day.

Summary

Each of these examples is intended to help set a gestalt. The virtual reality to be defined here is not a literary experience [4], a traditional computer session, or a simple television experience. It involves computer technology as an intimate mediator of the reality.

TERMS AND THEIR MEANINGS

The kinds of systems being discussed have been labeled in many different ways. This section provides some definitions and distinctions.

Definition

Some of the terms that have been used include:

- Virtual Reality
- Artificial Reality
- Alternate Reality
- Cyberspace.

Webster provides the following definitions:

Virtual, "being in essence or effect, but not in fact"

Artificial, "contrived by art (the conscious use of skill, taste, and creative imagination in the production of aesthetic objects) rather than nature"

Alternate, "a substitute, one designated to take the place of another"

Reality, "a real event, entity, or state of affairs"

While my Webster does not define cyberspace, it is perhaps not unfair to define it as:

"a place where the human nervous system and mechanical-electronic communication and computation systems are linked".

Examples

We need to cast a broad look as we think about virtual reality. Many different researchers from different fields are working on what might be called virtual reality. Some of the more often cited efforts include:

• Krueger's [5] "Videoplace" is a distinctly artificial reality with many of the characteristics of both a game and an art exhibit

• The multiple projects at VPL, NASA-AMES [6], and AutoDesk [7] that use Eyephones and DataGloves

• The Habitat project by LucasFilms Inc. [8]

• Interactive multimedia projects such as those undertaken at the Dartmouth College Interactive Media Laboratory. The potential use of virtual reality in medical applications both for training of physicians and for treatment has been discussed by Henderson [9]

• The use of virtual reality for architectural design has been suggested by several including Benedikt [10]

• ARK, the Alternate Reality Kit, developed at The Palo Alto Research Center (PARC) of the Xerox Corporation [11] allows the user to engage in "alternate realities" from their vantage point in "meta reality" and to engage in visual experiments that manipulate the laws of nature.

One might also include a whole series of efforts such as:

• Computer-supported collaborative work projects such as the Colab Project, also at PARC, [12] endeavor to provide a virtual meeting environment in a distributed network via public and private work spaces on the participants' screens

• Scientific Visualization efforts such as those described by DeFanti, Brown, and McCormick [13] create virtual or alternative realities. Likewise, hypertext browsers [14, 15, 16] endeavor to provide a visualization of reality. Our work at Pitt on the VIBE system falls in this area.

The kinds of efforts described include:

- computer/video games
- educational systems
- interactive art
- graphical and direct manipulation systems
- visual programming environments
- design systems
- simulation systems
- systems for scientific and document visualization.

DIMENSIONS

Clearly, the scope of these efforts defies any simple classification. There are some things that can be said about the efforts collectively. These are laid out in Spring. [17] Briefly, efforts can be classified along three dimensions:

- the naturalness of the interaction
- the kind of process/environment depicted
- the locus of the control.

Interaction

A quite observable difference exists between those efforts that use data gloves and eyephones and those that use keyboard or mouse input and a flat 2-dimensional display. The interface may be said to fall along a continuum from artificial to natural. Similarly, the interaction may be natural or contrived. Consider for example the following:

1. A data glove interface where glove actions are symbolic may not provide for a natural interaction.

2. A hypertext browser allowing natural interaction between the user and the hyper document, despite the fact that the input was keyboard-driven and the display two-dimensional, might in the last analysis be considered natural.

Having said this, it should also be clear that a clear correlation exists between sophisticated sensors and displays and simulated interaction.

Along the interaction continuum, we might find the following:

1. An artificial symbolic instruction set controlling an automaton that provides symbolic data in return.

2. A natural dialogue between the user and the system.

3. A simulated interaction between the user and the object of the system simulation—what is sometimes referred to as a "direct manipulation system."

Some interesting questions arise in discussion of the interface. Spring [17] explores the issue of creating virtual realities for processes that have no natural interface. These processes of concern were those that are primarily symbolic, bringing to mind another interesting question. Bruner and Piaget suggest a progression in learning from sensory motor, to iconic, to symbolic. My description is somewhat simplistic, but not inaccurate. Consider that we teach our children with things, and then with pictures of things, and then with verbal descriptions of things. Now consider that with computers, symbolic interfaces led to icon interfaces, and we are now talking about further modification to a sensory interface. This appears to be a rather unusual direction for the evolution of a new media. Consider, for example, the following points:

1. For at least four years, children view books as blocks, coloring paper, ripping experiences—lots of things other than symbolic interfaces.

2. We spend many hours as parents and many more through our schools teaching children how to work with the symbolic interface.

3. The failure of an adult to manage a very abstract book is viewed as a fault of the reader, not the book. The opposite is true in human/computer interactions.

It may be that the breadth of expressive capability of the new media is what is being explored here. With time, the truly capable users of computers may prefer less icon and more symbolic interfaces because of the compactness of the expression. Sensory and icon interfaces will be used primarily for early childhood education!

Reality

It makes me somewhat uneasy to imagine that one can conceptualize reality or develop a taxonomy of realities. Nonetheless, a continuum of realities that might be depicted appears to exist. Work now being done includes the development of computer-mediated realities, computer-developed virtual and alternate realities, and artificial realities. Thus, mediated, virtual, alternate, and artificial might be distinguished as follows:

- *mediated realities* are simply realities mediated through a computer—as an analog-digital-analog link. The experience may or may not be in real time. Every effort is made to maintain the laws of nature and the data basis of the experience. We might put much of the work at NASA-AMES in this category. There is a growing trend to equate virtual reality with telepresence and virtual workstations.

- *virtual realities* are like a simulation—it is reality as we know it but with selected dimensions abstracted. While all the laws of nature may not be in force, the effort is to maintain the reality base. Much of the work done in the architecture field could fall in this category.

- *cyberspace and alternate realities* are like simulation games. Selected rules of reality are suspended or replaced for the duration of the "game." Those existing rules deemed desirable for the simulation are allowed to remain in force.

- *artificial realities* are game-like. Reality as we know it is suspended in favor of a small set of carefully circumscribed rules that totally control the game's operation.

Control

The last dimension—control—in my view seems the most important and yet the most difficult to describe. While it is clear that this dimension is not orthogonal to the reality dimension, it is important enough to separate out.

How to best describe the control dimension has proven somewhat illusory. One possible explanation is found in the philosophy of Teilhard de Chardin. Teilhard distinguishes between entities of consciousness to the 0 power (inanimate entities), consciousness to the first power (animate entities), and consciousness squared (intelligent entities).

Given the types of objects that exist we might classify the realities along the control dimension as:

- a system containing only passive objects
- a system with many active and passive objects
- a system with multiple interactive or intelligent objects.

In each of these systems, the user is an intelligent entity exerting control over the system. In the first system, the user is the locus of control. In the last system, the user is clearly only one controller among many.

Summary and Dimensions

Control factors, reality base, and naturalness of user involvement provide three dimensions for the classification of efforts, as shown in Figure 1. Whether another context and other dimensions might better define the various efforts is a matter that will only become clear with further experimentation. For purposes of discussion, this classification will suffice.

Two classes of virtual reality projects are plotted against these dimensions depicted in the cube in Figure 2. The micro world types of projects are generally limited in how they accept user input and provide access to and control of "reality," and are governed by the rules set down for the system as well as by the user. In contrast, remote controlled sensing devices are more user controlled, provide access to reality as we know

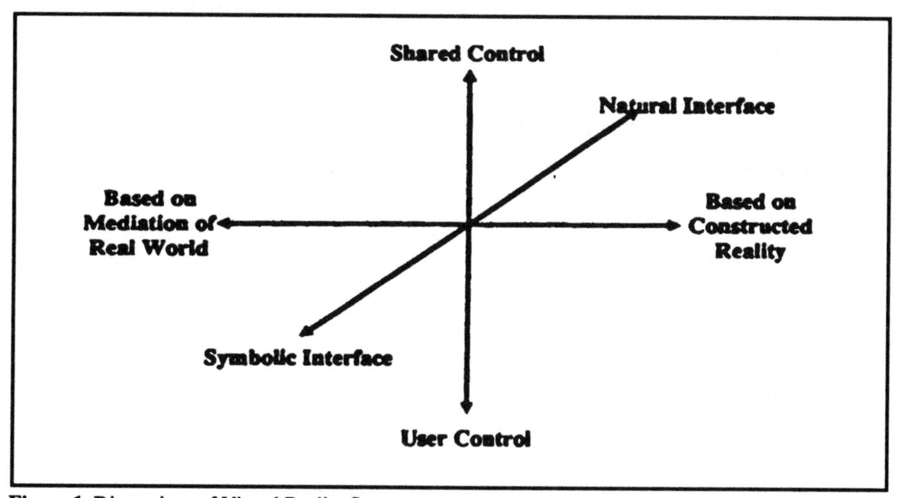

Figure 1. Dimensions of Virtual Reality Systems

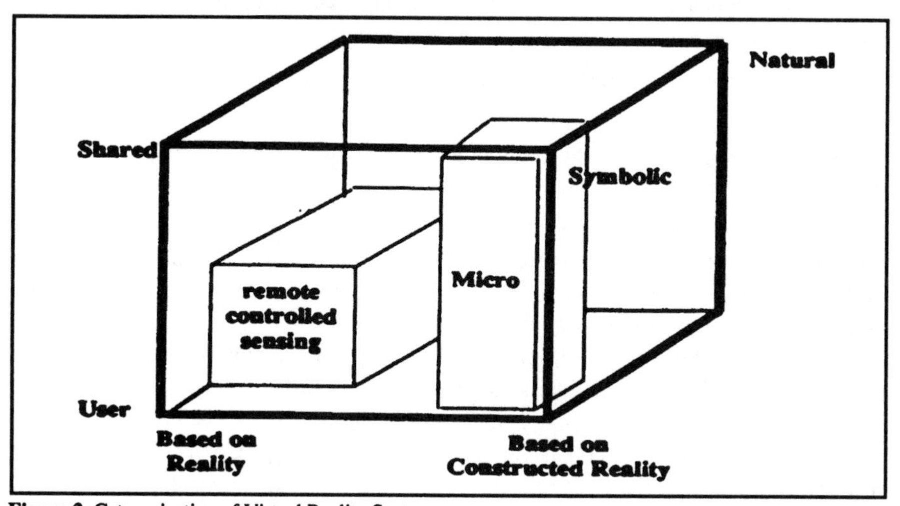

Figure 2. Categorization of Virtual Reality Systems

it, and provide a spectrum of involvement mechanisms that run the gamut from primitive computer controls to natural extensions of human action.

ALTERNATE MODELS

In order to build virtual realities, we need to have some model of what they should look like. Every researcher working in the field has a model but it would seem that few are explicit. A notable exception is Walser who has developed a very elaborate model.

The discussion to this point has provided some common ground for the use of terms. Based upon this discussion, we can then look at several "models." In each case then we will be looking for:

- the assumptions of virtual reality
- some superordinant concept or construct to provide guidance
- attributes or subconcepts that are important
- important principles. [18]

Below, a few assumptions common to most of the models are enumerated. Following is a discussion of possible models with an examination of two in particular.

Assumptions

In discussing the antecedents of virtual reality and in trying to describe it, a number of assumptions have crept into the text. These assumptions are made explicit below. Virtual realities:

- involve people as participants, or users, or actors. It is interesting to note Walser's notion of a human user as a patron of a puppet in the system. Here the puppet senses the human action and reacts to the human user, or patron
- involve computers, both as mediators of the experience and as originators of the reality
- in some way, shape, or form, provide a space in which we may exist for a period of time.

Thus, we have made several assumptions about what we are building: it is something for humans; it involves the use of a computer, potentially as the source of intelligent agents; and it involves participation in a "space" through an interface—unless we can create the equipment that was fictionalized in *TRON*.

We have mentioned several times how the computer exhibits some level of intelligence in and control over the interaction with the user. In primitive forms, we might imagine a simple context-sensitive help system as an example of such an effort. More sophisticated efforts in expert system design typify this stage. Control is now shared with the computer. As the systems become "more intelligent," control is shared more equally (indeed, in some situations some users perceived more control to reside with the computer, based on better knowledge representations and more sophisticated production rules in selected areas).

Intelligence is used here most informally—we simply suggest that systems the user feels are intelligent may be so defined, regardless of how the "intelligence" was achieved. A classic example of such an system is Eliza. Other examples abound and are governed by the general rule that science, when significantly advanced, is indistinguishable from magic.

Choices for Alternative Models

The many projects that bear the names virtual, artificial, and alternate realities, and cyberspaces are of some thing. We have suggested that virtual reality may be defined in the context of interfaces or perhaps, more broadly, human/computer interactions. There are actually many models being used to conceive and develop virtual realities. The model used will affect the kinds of questions we ask and the kind of framework we establish. More than one model may be valid or, perhaps, none of the models discussed here may be valid.

Nonetheless, we begin by suggesting that virtual reality may be considered as one of four things: tool, art, interface, or environment. This selection does not imply any judgment about other possible models. Other articulated models, such as Walser's [7] are not included simply because they have been addressed elsewhere.

The work of several authors would support virtual reality as a tool. Among these we might include the architectural design work of Benedikt [10]. Scientific visualization efforts such as those described by DeFanti, Brown, and McCormick [13] also would support this view. The work of others supports virtual reality as an art form of some type. Krueger [5] talks much about full body participation in the context of artificial reality. His discussion about teletouch and touching hands causes one to wonder if consumer interest in virtual reality will not be related in some way to the interests that initially spawned the VCR and pay phone service (900) markets; namely, pornographic films and dating/talk lines. Teletouch may offer a mechanism that allows users to interact intimately with minimal commitment and danger.

What could we learn about people in this kind of environment? Barlow [19] uses the analogy of drama to talk about cyberspace. To some extent it provides a way to erase the edge of the stage. The task is to create a designed space where members of the audience have coequal participative status with the actors. Laurel [20] points out that "their [designers'] notions of how to design the cognitive and emotional components of our experience lag far behind their ability to provide sensory and kinesthetic ones." And, "The key to virtual world-making lies in the domain of representation making, not in the emulation of reality. And the domain of representation making is art."

Other authors have alluded to virtual reality as an interface or interaction, or as a space or environment. We select these two perspectives for further examination below.

VIRTUAL REALITY AS INTERFACE OR INTERACTION

Several authors allude to issues that focus on the interface. Lewis [21] distinguishes anchored and unanchored visualizations—those grounded in some phenomenon and those grounded in some theory that is not manifest in a phenomenon. Hunt, Hunt, and DeLeon [22] define cyberspace as a form of active communication. Bonar [23] talks as well about important principles:

- depiction of logical operations as visual operations
- provision of visual cues
- replacement of abstract metaphors with concrete metaphors.

Bricken [24] describes his design paradigm in contrast to what it must be distinguished from:

- the interface is replaced by an inclusion mechanism
- mechanistic processes are replaced by intuitive ones
- simple visual interfaces are replaced by multimodal interfaces
- symbolic manipulation is replaced by experiential manipulation
- the metaphor is replaced by the virtual.

Below, we discuss this model for the virtual reality in terms of two major components—the interface itself and the interaction which takes place across that interface.

Interface

When we think about interfaces, we consider both the type of interface and its characteristics.

What does the interface connect—two software modules, two pieces of hardware, two humans, a human and some environment? This leads us to ask whether the interface is simple—a passive interface such as a car's windshield, or whether in some way the interface symbolizes or represents that which it is an interface to.

We can also ask about the characteristics of the interface. How it is constructed? What kind of distortion it introduces? Is it bidirectional? An interface provides a window, viewport, or symbolic representation of some thing or process.

For humans, the quality of the interface may be judged by what Don Norman calls "the gulf of evaluation" and "the gulf of execution." The nature of the interface might be classed by the degree to which it interposes itself:

- no interface—a human gazing at the heavens

- augmented interface—a human using a telescope
- mediated interface—a digitized image of a star.

Basically, there is an endeavor to model some process known to the user and depicted via the interface or to ease the transition from the known user model to a new system model.

Interaction

If we agree that virtual reality is an interaction, we must then be prepared to ask what it is an interaction between. It can no longer be a simple viewport or window. Indeed, there may not even be an interface as we usually think of it.

We may imagine several types of interactions. Between two humans, one form of interaction is called a conversation. A human interaction with the world is called experience. A human interaction with some nonmachine process via a machine is called telepresence. Human to another human via machine is mediated communication—a phone conversation. Human to some machine process via machine is often found in simulations and games.

As with interfaces, we might think about the role of devices in the interaction:

- none—a conversation
- augmented—a telephone conversation
- mediated—a natural language interface to a database, or an automatic translation system.

Looking forward, a major thrust may be discerned in the development of virtual and metaphoric realities that provide a new kind of link between the user and the problem environment modeled by the computer system.

We can talk about the style or approach taken to interaction; we can think about the actors, directors, etc.

1. Virtual realities will be created for those situations that provide some form of direct or indirect analog-digital-analog experience for users.

2. Alternate realities will be created for those situations that benefit from a rich multisensory interface to depict symbolic data or data not available to the human senses.

Virtual reality systems use very immediate computer mediation of the user's sensory and motor activities. If we use the interaction model, it is possible to use some of the completed work in human computer interaction to provide some boxes within which work on virtual reality can be done: interface and dialogue.

The interface was further analyzed into the various sensory modalities: visual, auditory, gustatory, olfactory, touch, and kinesthetic. The dialogue was further broken down into levels for analysis: physical, lexical, syntactic, and semantic.

In the case of virtual reality interactions, the computer plays a dual role. Not only is it involved in the mediation, but it may serve as the source of one of the endpoints. This concept is perhaps easiest if we think about multiple computers. One plays the role of controlling the interface. Another manages the dialogue that is passed across the interface. Finally, several others may serve as origination and termination points for the interaction—serving as the principles engaged in the interaction.

VIRTUAL REALITY AS ENVIRONMENT

Virtual reality is a space for many authors. Farmer [8] states very clearly that "Cyberspace is a place, not just an interface or a metaphor." The problems that have to be addressed to make progress include bandwidth and graphics resolution limitations, user interface and data communications standards, event integrity, and the need for more computer horsepower. Farmer also refers to Gibson's definition of cyberspace as "a pseudo-physical realm in correspondence to data structures and processes of a large computer." Benedikt [10] suggests several important principles for the design of virtual reality: dimensionality, continuity, density, and limits. Gaines [25] identifies the structural criteria, implying a space, as connectedness, reflexivity, transitivity, reversibility, and continuity. He suggests three levels of being that need to be considered:

- physical being—space, time casualty
- psycho-social being—convention, anticipation
- logical being—rationality, coherence

Heim [26] discusses the ontology of cyberspace—the way phenomenal entities exist as realities in cyberspace. He also indicates a need to address the ontological status of cyberspace itself. Hjerppe [27] discusses the problems of (dis)orientation in hypermedia and cyberspace. McFadden [28] makes several points about cyberspace. Two are selected as examples. First, the logical structure of cyberspace is non-Euclidian; it is recursive, almost fractal. Second, neither a natural direction or flow of time nor entropic flow exists.

If we think about virtual reality as environment, then we must be concerned with:

- space
- objects
- the laws governing the space and the objects.

In thinking about realities, spaces, or environments, we need to consider such things as:

- the system ontology
    - a. theory about the nature of being and the kinds of existence
    - b. theory about the nature and relations of being
- the system epistemology

a. the nature and grounds of knowledge

b. the limits and validity of knowledge

In this case we are less interested in how we observe or participate in the environment than we are in the rules that govern and control the operation of the environment and the objects in it.

The proponents of cyberspace see this as the most appropriate model. In this environment, the computer serves several roles. Again we might imagine multiple processors playing different roles:

- One or more serve as the puppets that absorb information from the human actor and provide feedback to control the actor
- Others serve as nonactor-based entities in the environment
- Other computers serve as the laws of the space, monitoring and controlling the actions taken by the actors and nonactors.

SUMMARY

This concluding chapter has reviewed the literature on virtual reality and suggested a variety of definitions for the different terms employed. A classificatory model for virtual reality is suggested along with two operational models that seem to offer some significant promise for analysis and design of virtual realities. These include:

- A model of the interface to the system based on the notion that it is an interactive interface
- A model of the system process based on the notion that it is a space governed by an ontology and occupied by objects that are passive, active, and interactive. Interactive objects are governed by a set of laws that comprise their epistemology—a set of rules that govern how they learn about the space.

NOTES

1. Spring, M., Jamison, W., Fithen, K., and Thomas, P. *Preliminary Notes: Human Computer Interaction Reference Model*, SLIS Research Report LIS032/IS90010; December, 1990.

2. Brand, S., *The Media Lab: Inventing the Future at MIT*. New York: Viking, 1987, p. 104.

3. Zuboff, S., *In the Age of the Smart Machine: The Future of Work and Power*. New York: Basic Books Inc., 1984.

4. Virtual reality may end up being a literary tool, but it is not literary in the sense discussed above.

5. Krueger, M., "What Should You Wear to an Artificial Reality," *The First Conference on Cyberspace*, Sponsored by The School of Architecture and the Department of Computer Sciences at The University of Texas at Austin, May 4th and 5th, 1990, pages, 54, 55

6. Fisher, S., "Virtual Environments: Personal Simulations and Telepresence," *Multimedia Review*, Vol. 1, No. 2, Summer, 1990, pp. 24-31.

7. Walser, R., "The Emerging Technology of Cyberspace," *Multimedia Review*, Vol. 1, No. 2, Summer, 1990, pp. 42-46.

8. Farmer, R., "Cyberspace: Getting There from Here," *The First Conference on Cyberspace*, Sponsored by The School of Architecture and the Department of Computer Sciences at the University of Texas at Austin, May 4th and 5th, 1990, pp. 27-30.

9. Henderson, J., "Designing Realities: Interactive Media, Virtual Realities, and Cyberspace," *Multimedia Review*, Vol. 1, No. 2, Summer, 1990, pp. 47-51.

10. Benedikt, M., "Cyberspace: Some Proposals," *The First Conference on Cyberspace*, Sponsored by The School of Architecture and the Department of Computer Sciences at the University of Texas at Austin, May 4th and 5th, 1990, pp. 5, 6.

11. Smith, R.B., "The Alternate Reality Kit: An Animated Environment for Creating Interactive Simulations," *Proceedings of the 1986 IEEE Computer Society Workshop on Visual Languages*. June 25-27, 1986, Dallas, Texas, pp. 99-106.

12. Stefik, M. et. al., "Beyond the Chalkboard: Computer Support for Collaboration and Problem Solving in Meetings," *Communications of the ACM*, Vol. 30, No. 1, January, 1987, pp. 32-47.

13. DeFanti, T., Brown, M., and McCormick, B., "Visualization: Expanding Scientific and Engineering Research Opportunities," *Computer*. Vol. 22, No. 6, August 1989, pp. 12-26.

14. Conklin, J. and Begemen, M.L., "gIBIS: A Hypertext Tool for Team Design Deliberation," *Hypertext'87 Proceedings*. November 13-15, 1987, Chapel Hill, North Carolina, pp. 247-252.

15. Crouch, D., "A Pictorial Representation of Data in an Information Retrieval Environment," *1987 Workshop on Visual Languages*. August 19-21, 1987, Linkoping, Sweden: Tryck-Center, pp. 177-187.

16. DeRose, S.J., "Expanding the Notion of Links," *Hypertext'89 Proceedings*. November 5-8, 1989, Pittsburgh, Pennsylvania, pp. 249-258.

17. Spring, Michael B., "Informating with Virtual Reality," *Multimedia Review*, Summer 1990, **1**(2), pp. 5-13.

18. In this context, principles are relations between or among concepts.

19. Barlow, J., "Music in Cyberspace; Cyberspace as Place," *The First Conference on Cyberspace*, Sponsored by The School of Architecture and the Department of Computer Sciences at the University of Texas at Austin, May 4th and 5th, 1990, p. 4.

20. Laurel, B., "Theater and the Art of Designing Virtual Worlds," *The First Conference on Cyberspace*, Sponsored by The School of Architecture and the Department of Computer Sciences at the University of Texas at Austin, May 4th and 5th, 1990, p. 56.

21. Lewis, C. M., "Cyberspace and the Two Gibsons," *The First Conference on Cyberspace*, Sponsored by The School of Architecture and the Department of Computer Sciences at the University of Texas at Austin, May 4th and 5th, 1990, pp. 58, 59.

22. Hunt, J., Hunt, E., and DeLeon, T., "Virtual Communities: Perspectives on the Implementation and Ramifications of Shared Virtual Realities," *The First Conference on Cyberspace*, Sponsored by The School of Architecture and the Department of Computer Sciences at the University of Texas at Austin, May 4th and 5th, 1990, pp. 49, 50.

23. Bonar, J., "Proposal for the First Conference on Cyberspace," *The First Conference on Cyberspace*, Sponsored by The School of Computer Sciences at the University of Texas at Austin, May 4th and 5th, 1990, pp. 9, 10.

24. Bricken, M., "Virtual Worlds: No Interface to Design," *The First Conference on Cyberspace*, Sponsored by The School of Computer Sciences at the University of Texas at Austin, May 4th and 5th, 1990, pp. 11-13.

25. Gaines, B., "Modes of Being: A Logical, Psychological and Ontological Analysis of Cyberspace," *The First Conference on Cyberspace*, Sponsored by The School of Architecture and the Department of Computer Sciences at the University of Texas at Austin, May 4th and 5th, 1990, pp. 33, 34.

26. Heim, M., "The Erotic Ontology of Cyberspace," *The First Conference on Cyberspace*, Sponsored by The School of Architecture and the Department of Computer Sciences at the University of Texas at Austin, May 4th and 5th, 1990, pp. 38, 39.

27. Hjerppe, R., "Lost and Found in the World in Hypermedia and in Cyberspace: Exploration, Navigation and (DIS) Orientation in Three Worlds," *The First Conference on Cyberspace*, Sponsored by The School of Architecture and the Department of Computer Sciences at the University of Texas at Austin, May 4th and 5th, 1990, pp. 43, 44.

28. McFadden, T., "The Structure of Cyberspace and the Ballistic Actors Model—an Extended Abstract," *The First Conference on Cyberspace*, Sponsored by The School of Architecture and the Department of Computer Sciences at the University of Texas at Austin, May 4th and 5th, 1990, pp. 60-62.

Michael B. Spring
Department of Information Science
University of Pittsburgh
Pittsburgh, Pennsylvania 15260

INDEX

B

C

D

E

M

N